STORY OF MY LIFE AND WORK

BY

G. FREDERICK WRIGHT

D.D., LL.D., F. G. S. A.

*Surely there are in every man's life certain rubs,
doubtings, and wrenches, which pass awhile under the effects of chance, but, at the last, well
examined, prove the mere hand of God.*

—Sir Thomas Browne

Oberlin, Ohio, U.S.A.
Bibliotheca Sacra Company
1916

The News Printing Co., Oberlin, O.

TO

The Many Generous Friends

WHOSE INTEREST
THROUGH ALL THESE YEARS HAS BEEN
AN INSPIRATION,
THIS VOLUME IS AFFECTIONATELY
DEDICATED

PREFACE

THE sixty years of my active life cover a period of
unexampled intellectual as well as of mechanical readjustments. To the discussion of the intellectual problems which have special bearings on our religious life
Providence has given me a call which I could not decline. The chief reason for the preparation and publication of the present volume has been to keep in the
foreground of the public consciousness the new arguments and recently discovered facts (some of which I
have contributed) supporting reasonably conservative
views concerning the relation of science to the Bible.
This I do at the present time, not because I think my
work is all done, but because this survey should be
made while my powers are still unabated.

A minor reason for the publication of the volume
is that as an autobiography (which it really is) it will
serve to bring before the minds of the present generation a vivid picture of the conditions of life during
the last half of the nineteenth century, when most of
these readjustments referred to were being made.

I am encouraged to make this venture from the fact
that more than 40,000 of my contemporaries have purchased the books I have written, and a still larger

number have read my numerous contributions to the current periodicals of the time, a partial list of which is given in the appendix. A glance at this list will tell better than words how constantly the subjects on which I have written have been before my mind, and how wide has been the range of investigations upon which my conclusions have been based.

By permission of the Publishers of the *Nation* I have made free use of letters published in that periodical, relating to my trip across Asia, but for the most part the form of these communications has been somewhat changed.

With strong assurance that the fundamental truths which I have attempted to define and defend will ultimately prevail, notwithstanding the eclipse into which many of them have fallen, I offer the volume for the consideration, both of the general public, and of the scientific and theological fraternities to which it has been my privilege to belong.

G. FREDERICK WRIGHT.

Oberlin, Ohio, November, 1916.

CONTENTS

CHAPTER I

CHAPTER II

CHAPTER III

CHAPTER IV

CHAPTER V

CHAPTER VI

CHAPTER VII

CHAPTER VIII

CHAPTER IX

CHAPTER XII

The essence of intellectual living does not reside in extent of science or in perfection of expression, but in a constant preference for higher thoughts over lower thoughts. Here is the true secret of that fascination which belongs to intellectual pursuits, that they reveal to us a little more, and yet a little more, of the eternal order of the Universe, establishing us so firmly in what is known, that we acquire an unshakable confidence in the laws which govern what is not, and never can be, known.—Philip Gilbert Hamerton.

Story of My Life and Work

CHAPTER I

HAPPY DAYS OF CHILDHOOD

ENOCH WRIGHT, my grandfather, was born in Pittsfield, Massachusetts, in 1763. His parents came from Northampton, Massachusetts. What their name was I have not been able to learn, for the Wrights were at that time a numerous family in the Connecticut valley.

At the close of the Revolutionary War we find Enoch, at the age of sixteen years, enlisted as a teamster in the campaign which ended in the surrender of Cornwallis at Yorktown, an event which he was permitted to witness. His discharge from the service was dated on the field, and reads as follows:

> Camp York Town, Virgine: Oct. 10: 1781
> this Certifyes that Enoch Wright is Discharged the wagon Servis on Account of Inebility of helth & not having Any Teme of his own thot Best So to do
> Jos Cogswell W. M. G.
> Sd Wright hath Purchesd him Self a Hors & hath Liberty to take it home.
> all Isuing Comiss are Desird to furnish the Barer With Provitions to Connecticut.

Why he should have gone to Connecticut is not

certain, but it is surmised that he was attracted thither by the presence of Tryphena West, whose family was originally from Connecticut, but was found not long after residing in Pittsfield. Among her brothers were Ichabod, and Frederick, after whom I was named.

In 1783 Enoch Wright and Tryphena West were married, much to the displeasure of the bride's parents, on account of the groom's lack of worldly goods. But Tryphena was courageous and confident and boldly set out on horseback with her young husband to make a home near Skenesboro (now Whitehall), New York, at the head of Lake Champlain. Here he purchased from a Mr. Carver a tract of land five miles northeast of Whitehall village. The boundary line between Vermont and New York is here formed by East Bay, and Poultney River, which, after running some miles to the north, bends around to the south and leaves a projecting point of the town of West Haven, Vermont, extending between the river and Lake Champlain, almost to Whitehall village. Thus Vermont was upon three sides of my early home, from which resulted the fact that my early associations were much more intimate with Vermont than with New York. The towns of Poultney, Fair Haven, West Haven, Benson, Castleton, Rutland, Hubbardton, and Middlebury were much more famil-

iar to me than any places in my native state, except
Whitehall.

Skenesboro and the immediate vicinity are connected with many of the most thrilling scenes of
American history. For many days Skenesboro was
the headquarters of Burgoyne's army; the battle of
Hubbardton occurred but a few miles to the northeast;
and the bateaux of Burgoyne's scouting parties went
up East Bay to Carver's Falls, two miles to the north;
while, only seven or eight miles to the west, after
crossing Lake Champlain and Dresden Mountain, an
unfrequented road led us to the Bosom on Lake
George at the foot of Black Mountain and opposite
Sabaday Point, and brought to our attention the many
thrilling scenes in Colonial history when the French
and English were struggling for the possession of that
most important line of early communication.

My grandfather built him a log cabin a short distance back from the home where I was born, and
where in my childhood's days were the decaying trees
of the apple orchard which he had planted with his
own hands. I well remember the heap of stones
which marked the foundation of this cabin, and the
spreading roots of the stump of a hollow pine tree
concerning which my grandmother often gave me a
thrilling story of her pioneer experience. When in
due time they had become the possessors of a flock of

eight sheep, it was their custom to shut them up at night in this hollow stump to protect them from the wolves. But at last these ravenous beasts effected an entrance and killed the entire flock, the remnants of whose bodies were found scattered around in the inclosing forest. Painfully my grandmother collected the locks of wool lying around, and carded and spun them into yarn, and from it knit stockings for her children.

My grandmother lived to be eighty-seven years old, and for some years I was her intimate companion, sitting by the fireside to keep her company while she regaled me with stories of her pioneer life. Children were born to her in rapid succession, until there were ten in all. But she was a thrifty housekeeper, and, though slight in frame, had a vigorous physical constitution. She delighted to tell me that after the first year, when she brought up a calf on hay tea, they never ceased to have fresh milk in the household. The unfailing spring of water to which they resorted in dry seasons was a quarter of a mile away. Not daring to leave her children at home alone, she would often bring water this distance for household use, with one babe in her arms and another trudging along with unequal steps at her side. At one time as she was combing her hair in the door of her cabin on a pleasant day, she thought she saw one of the neighbors' cattle in the wheat field near the house, and hastened to drive the creature away; but was surprised to see it push through the brush fence in a manner unlike that of a domestic animal, and on looking closely discovered that it was a bear. These and other stories told me by my grandmother relate to events which occurred one hundred and thirty years ago, and illustrate the length of time through which evidence of the first order may be transmitted by tradition. On visiting this region at the present time, all evidence of the conditions existing in the early years of my grandfather's settlement have disappeared; but of these things I have no more doubt than I have of any other fact that is made known to me by human testimony; while I doubt not that by repeating them here those who read this account will believe them as firmly as they do any facts of history.

Unfortunately a part of the land which my grandfather purchased lacked a good title. He had bought it originally of the New Hampshire grant, which was supposed to own the land to the head of the lake. Hence he was compelled to pay a second time for it. Nevertheless, his business capacity was such that he prospered greatly, adding farm to farm until he must have been in possession of nearly one thousand acres. The region was heavily covered with timber, much of it being pine. The immense stumps of these

trees were so saturated with pitch that many of them
remained in the ground for a century, while others,
after being violently wrenched from the ground, were
set up on edge to make fences which still endure.
The land was cleared of the forests in the shortest
possible way, the trees being felled and piled in heaps
where they could be burned and the ashes saved,
from which potash was made,— the ashes being
leached and the liquid boiled down in huge kettles of
well-known shape, tapering inwards from top to bottom. It is from similarity to the shape of these kettles that the numerous well-known depressions and
lakelets in the glaciated region are named " kettle
holes." At first potash was almost the only market-
able product that could be sent from the land. But
as soon as even a small area was cleared immense
crops of wheat could be procured from the virgin soil,
and this found a ready market at Troy and Lansing-
burgh, at the head of navigation on the Hudson
River, about one hundred miles south. But over that
distance it had to be hauled by teams. This necessi-
tated the establishment of innumerable small taverns
along the route. Some of the houses put to this purpose in that heyday of hotel life are still standing,
but in many more instances a bed of tansy is all that
marks their former location. Those were the days
when it was not thought imprudent to take a dram,

and indeed when "morning bitters" were supposed to be a necessity. Hence the tansy bed by the side of every public house. In looking over my grandfather's papers, I find regular account of small amounts of rum among the articles for which his wheat was exchanged.

After a few years the log house in the orchard was exchanged for one of more considerable pretensions, built just in the rear of the one which at a later date my father built, and in which I was born. This second house was a frame building covered with clapboards which, if I remember aright, were split from the straight grain of pine trees and given a smooth surface by the shave. They were fastened with wrought nails. The home stood long after my remembrance and was a favorite place for the storage of corn and apples, and for the games of hide and seek which we children played with each other.

Though they had been brought up under the strict religious influences prevailing in New England, my grandparents were so engrossed in their pioneer life that for twenty-one years they were entirely neglectful of their religious duties, but at this time an event of great significance occurred. Upon reaching his majority their oldest son, my uncle Orin (a name of blessed memory to all the children of the neighbor-

hood who enjoyed rambling with him in his old age
through the forests in search of ground nuts, saxi-
frage, and wintergreen, and along the streams and
lakelets, where fish were caught), went back to Pittsfield to attend school at the ancestral home. There
he fell under the influence of a powerful revival of
religion conducted by the erratic Lorenzo Dow, and
experienced a change of heart which made him ever
afterwards a pillar of the church and a witness for
everything that was noble and true. His first impulse upon his conversion was to set out for his home
to give his testimony to his parents and brothers and
sisters. He hastily walked the one hundred and
twenty miles that separated him from them, arriving
at night after all had retired, but his mother, recognizing his step, called, "Orin, is that you? What is
the matter?" He replied, "I have found the Saviour and have come home to tell you. I want the
whole family aroused that I may tell them of my
experience." Consequently all the children were
aroused and gathered about the fireplace.

The effect was instantaneous, my grandfather and
grandmother at once acknowledged their error in so
long neglecting their religious duties and entered
upon a new and joyful life of Christian experience. The influence rapidly spread throughout the
neighborhood and it was but a short time before a

Congregational Church was formed, of which my grandfather was the clerk and leading member. In those days the practice of infant baptism was more scrupulously observed in Congregational Churches than it is at the present time, and it is affecting to notice that at the communion following the organization of the church all my grandfather's children were presented for baptism, though as my father told me the consent of the older ones was obtained.

In a few months a meetinghouse was built about three miles to the southeast of our house, where it would accommodate a large circle of families interested in the movement. My grandfather was chairman of the building committee and kept the records of the society as well as of the Church. On seeing how carefully these were kept, one does not wonder at his success in business, for note was made of everything purchased and of every day's work employed.

But shortly after, in 1808, he was seized with a violent fever, and cut off in the midst of his activities, leaving my grandmother with the cares of her family and a large landed estate. The older children, however, were so well developed that she could shift most of the burden upon their shoulders, and this she did, until one by one they were all married, and seven of them were settled on farms adjoining the old

homestead, she making her home there with my father
until her death in 1847.

My mother's maiden name was Mary Peabody
Colburn. She was descended from a family that
came to Boston about 1640, living for the most
part in the vicinity of Lowell. Her mother was a
Peabody, one of the numerous family of that name
living in Salem. She was related also to the
Spoffords, some of whom are still living in North
Andover. But she herself was born in 1800 in
Fredericktown, New Brunswick, whither her father
and mother had gone in connection with the loyalist
emigration at the close of the Revolutionary War,
preferring the rule of the King to that of the new-
born Republic. In 1808, however, they came back to
the United States and settled in Fairhaven, Vermont,
which was only five miles east of the Wright homestead. My grandfather Colburn also had a large
family, the oldest of whom, my uncle John, was at
one time interested in the establishment of an iron
foundry at the head of East Bay just below Carver's
Falls. Some of the remains of the foundry are still
in existence. The failure of the enterprise was due
to a singular and very instructive geological event,
the marks of which are still visible.

At the time of Burgoyne's campaign and until the

time of my uncle's adventure, East Bay was navigable
up to Carver's Falls, and so could be depended upon
as an outlet for the product of their forge. But two
or three miles above the Falls, Poultney River was
running in a very unstable channel, determined by
the unequal melting of the ice of the Glacial epoch,
which conducted the stream to a waterfall which furnished prospective power of considerable value. A
mile or two above this waterfall the stream was prevented from flowing into a partially filled preglacial
channel by a narrow embankment of gravel and sand.
An enemy of the owner of the waterpower conceived
the plan of taking vengeance upon him by turning
the course of the river at that point. This he carried
into effect one dark night, and in the morning the
rushing water had so enlarged the breach that it was
too late to be remedied and a permanent change in
the channel was effected. "The dry falls" (near
which for a time Horace Greeley had his home) and
the elevated abandoned channel were left to the geologist as permanent records of the change, while the
manner in which it was effected is known only
through this tradition which I desire to perpetuate.
As my memory joins itself on to that of those who
were contemporaneous with the event, there need be
no doubt of the truth of the story.

As a result of this change in the channel an immense amount of fresh sand and gravel was washed down the stream and over Carver's Falls to fill up the channel of East Bay and render it permanently unnavigable. Thus my uncle's promising plan was "nipped in the bud" and the remnants of the buildings in a lonely and inaccessible place were all that remained of the venture at the time of my childhood, to excite the curiosity of visitors.

Two other facts relating to this insignificant stream, with which I became familiar, were of great assistance in later years in helping me to solve difficult geological problems. From them I learned how water can be made to run up hill. The headwaters of Poultney River were twenty or twenty-five miles southeast of our house. Hubbardton Creek entered East Bay, the continuation of the river, a short distance northwest, coming from the north. At one time a series of thunderstorms passed over the headwaters of the river, raising it, opposite the mouth of the creek, as much as forty feet above its ordinary level. At the same time there had been no rain in the valley of the creek. The water of the river, therefore, when it passed the mouth of the creek rushed up into it and carried upstream a dam which had been constructed to furnish power for a grist mill. As I had often ridden to this mill with grists of corn to be ground, the story of this dam's floating up stream made a deep impression on me, and, as I found many years later, helped me to the solution of a most difficult problem in glacial geology.[1] The other fact was that in going to the village of Whitehall one road crossed a causeway, which was near the level of the water at the head of Lake Champlain. Ordinarily this was dry, but when strong north winds blew for some time the water used to rise and cover the road so as to make it impassable, thus illustrating the power of the wind in affecting water levels, and helping one to understand the story in Exodus where the " strong east wind " is said to have opened the Red Sea for the passage of the Children of Israel, while a change of wind had overwhelmed the Egyptians who ventured to follow them.[2]

During the years of her girlhood, following their return, my mother's family lived in West Haven and Benson. During a portion of this time they kept a toll gate on a turnpike which led from that section of the country to the great market place at the head of navigation at Troy on the Hudson River. Many a day she was left in charge of the gate, which gave her opportunity not only to become familiar with the faces of a great number of people but also to satisfy her insatiable love of reading, which followed her to the end of her life. My mother's education, like that of most young women of the time, was limited to the three R's and fancy needlework, while in arithmetic she was scarcely taken beyond fractions, but she knew Watts' Hymns, the Bible, Young's " Night Thoughts," and Pollok's " Course of Time " almost by heart, and had largely devoured all the choice literature that came within her reach. She had read Shakespeare, " Scottish Chiefs," and Baxter's " Saint's Rest " while in New Brunswick before coming to the States. A young lady of her acquaintance, who was desirous of emulating her in some respects that she might make herself agreeable to her gentlemen friends, begged of her at one time to lend her for a few days her " Young Man's Night Thoughts," things with which my mother thought she was already too well acquainted.

In the powerful religious revivals which swept over that region in the second decade of the last century, my mother became deeply interested, and in the year 1818, in the company of one hundred others, joined the Congregational Church of Benson, a town which then had twice the population which it now has. About this time a proposal of marriage was made to my mother by a young minister, which it would have seemed natural for her to accept, but at the same time a plain-spoken, honest farmer, in the person of my father, was competing for her affections and secured the prize. Thus the train of events that led up to my own existence hung for a time in the most delicate balance. Fortunately for myself it turned in my favor and in due time I with four brothers and a sister came into the world to struggle amid its vicissitudes, and to leave our footprints on the sands of time.

The letter in which my father made his final proposal illustrates better than almost anything else, both his own sterling qualities and the formalities of the time.

" The winter is past and gone the spring has now returned which now animates all around us and awakens in man a spirit of joy and gladness and all the social passions of the mind: for man is formed for asocial being and not for solitude capable of enjoying sweet intercourse with his fellowbeing; for it is written two are better than one and a threefold cord is not quickly broken. May I not use freedom while conversing with one whom I trust hath the spirit of Christ, for I also have this consolation, that Christ hath formed in me the hope of glory; how strong the friendship when formed on right principles: and how hardly to be broken. I need the council of one who can sympathize in my afflictions and share in my pleasures, one in whom I may ever find new delight. After haveing some personal acquaint-

ance with you, I am led to believe the report I have
so frequently heard of you. I shall hope for afriend
in you for I trust you will find afriend in me; where
true friendship is existing happiness will exist in
the pleasure of afriend; the generous heart will
not wish to make himself happy in the misery of his
friend; but will make happiness consist not in the
good of one but all. Shall I find you like minded.
After careful examination and investigation of the
subject from our first acquaintance, I am convinced
that amore particular acquaintance would be interesting to me. Much however depends on your choice;
and the freedom of your situation. I hope you will
not be delicate about giving your mind on the subject, trusting you will find a generous heart to deal
with one, who will not be outdone in generosity. I
will acknowledge you my equal, and, I trust your generous heart will ask no more. I will conclude by
refering you to the 2. Epistle of John 12th.

"Whitehall April the 10th

    W [ALTER] WRIGHT.

"M. C."

It was my father's lot to settle on the old homestead and to have the care of his mother until her
death in 1847. On this account our house was the center for the family gatherings, which were frequent and

iumerous; for I was blessed with an unusual num-
)er of cousins, all of whom were pleasant and worthy
.ompanions. As I have already said, five of my
'ather's brothers and one of his sisters were married
ind settled upon adjoining farms.

I was born on the 22d of January, 1838. When
[was twelve years old there were forty-seven cousins
n the Wright family in the neighborhood and twelve
or fifteen upon the Colburn side. One of my father's
sisters had married Perez Chapin, a Congregational
minister of the old style, who settled for life in Pow-
ial, Maine. There were five cousins in this house-
nold. The only brother of my father who had
strayed from the fold was my uncle Ira, who was a
physician and had been a surgeon in the war of 1812,
but was now settled in Watertown, New York. A
brother and two sisters of my mother had removed
to the vicinity of Warsaw in central New York.
The cousins in all these families periodically visited
the old homestead and brought with them ideas from
the outside world. We all belonged to the Puritan
stock and our amusements were of the most innocent
character, but a happier society than that in which
I spent my childhood it would be difficult to imagine, and here I may say that of these seventy or more
cousins all have had honorable and useful careers,

while a number of them rose to positions of marked importance.

Moses Colburn was a very learned and efficient clergyman for many years in South Dedham, Massachusetts. Jarvis Adams, son of my father's youngest sister, was a lawyer of eminence and became president of the New York, Pennsylvania, and Ohio R. R. Simeon Wright became prominent in educational matters in Illinois, and his brother Grove a horticulturist, who made distinct additions to the world's knowledge of the processes of vegetable life, and was withal a poet widely recognized among the poets of Illinois. Albert Colburn graduated from West Point and was chief of McClellan's staff, at the time of his death in the midst of the Civil War, while my brothers Johnson and Eugene had long and successful careers as professors in two of the most useful western colleges.

It is interesting and instructive in this connection to call attention to other men of note who in their boyhood received the impress of the influences which permeated "the Wright neighborhood." Rev. Joseph Mansfield, for many years a prominent minister and presiding elder of the Methodist Church in the Boston district, and Reverends Allen Clark and Henry Skeeles, for a long time most useful home missionaries in the West, were one with us during all the days of their boyhood. Honorable William Pitt Kellogg, military governor of Louisiana during the Civil War, and senator from that state, through whose effective stand the electors from that state were recognized in the presidential canvass of 1875, thus securing the election to the presidency of Rutherford B. Hayes, was the son of one of the ministers who for considerable time during my childhood occupied the pulpit of our church. Honorable Solomon Spink, appointed by President Buchanan as the first governor of the territory of Dakota, and whose name is perpetuated in "Spink" County, South Dakota, was another familiar companion in those halcyon days.

The influences which led to the dispersion of this numerous company of relatives afford an instructive illustration of the powerful forces at work in shaping the course of our national history and in raising new and difficult problems in our social, economic, religious, and national life. The opening of the Erie Canal, and later the development of our railroad system, brought the markets of the East and the West closer together, so that products of the farms raised in Whitehall had no special advantage over those in central New York and in the region of the Great Lakes. Besides, it was impossible that forty-seven children, which was the number of the Wright cousins in and near the homestead, should get an honorable living from a tract of land that was only sufficient for seven families. Dispersion was therefore an absolute necessity and everything was beckoning them to the West. One after another they began to settle in Ohio, Michigan, Wisconsin, Illinois, Iowa, and Nebraska. This process has now gone on so far that only the son of one cousin remains in the neighborhood. But they have not been lost to the nation. One of my cousins has sixty descendants in Ohio and Michigan, and altogether the progeny of the enterprising couple who set out from Pittsfield for Whitehall with all their belongings on horseback in 1783 has increased until it numbers nearly 300, or 75 fold in a little over a century. If this increase should go on without interruption during the next ten centuries the blood of my grandparents would mingle with nearly half of the nation; but of course the principle of natural selection comes in to limit the growth of any one scion of the human species and it remains to be seen how well equipped in the struggle for existence our family is, and I am bound to admit that many tendencies are at work which will prevent their filling the land as the mathematical calculations in geometrical progression would show that they might do if they were unrestrained. To a large extent they have abandoned agriculture. Many of them have chosen not to marry, and the

families of nearly all are less than half the size of
that of their grandparents.

During the period previous to 1850, in which we
were clustered about the old homestead, life went
on in the even tenor of its way, still with variety
enough to make it seem like a golden age in the past.
The life upon the farm is necessarily varied, and
dealing as it does with living objects in both the
animal and the vegetable world, it never can settle
down and become mere mechanical humdrum. In
the early spring the maple trees were to be tapped,
the sap collected, and boiled down to that most delicious of all sweets, maple sugar. Much of this was
for home consumption, being packed away in firkins
or in the form of syrup sealed in jugs and jars; but
a considerable portion, especially in the early part of
the season, was taken to market. With the market-
ing I was often entrusted at a very early age. My
father had, and maintained, the reputation of getting
the earliest sugar, which is the most delicious, into
the market. When I would appear in the village
with a basket of small cakes of sugar obtained from
the earliest " run " of sap there was eager rivalry to
secure at a high price the small portions of the coveted sweet which were doled out.

My father made some marked improvements in

the manufacture of maple sugar. Formerly the sap was boiled down in the big potash kettles, which were either swung on poles over the fire or set up in an arch of more or less imperfect construction. By this process some of the sugar was sure to be burned on the upper edges of the kettle, discoloring the whole and giving to it an unpleasant taste. Besides, in order to keep it from boiling over when the syrup was approaching the desired thickness it was necessary to pour some kind of oil upon the surface. This was usually accomplished by hanging a piece of fat pork on such a level that whenever the foaming liquid reached above a certain point it would automatically obtain the requisite regulating film of fatty material. This, added to the dust and smoke which became incorporated in the liquid, gave a dark color to the whole which greatly deteriorated its value.

But my father, anticipating later inventions, made evaporators out of sheet iron nailed upon the bottom of boards turned upon edge to form the sides. This prevented all burning and, being carefully housed, protected the delicate syrup from the incorporation of dust and smoke. At the same time it obviated the necessity of mingling the fatty substance with the liquor to prevent the boiling over.

Everything living has an individuality. This is as true of maple trees as of anything else. There

were favorite monarchs of the forest which poured
forth their liquid treasures early and late in large
quantities and of especial sweetness. For these we
came to have a special affection and it was a coveted
privilege to gather the sap from the over-running
buckets which caught the fruits of their labor. Both
the buckets and the spouts were home-made, the
buckets being made of cedar staves so bevelled that
they were larger at the bottom. The buckets varied
in size, the larger ones being assigned to our favorite
trees. The spouts were usually made from sumac, a
section of the stem of the proper length being sawn
half way through on opposite sides of each end, so as to
leave two plugs which could be whittled down to the
size of the holes bored in the tree. Cleaning out the
pith of the stem left a hole through which the sap
could find an exit and a channel through which to
conduct it to a distance from the tree sufficient to
ensure a firm foundation for the bucket which was
to receive it. The gathering of the sap after a fine
" run " was most exciting business, and furnished a
delightful recreation for numbers of my cousins
whose parents had no sugar orchard, and who regularly visited us at this season of the year. And oh
the delights of " sugaring off " the precious sweet,
of " waxing " it on snow and of making it into cakes
of fantastic shapes, filling ourselves with it mean-

while to our utmost capacity! There is no sweet like early made, fresh, pure, maple syrup.

But each season of the year had its appropriate recreations as well as its duties. The Puritanism of my childhood was not depressing by any means. In the late spring and early summer fish abounded in East Bay, where they came up from Lake Champlain to spawn, being finally entrapped in the basin below Carver's Falls. Nothing could be more exciting than to go with the grown-up relatives, who often came from near and far to fish with seines for the lively pike and shad which filled the waters of this stream. Later we were taken by Uncle Orin in his old age to fish for perch and bullpouts in the ponds which sheltered them. On the way to and fro this good uncle told us the names of the trees and shrubs which we passed, and gave directions where to find the bloodroot and sassafras and sarsaparilla and peppermint and wintergreen which grew in protected places. These were our first lessons in botany, and they were better than those we afterwards got in college. We learned to know every tree of the forest by its bark as well as by its leaf. As I was less robust than the other boys, this good uncle would frequently take me up under his arm and carry me a long distance over the roughest ground. Oh happy days of childhood!

In the autumn there were husking bees and apple parings which brought all the neighbors together and made work a play. It was great fun on a moonlight evening to compete with one another to see which could husk a shock of corn the quickest. As the apple parings were in the house they were not dependent on the weather. It was fun to see the older boys pare the apples on their rudely constructed machines, and the girls quarter and core them, while we younger ones strung the quarters on long cotton strings preparatory to being hung up for drying. And the product was far better than that produced by modern processes.

In the winter there were spelling matches and skating parties, which gave us all the variety that a boy or girl could well ask. With all these diversions we did not feel robbed of pleasure because we were not permitted to attend dances and circuses, and take promiscuous rides to various pleasure resorts of ill repute.

Nor in this connection should I fail to pay a proper tribute to the little country church which our family habitually attended, and of which I early became a member. This was two miles and a half away, so that the family team was got in order every Sunday morning to take all but one of the family to the ser-

vices, which consisted of a sermon in both the forenoon and afternoon, with a Sunday School between,
and time to eat a frugal lunch. The duty of the
one who stayed at home was to guard the premises,
watch the bees which were likely to swarm in their
season, and to prepare a bountiful meal for the hungry worshipers on their return in the middle of the
afternoon. Those who failed to attend the church
services missed a most valuable and important social
occasion. For, at the church were gathered the best
people for miles in every direction, who would rarely
meet but for this. Thus I came to know and be
interested in all the principal families of the vicinity,
and to know what was going on around me. This
enlargement of my mental horizon was of incalculable service. The ministers, as became a Congregational church of Puritan connection, were highly
educated men, who preached over the heads of the
children, but even so left an indelible impression on
my mind. I distinctly remember, after more than
sixty years, many of the sermons of those days.

Just here I want to pay my tribute to two of these
cultivated clergymen, whose influence was deep and
permanent upon all our lives. Rev. Mr. Herrick
was a Yale graduate, and his wife was a sister of
Dr. Dutton of New Haven. This family brought
cultivating influences of the highest sort into the

church and community, and, fortunately for me, could find no house vacant in which to live except in our immediate neighborhood, thus intensifying his influence upon our family. It is interesting to note, also, that on leaving our little church, Mr. Herrick went to Ticonderoga and became the pastor of Joseph Cook during the most impressionable years of his boyhood. Mr. Finch, who followed Mr. Herrick, was likewise a most scholarly and cultivated man, whose sermons were all carefully written and who never dared to speak without his manuscript, but even so; the impressions he left upon my mind were indelible. Little did either of these men know how vital were the seeds of truth which they planted in the hearts of their youthful auditors. But we did not always have our regular preachers. Among those who occasionally filled the pulpit was Elder Grant, an uncle of the celebrated Joseph Cook, a man who had much of his nephew's genius. But he was illiterate, and was devoting his life to missionary work among the sailors who, at that time, before railroads, thronged Lake Champlain and its connecting canal. His wit and readiness to turn any untoward event to a good purpose was proverbial. At one time he was announcing at the close of his discourse the subject of his sermon on the next Sunday. To illustrate his point and make it emphatic he took up the pulpit Bible and said he was to prove his points from within the lids of that book. But unfortunately it was in a very dilapidated condition and the leaves fell out and were scattered far and wide by the breeze that came in at a window. He made no further remarks, except that he guessed it was all there, and with a broad smile, which spread over the whole congregation, closed the services. It is needless to say, that on the next Sabbath there was a new Bible on the desk.

It not infrequently occurred that there was no preacher provided for a series of Sundays. But services were not discontinued on that account. At such times we had " deacons' meetings," when one of these officials conducted the service and had a sermon read. From my twelfth year and upwards I was frequently called on to read the sermon. So early was I introduced to the work which I afterwards chose as my calling.

My mind often recurs to the scenes connected with my uniting with the church, and the lessons it teaches with reference to the significance of such a transaction. I was barely twelve years old, but had been moved in a very quiet way to desire to make a public confession of Christ. I confided this to my sister on a long horseback ride in which I accompanied her. She in turn confided it to my mother. And so it

came about that I was invited to attend the afternoon
meeting, which was preparatory to the communion.
There I was questioned by the staid members who
were present as to my motives in wanting to unite
with the church, and was duly propounded for membership. Upon the following Sabbath, as we had no
regular minister, the Rev. Lewis Kellogg, of the Presbyterian Church in the village, officiated. I stood up
alone before him to assent to the creed of the church,
which I had never read, and to the dismay of the
deacons the creed could not be found. But Mr. Kellogg came to their relief by saying that he would
repeat it from memory. This he did without a
break, and to this I assented. All that I knew was
that it was the faith of the best people with whom I
was acquainted, and I judged the tree by its fruits.
The experiences of a long life have not changed the
conviction formed upon that primitive evidence.

In this connection I must pay my tribute to the influence of one of the church members who was so
much of an invalid that she never left her house, or
indeed her room, for the many years that I remained
at home. This was Celinda Manville, who lived
with an unmarried brother about half way between
the church and the village of Whitehall. Her room
looked out on the road which we usually took in
going to market, so that she could see every one who

passed. Thus she kept herself informed of what was going on, and noted the growth of all the children of the neighborhood. Occasionally my mother took me in to see her. There I learned that she made it her business to pray for all the children of the community by name. Who can tell but she occupied the most influential position of all? I may add also here, that the only signature of my grandmother in my possession is as a subscriber to a pledge that she, with other women who formed the original church a generation before I was born, made that they would spend an hour each week in private prayer for their neighbors and friends and those who should come after them.

My education began in the country schoolhouse a half mile from home, where we gathered for three months in the summer and an equal period in the winter to spend the time from nine in the morning till four in the afternoon, taking our lunch with us. The games we played during the recesses and the noon hour were many of them rougher than they should have been, but served to develop my physical strength, which was none too great at that stage of my life. The schoolroom was rude in all its furniture and conveniences. There was a stove in the middle, with broad desks fastened to the wall on three sides, upon which we placed our books when studying or writing, and against whose serrate edges (for they had been deeply cut into by boys whose idle hands found nothing else to do) we braced our backs when not engaged in study. In the summer the school was taught by some well-known young lady of our family acquaintance, and in the winter by an equally familiar young man. With these we had perhaps the year before been companion pupils. But usually they had little difficulty in establishing order, and gaining our respect. The teaching was rudimental, but effective in giving us a knowledge of the three R's sufficient for all practical purposes.

' The schoolrooms were not provided with sanitary drinking cups, but with a tin pail, from the side of which we drank as well as we could. When Mary White came to school with the measles I took pains to see which side of the pail she drank from so that I should not take the disease from her. But my effort was in vain. I caught the measles and gave them to the rest of the family that had not had them, much to their advantage in after life.

The schools usually closed with some sort of an exhibition, in which both the girls and the boys took part. My very earliest remembrance is of attending one of these when my sister, several years older than

I, with feeling gestures and trembling voice recited
the little poem beginning

> "Twinkle, twinkle, little star,
>   How I wonder what you are."

My own most memorable effort in this direction
was the part I played in a dialogue with George Jackson, which involved a whale-fishing scene, in which
I was the whale and he the harpooner. We made it
as realistic as we could. I filled my mouth with
water from the tin pail and floundered around on
the floor, spouting water now from one side of my
mouth and then from the other while he endeavored
to harpoon me with a stick which had a pin stuck in
the end. When water failed I interrupted the scene
by getting up and running to the tin pail to get a
fresh supply. I need not say that we created a sensation, especially as we took both the teacher and the
pupils by surprise.

The school district was provided with a library,
which had been partly purchased by subscriptions several years before, and was partly paid for by public
funds appropriated for that purpose. It is affecting
to read over the names of the original subscribers,
several of whom I only knew as men who had made
wrecks of themselves in later life, yet whose good intentions had provided me with a most important

means of securing a broad education. The library was kept at a shoemaker's house half way between the school and home. The number of books was small, but the quality was good. Before I was twelve years old I had drawn and read all the volumes of Rollins' "Ancient History," Stevens' "Travels in Egypt, Arabia and Palestine," and Fremont's report of his expedition to the Pacific Ocean, as well as some others. Stevens' Travels was read aloud to my mother winter mornings before light, after I had fed the horses in the stable, and while she was getting the breakfast.

But, better than all, a trying calamity to my father worked greatly to my benefit. When somewhat past middle life he suffered from an inflammation of the eyes which, while it did not prevent his seeing sufficiently to attend to his general duties, did make it impossible for him to read with any satisfaction. The result was that I was set the task of reading the papers aloud to him. The paper which I read most faithfully was *The National Era,* published at Washington and edited by Gamaliel Bailey. This paper contained full reports of the great speeches made in Congress by the unrivaled political leaders of that time, such as Daniel Webster, John C. Calhoun, Henry Clay, Thomas Benton, John P. Hale, and others of less renown. Whittier was a contributor, and, best of all, Harriet Beecher Stowe was contributing her masterpiece, " Uncle Tom's Cabin," which I then read aloud and have never dared to read since, lest the first flavor should be lost. *The Emancipator,* edited by Joshua Leavitt, was another invaluable paper which had to be read, also the *Oberlin Evangelist,* with the regular sermons of Professor Finney. We also took *The Independent* from the beginning of its publication. All this, with the Bible, which was read daily at family prayers, and which I read through in course more than once, furnished no small part of a liberal education.

To supplement our district schools there were " select schools " taught every autumn by more advanced teachers, who were able to carry the pupils farther along in their studies than could be done in the public schools. These were attended by the older boys and girls. I think I never but one season had the privilege of attending them. But incidentally I received much advantage in associating with the pupils and teachers, some of whom boarded at our house. One of these teachers, Michael R. Kelley, an Irishman of broad education, exerted a strong influence on a number of the older boys and got several of them started on the way to college. He made his home at our house, and took much interest in helping me to understand a book on natural philosophy which fell into my hands. Mr. Kelley afterwards went to Illinois, where he became prominent in shaping the educational institutions of that State.

My grandfather showed his interest in the education of his children by building a house in Castleton, Vermont, ten miles away, where his children could live during a portion of the year in proximity to an Academy which was established there at an early date. This house ceased to be occupied by the family when his grandchildren came to need its advantages, but the reputation of the school drew them there in large numbers. Here many of my cousins went to carry on their education to fit themselves for college, or for more immediate entrance into the duties of later life. The school had a wide reputation and was patronized by both girls and boys. But when I came of an age that I needed the privileges which the school afforded, it had been transformed into a female seminary. So great, however, was the pressure from certain families to send their boys there, that a dormitory was built in close proximity to the main building and fifteen or twenty boys were admitted to the school. I was among them, and there carried on my preparation for college. As I was too young and bashful to care much for the society of young ladies, their presence did not interfere with my progress in study. We had good teachers, all of whom have since filled prominent places in the educational work of the nation. I could not ask to have been associated with nobler men, or more accomplished teachers. Among them were the distinguished brothers, George N. and S. W. Boardman, graduates of Middlebury College, Professor Aikin, of Dartmouth, and Rollin Ballard, of Vermont University.

Following the usual course, I was engaged to teach a district school as soon as I had got a little ahead of the younger children of the neighborhood. To me this invitation came before I was seventeen years old. The school was two miles from home in the district where William Miller had lived, who created such a commotion throughout the country from 1830 to 1848 in prophesying that the end of the world was to occur between those dates. He was not living at this time, but I boarded with his son, in the old homestead, and had several of his grandchildren among my pupils. He had died so recently, however, that I had a distinct remembrance of his personal appearance. He was a dignified, serious looking man, who was evidently sincere in the belief that he had found the proper interpretation of Daniel's prophecy, and, by making a day in prophecy always equal a year, he was persuaded that the second coming of Christ and the end of the world was to take place in 1843. It is said that as many as

40,000 persons became convinced of the correctness of his interpretations and prepared themselves for the soul-searching event. Large numbers, clothed in ascension robes, gathered in the little church near Mr. Miller's house, and in other places throughout New England. The largest number of all was assembled in Boston. Excitement was increased by the appearance in the heavens of a flaming comet, which was naturally supposed to be a harbinger of the approaching catastrophe.

But the interpretation proved to be fallacious. Mr. Miller, however, accepted the disappointment as became the sincere man that he was, and said that the Book must be true, though all men were liars, and settled down in the expectation that the event was near at hand, though no man could tell the exact hour or day. Thirty years later, in 1873, while on a vacation tour through New Hampshire, I came upon an encampment of Millerites on Lake Winnepesaukee, who fully believed that they had found the mistake in their leader's calculation. They believed that he should have reckoned from the beginning of Christ's ministry rather than from his birth, and so had made a mistake of exactly thirty years. When I remembered the shock to faith in the Bible in our neighborhood in 1847, when Prophet Miller's calculations were proved fallacious, my heart sank within me as

I looked on this great company of earnest men and women who were clinging to this delusion. It is to be hoped that they joined the large number of more moderate interpreters who look for the second coming some time in the near future, but are not willing to set any definite date. I have never ceased to be thankful for the influence exerted over me and the others who attended the little Congregational church in East Whitehall, by the educated ministers who restrained us from unprofitable speculation concerning the interpretation of prophecy.

CHAPTER II

COLLEGE DAYS AT OBERLIN

THE close of the first district school which I taught, brought me at the age of seventeen to the great crisis of my life, when I was to leave home to enter upon a collegiate education. The question where I was to go was easily determined. Though I had the greatest regard for my teachers from Middlebury, Burlington, and Dartmouth, who instructed me at Castleton, it was foreordained that I should go to Oberlin College, in Ohio, 700 miles from home. The providential influences which brought this about were numerous and imperative. The Institution at Oberlin was founded in 1833 by two remarkable men from our neighborhood, John J. Shipherd and Philo P. Stewart. Through their influence my father and my uncle William became interested in the enterprise and contributed to its establishment. My uncle William, I think, gave $500 and sent one of his neighbor's children there to be enrolled in the first classes that were formed. Later two of his own children were sent there for a time, though neither of these stayed long.

Several things kept up our interest in the Institution. First, there was the anti-slavery agitation which had won over our families. The conversion of Uncle William to anti-slavery views came about in an interesting way. While he was engaged in holding a scythe to sharpen it on the grindstone, which his hired man (a Mr. Saunders, for whose intellectual ability he had little respect) was turning, a heated discussion arose between them over the rights of the Negroes, and the responsibility of the North for their emancipation. In this discussion the ignorant hired man evidently had the best of the argument. Uncle William wisely concluded that if such an ignoramus as Saunders could keep ahead of him in an argument, he must have the best side in the case. The result was the addition of a gallant champion to the anti-slavery cause. But my father and mother needed no such accident to make them take the side of the oppressed.

A second reason for our attachment to Oberlin was sympathy with the religious influences which were prominent in giving character to the Institution. My father, though a man of few words, was a profound thinker on theological and philosophical subjects, and early took sides with the New School party in the Presbyterian and Congregational churches, led by Albert Barnes, Doctor N. S. S. Beman of Troy,

Doctor Joshua Leavitt (editor of the New York Evangelist), and especially by Charles G. Finney, whose agency was supreme in promoting religious revivals in central New York and elsewhere during the ten years previous to the establishing of Oberlin. The removal of Finney to Oberlin in 1835, and the establishing of the theological department there with him as its leading professor, greatly intensified the original interest in the institution. Therefore the *Oberlin Evangelist* with its sermons of Finney and other kindred matter became a regular visitor, and continued such as long as it was published, a period of nearly thirty years. As already remarked, sermons from the *Oberlin Evangelist* were frequently read on Sunday at the deacons' meetings at the little white church when there was no preacher present.

Politically my father sympathized in general with the principles of the Democratic party, but in 1844 voted for James G. Birney on the Free-soil ticket, and ever afterwards acted with the Free-soil party, in this respect following the lead of the men at Oberlin, who never joined with the ultra, or Garrisonian, abolitionists, who refused to take part in the government because of its connection with slavery. My memory of political discussions before I was twelve years old is limited to two utterances made in my hearing concerning diverse subjects. One was by my

brother Johnson to the effect that if war was declared
on Mexico it would be the " death knell " of slavery.
I could not have been more than six years old at that
time. It is needless to say that I looked long for the
fulfillment of that prophecy. Another political bit
of wisdom illustrates how mistaken political shibbo-
leths are wont to be. I do not know how I should
remember it, since I was so young when it was
made, but I do remember that one of my uncles be-
rated Lewis Cass in my presence for asking for appropriations to improve St. Clair Flats. The contempt
that he threw into the words " St. Clair Flats " was
most impressive. When now I pass Detroit and go
through St. Clair Flats and note that the tonnage
passing through the canal which Cass with such fore-
thought promoted, is many times that passing through
the Suez Canal, this mistaken political shibboleth always comes to mind.

With this interest in Oberlin it was natural that
the children should one by one go there for their
education. So in due time, my oldest brother, Johnson, of blessed memory, went there to graduate from
college in 1855, and theology in 1859. My only
sister, Marcia, graduated in 1854. I entered the
college class of 1859, and graduated from theology
in 1862. My youngest brother, Walter Eugene
Colburn, graduated in 1865. Meanwhile another

brother and an adopted sister were students there for a short time.

It was in the spring of 1855 that I left home to join my class in Oberlin. Instead of the through trains which now run with such regularity and speed through the state of New York from Boston to Chicago there were several separate roads, having no connection with one another, hence we were compelled to change cars several times. Magnificent steamboats, however, were running from Buffalo to Cleveland, which might be taken for that part of the distance. But on my first attempt to go by steamer, there was a collision with a sailing vessel soon after leaving the port at Buffalo, which came near sinking us. But we were able to get safely back and were put on board a railroad train which would take us to Erie, Pennsylvania, where the trains were so scheduled that the night had to be spent in that town, to the advantage of the hotel keepers. Later, when it was proposed to obviate this difficulty and enable passengers to go through Erie without change, there was a railroad war which attracted attention throughout the country.

On reaching Oberlin my future was greatly influenced by the boarding place which my brother had selected for me. This was with a most worthy and motherly widow living a mile west of the village, and had been the home of both my sister and brother during much of their time in Oberlin. Mrs. Delia Shepard, who took the place of a second mother to me, was sister-in-law to Lorenzo D. Shepard, an eminent lawyer, then the city attorney of New York City and the father of Edward Morse Shepard, who later became so prominent a factor in cleansing the politics of the Democratic party, to which he was, after the example of his father, devotedly attached. Lorenzo Shepard was a delegate to the Democratic convention at Cincinnati in the summer of 1855 which nominated Buchanan for the presidency. This led to a short visit of his wife to her sister in Oberlin, while Mr. Shepard was in attendance at the convention. It was then that my acquaintance with Edward M. Shepard began, an acquaintance which was continued later when he spent a year in Oberlin with his aunt, and which ripened into a lifelong friendship which had a profound influence upon both of us. To this I will return later.

It was one of the admirable things in the life of Oberlin at this time, and I am glad to say is still so to a considerable extent, that the students for the most part boarded in homes, and not in dormitories. The opportunity this offered to middle-aged women, left to provide for the support of their families by making a home for students, was of great advantage both to them and to the life of the place. The names of the numerous matrons where we boarded became household words, which bring up pleasantest memories whenever the students of that time meet in after years. To Mrs. Delia Shepard and her family my attachment was next to that which I cherish for the members of my own home, from whom school life had sundered me.

Oberlin in 1855 was but twenty-two years old, but it was more mature than its years would indicate. The institution really came to its maturity in 1835 when a large body of theological students who had seceded from Lane Seminary because they were not permitted to discuss the slavery question either in public or in their boarding houses, came to Oberlin, where the freedom which they desired was granted to them. In all there were thirty-seven of these students, most of whom were of exceptional ability. They had been drawn to Lane Seminary in Cincinnati by the reputation of Lyman Beecher, Calvin Stowe, and other of the best representatives of New England theologians and teachers. At this time Henry Ward Beecher was a student there and Harriet Beecher Stowe was preparing to write "Uncle Tom's Cabin." When the trustees passed the obnoxious rule which barred the slavery question from dis-

cussion, Lyman Beecher was absent in New England,
so that he had no voice in the matter. On his return it was too late to remedy the error, for other
influences of a most singular order had come in to
render the move of the students irrevocable.

A benevolent friend of the students living in
Cumminsville, near by, opened a vacant building
to them; and here they were gathered, for some time
carrying on their studies by themselves, with the aid
of John Morgan, a graduate of Williams College,
and a crony and lifelong friend of Mark Hopkins
and of the celebrated Field brothers. Morgan was
a scholar of the finest type, and was resolved that
come what might he would cast in his lot with the
protesting students. Meanwhile, Rev. Asa Mahan,
a Presbyterian pastor in the city and one of the trustees of Lane Seminary, took the part of the students,
and was looking around for some way to help them.
He was already negotiating with Arthur Tappan,
then a prosperous merchant in New York City,
and an ardent abolitionist, for help in the matter
Charles G. Finney was then preaching in New York
City and was at the height of his influence as an
evangelist.

Tappan was one of his ardent supporters, and was
on the point of sending Finney on to Cincinnati for
a few months to give instruction to the rebellious

Lane 'students in Cumminsville, when there occurred one of those mysterious turning points in history in which the greatest events often hang on the
slightest of circumstances.

Oberlin had been started by two visionary men of
remarkable ability each in his way, for the purpose
of promoting general education of a collegiate character which should be open to both sexes, and which
should be combined with manual labor sufficient to
furnish self-support to the students. The school was
opened in 1833, and had made small progress in 1835.
In fact the promoters were at their wits' end to find
means for accomplishing their purposes. At this
juncture " Father Shipherd," as he was called, started
in the late autumn for New York City to try to collect funds. The National Road from Philadelphia
to Alton on the Mississippi River was then built,
and furnished the easiest way to reach the Atlantic
coast from all the central west. So Mr. Shipherd
went from Oberlin to Columbus to take advantage
of this new line of communication. At Columbus
he chanced to meet Theodore Keep, a son of one of
the earliest friends of Oberlin, who was coming from
Cincinnati, where he had been one of the seceding
students from Lane Seminary. Keep told Mr. Shipherd of the situation at Lane, and urged him to go
down to Cincinnati and see if some arrangement

might not be 'made for the advantage of all parties
concerned. Though suffering from a temporary ill-
ness, Shipherd changed his original plan, and rode
the one hundred and fifty miles with the mail carrier
in an open wagon, and through fathomless mud, to
the Queen City on the banks of the Ohio, up which
river he might later find his way to the National
Road again at Wheeling, West Virginia. Mr. Mahan at once fell in with Shipherd's proposition that
the Lane students should come up to Oberlin and
form a theological class which should be the beginning of a theological department. And Professor
Morgan agreed to go with them if suitable arrangements could be made for their accommodation.

Immediately Mr. Shipherd and Mr. Mahan set
out on an expedition to find suitable teachers and to
secure adequate funds for the establishment of a theological department at Oberlin. They went first up
the Ohio River to Ripley, where they called on Rev.
John Rankin, a distinguished abolitionist, and were
taken by him thirty miles across the country to Hills-
boro, to see the brilliant Theodore Weld, who was
then lecturing in that place. To him they made the
offer of the chair of Systematic Theology at Oberlin
as soon as funds could be raised. As Weld had been
one of the Lane Seminary students, and was most

highly regarded for his great ability as a lecturer, and for his general intelligence and nobility of character, it was hoped that he might accept the position, and be of service in raising the necessary funds for endowing the chair. Weld, however, replied at once that he did not feel himself qualified for the position, but said that the man they needed was Charles G. Finney, who was then preaching in New York City, and he had reason to believe that Finney would listen favorably to such a call. It should be said that Weld was a convert of Finney's during the revivals which attended his preaching a few years before, in central New York.

In accordance with this advice, Mahan and Shipherd went on at once to New York and had a conference with Finney and his chief supporter, Arthur Tappan. But they were met with the condition that their proposition would not be considered unless the trustees of Oberlin College would vote to receive colored students on the same terms as those granted to whites. This, however, the Oberlin trustees had just voted not to do. Whereupon Shipherd wrote them a most urgent letter, assuring them that if they did not reverse their decision they could not secure the help needed, and that he should feel it his duty to cease his relation to the Oberlin enterprise which he had done so much in founding. This brought the trustees to terms and ¡by the casting vote of "Father Keep," the chairman, Oberlin was formally opened to colored students. While there were no colored students clamoring for admittance, they gradually turned to Oberlin in small numbers, and have continued to do so up to the present time, but never so as to form more than a small per cent of the general body. The mere fact, however, of their admittance created great interest in the institution among the anti-slavery element throughout both the United States and Great Britain, and drew to it both students of a high character and the much-needed funds for carrying on the school.

As a result of this tie vote by the Oberlin trustees, Arthur Tappan and his friends raised a fund sufficient to pay eight professors a salary of $600 each, and gave outright enough to erect two buildings costing $10,000 each. So at once Finney, Mahan, and Morgan began their work at Oberlin with the Lane "rebels" as 'the nucleus of classes which were reinforced by many others of like mind. Other teachers were added as soon as they could be found. A slab hall was built for the temporary accommodation of the students, and Oberlin received the impulse which has not ceased to give it momentum to the present day. In consequence of giving equal educational advantages to women and the colored race, students were attracted to Oberlin from far and near, so that the college has been one of the most cosmopolitan institutions in the world.

When in 1839 Livingstone was waiting in London to set out on his missionary career, and his first quarter's salary was sent him, he forwarded it immediately to his brother Charles in Scotland and told him to go to Oberlin and get an education. This his brother did, graduating in 1845. In 1885 Miss Barbara I. Buchanan from South Africa presented herself to enter college, and on being asked how she was influenced to come to Oberlin, at once answered, "I am not a missionary's daughter, but the daughter of a barrister who married a cousin of Florence Nightingale, and I asked her where I should go for an education, and she sent me here." Miss Buchanan is now Lecturer in the Normal College at Johannesburg. These illustrations bring out the fact that what was Oberlin's extremity during the financial crash of 1837 really became her opportunity. To save the institution from collapse, the trustees sent two agents (Rev. John Keep and Mr. William Dawes) over to England to present their cause to the anti-slavery people there, especially to those of the Quaker order. From these they succeeded in raising enough money to secure the continuance of the school.

Among the contributors were the members of the Florence Nightingale family.

At the time of my entering college, Oberlin was a seething pot of religious, social, educational, and political reforms whose ebullitions were kept in check by a remarkable body of able and level-headed professors and trustees. Though for the first time opening the doors of a college to women on equal terms with men, the authorities kept aloof from the women's rights movement so far as it tended to break down the distinction between the spheres of duties appointed by nature to the two sexes. Several of the leaders of the women's rights movement, however, came to Oberlin for an education and were warmly received, and welcomed to free expression of their opinions. Among the most prominent of these were Lucy Stone and Antoinette L. Brown, of the class of 1847. Notwithstanding their strong anti-slavery position the Oberlin leaders did not join the radical abolitionists, who stood aloof from the government; but were prominent in forming the Republican party, and were faithful to its principles to the end. President Mahan was a delegate to the Buffalo convention which nominated Van Buren in 1848. Though honoring manual labor by incorporating it in their curriculum, they never advocated communism; and when the manual-labor provisions became impracticable they were quietly dropped. Religiously they were led by the most noted evangelist of the century, Charles G. Finney, yet he remained as pastor of the First Church for thirty-five years and adjusted himself and his preaching to the permanent wants of both the students and the citizens.

The personnel of the Oberlin faculty in 1855 was remarkable. President Asa Mahan, who had come to Oberlin with the Lane rebels at the outset, had retired from the presidency a short time before. He was succeeded by Finney, who continued to give instruction in systematic theology, and to fill the church pulpit. But the active duties of the presidency were for the most part performed by other members of the faculty. Besides, from the beginning Finney was habitually absent for a considerable part of each year conducting revival meetings in various parts of this country and of Great Britain. I was never in any of his classes, as he had retired from teaching before I reached my theological course. But his preaching never failed to pierce my heart to the very center, opening up its secret motives and moving me to consecrate my all to the work of helping to redeem mankind from its burdens of ignorance and sin.

Finney had been a lawyer, and always aimed in his preaching to convince the reason so that his ap-

peals could not be resisted except by wilful disobe-
dience. Starting from the axiomatic assumption that
the fundamental obligation of a rational being was
to "choose the good of being," he so stated specific
obligations, and so unveiled the deceitfulness of the
sinful activities of the human heart, that there was no
escape from response to his exhortations. Besides, he
so presented the limitations under which God had
placed himself in the creation of the human race with
all its moral powers, including the freedom of the will,
that the doctrine of the atonement as presented in the
Bible appeared most reasonable, and appealed to one's
conscience with irresistible power. His equal as a
convincing preacher I have never heard since.

Both in his preaching and in his public prayers
Finney was so straightforward and simple that all
could understand him, and often so childlike that only
his marvelous personality saved him from appearing
ridiculous. For example, on one occasion he preached
on the same day, forenoon and afternoon, two sermons on "Signs of a Seared Conscience." The sermon in the morning had eighty-five heads, each a
sign, and the sermon in the afternoon eighty-seven,
as reported in long hand by Professor Cowles in the
Oberlin Evangelist. The sign on which he dwelt
longest was the borrowing of tools and not returning
them. In the sermon as reported the individual ap-

plications were omitted, and only the statements preserved, in which the preacher showed how mean and wicked it is to borrow an axe or a coat and neglect to return it in as good order as it was when obtained. If one borrowed money he was expected to return the principal with interest, but when he borrowed tools he often would not return them at all, or when he did they were in a damaged condition. As reported the sermon made it seem that society could not hold together if there were not a reform in the habits of the people with reference to their responsibility for borrowed tools.

The sermon as preached was adorned with many illustrations which were omitted in the *Oberlin Evangelist*. As reported to me by his son Norton, it appeared that on the Saturday previous Finney had engaged several workmen to prepare his garden for planting, but when they came on the ground and were ready to work, he found that his various farming tools were not in their accustomed places. With some impatience Finney told them to go home and come again Monday. Whereupon he went into his study to finish the preparation of his sermon for the next day. In preaching it on Sunday, when he came to the sin of borrowing tools without returning them in good order, the point was illustrated by his experience of the day before. "Why," he said, "when

I went to my tool house yesterday with the men on hand to do my work I found it practically empty. President Mahan had borrowed my plow and never sent it back, Professor Morgan had sent for my spade and I do not know where it is, Deacon Beecher has had my monkey wrench for so long a time that the memory of man cannot recall how long ago it was. What does it mean that among the best of us there is such carelessness concerning our fundamental obligations?"

The sequel was interesting and significant. On Monday morning before daylight Finney's watchdog was making a great commotion, so that Finney called his son Norton to dress and go out to see what was the matter. This he did, and found that a neighbor across the way had a sawhorse belonging to Finney, which had been borrowed for some time and not returned. Thinking to get it back without detection he had come into the yard at this early hour, but before he had deposited the borrowed object in its proper place the dog had seized him and prostrated him to the ground, where Norton found him. But the sawhorse was near by to show what was the occasion of this early irruption into the premises. From that time on all through the forenoon borrowed tools kept coming in, from every side. Some of them were recognized as belonging there, but many of them had been so long borrowed that the holders had forgotten where they were from and returned them here on general principles to relieve their consciences of the burden which rested on them.

This incident is but one of many which illustrate the adage that there is but a step between the sublime and the ridiculous. The many stories that are told about Finney's eccentric remarks and actions, are grossly misleading without one takes into consideration the personality of the man. So great was he and such was his personality that nothing seemed unnatural in the introduction into his sermon of the incidents above related. Nobody took offense, and no one who was present thought there was anything out of place in pointing his moral as the preacher did. The only evil possible to result arose from the occasional attempts of small men to imitate him in such matters. Such attempts invariably resulted in ridiculous fiascoes.

At the period when I was in college the professors throughout the country were not mere specialists, as is generally the case now, but broadly educated men, who were able to speak with intelligence and effect upon almost any topic of public concern; at the same time their knowledge of the special subjects they were to teach was ample for the instruction of the raw students who sat at their feet. Specialization could come

later, and as illustrated in any number of cases did
come later and with the best results. F. C. Hayden
and Major J. W. Powell, the two most prominent
pioneers in the United States Geological Survey;
Elisha Gray, generally recognized by electricians as
the inventor of the telephone, and various other most
important electrical devices; and Charles Hall, the
inventor of the processes now exclusively used for the
cheap production of aluminum, all were the product
of the teaching of the days before specialists had super-
seded all-round professors in college chairs. J. Dol-
son Cox, also, became one of the most efficient generals
in the Civil War, and was afterwards Governor of
Ohio, for several terms a member of Congress, and
finally Secretary of the Interior. He always spoke in
praise of the education he received at his Alma Mater.

Of the teachers at Oberlin during my years of study
there, I would make special mention of the following,
whose influence on me was marked.

James H. Fairchild was peculiarly an Oberlin
product, having been enrolled as a student in the first
class that entered, in 1833. In due course of time he
taught in almost every department. For some time
he was teacher of Hebrew. He was also for five
years tutor in Latin and Greek, then for three years
Professor of Languages, and then for twelve years
(covering my college course) Professor of Mathematics

and Natural Philosophy. Later in my course he was my teacher in Moral Philosophy and in Theology. Like all his pupils I felt profoundly the influence ot his clear-cut methods of instruction in everything which he undertook to teach. He taught nothing that he was not fully prepared to teach, and there was not a superfluous element allowed to come in to distract our minds, and cloud our conception of the subject taught. In Moral Philosophy especially his teaching was clear and convincing. With President Finney he regarded obligation as an intuitive perception of the mind, and maintained that the whole law is included in the statement that we are under obligation to " choose the good of being," this phrase being all-inclusive. Every being that is capable of a thrill of happiness, from the Creator down to the worm that crawls beneath our feet, is to be valued in the calculation according to his worth. But in deciding what is our duty in specific acts of our wills we are to be guided both by experience and the testimony of others, the revelation of the Bible being foremost in giving us light. After being once grounded in the main features of this system of ethics, one can but be amazed at the cloudy conception of the subject which characterizes most of the systems of ethics that are now taught in our schools and colleges.

Professor James Monroe had been as a young man

in Connecticut a devoted and successful anti-slavery
lecturer, but he came to Oberlin for his college education.   He was my teacher in rhetoric and belles-let-
tres.   Into this department he brought the rich results
of his early experience in presenting truths in the most
convincing manner to the cultivated audiences he had
been accustomed to face in New England.   In voice
and manner, and in richness of thought, he could not
be excelled.   Naturally he continued to be interested
in the anti-slavery cause, and as the war approached
he was elected to the State legislature, and became one
of the most influential members in shaping the course
of the State in those troublous times.

President Finney, however, was much exercised in
his mind over Professor Monroe's entering the political arena, and at one time preached a most powerful
sermon to try to dissuade him from running as candidate for the State Senate.   The scene was one of
the most memorable of my experiences in Oberlin.
Professor Monroe sat in a conspicuous place in the
church, and listened with rapt attention as the elo-
quent preacher endeavored to prove that a man of
high moral principles who had entered the arena of
moral reform could not run for office without lowering
his standard and compromising his character.   Such
a man cannot get the votes of the people except he
come down to their level.   Professor Monroe, he con-

tended, is too good a man to do this. He can't afford to do it. He should remain on the high pedestal of moral principle where he now is and strive to draw all men up to it. If he gets down to the level to which he will have to fall if he gets the votes of the people, he never will rise again to his original high standard. " Professor Monroe," said the preacher, " is too good a man to run for the legislature of Ohio."

Just then Professor Peck, who sat near, rose in his place and lifted his hand in token that he wished to speak. President Finney turned his great eyes toward him, and perceiving what was wanted, said, " Speak on, Brother Peck," and sat down while Professor Peck finished the sermon in trying to show that we were not going to lose Professor Monroe from the ranks of high moral reform, but were going to have him in both capacities as reformer and legislator. When Professor Peck finished his well-chosen remarks, Finney, with tears in his eyes, prayed that we might all be led aright, and dismissed the meeting.

Professor Peck's previsions were correct. Monroe was elected, and never betrayed his trust. Indeed some have surmised that Finney, in his sermon, was trying to secure Monroe's election by showing that he was so good a man that his constituency would honor themselves by voting for him, thus showing that their level was higher than was generally supposed. Later Monroe was sent for many years as consul to Rio de Janeiro, being there all through the Civil War and for some time after. On his return he was elected and re-elected to the National House of Representatives for five successive terms (from 1870 to 1880). Very appropriately he spent his last years in Oberlin as Professor of Political Science and Modern History.

Professor Henry E. Peck was not so purely an Oberlin product. He was a graduate of Bowdoin College and of Oberlin Theological Seminary. During my college course he was Professor of Mental and Moral Philosophy, and in the Seminary, of Sacred Rhetoric. His was one of the most facile and suggestive minds that I ever came in contact with. He too was prominent in promoting moral reforms, especially the anti-slavery cause, and in stimulating the patriotism of the country during the Civil War. He was one of the most effective political speakers I ever heard. For supposed connection with the actors in the Oberlin-Wellington Rescue Case, he was arrested and held in jail at Cleveland with twenty-seven others while some of their number were tried for violation of the Fugitive Slave Law. In recognition of his interest in the Negroes, Professor Peck was appointed by Lincoln the first Minister Plenipotentiary to Hayti, where he died in 1867.

Doctor James Dascomb came to Oberlin on the opening of the school, and was the Professor of Chemistry, Botany, and Physiology for forty-four years. He was a graduate of Dartmouth College, and of the medical department of that institution, then one of the most flourishing in the country. His teaching was not after the minute laboratory methods of the present time. The experiments were all made by the teacher in presence of the pupils, and the explanations were sufficiently lucid to fix the facts in our minds. If we wished to specialize, as comparatively few did, the teaching we had under him was a good foundation from which to start. But as taught at the present time the pupil is so held down to minutiæ that often he gets no comprehensive knowledge of the subject, unless he goes on to be a specialist.

But Professor Dascomb's teaching was adequate for the purposes of a general education. He taught us to be accurate in all our statements and investigations, and to avoid all superfluity of words. If he asked us to define specific gravity, and we began, " It is where," we were held up at once and told that specific gravity was not " where." If then we began, " Specific gravity is when," we were told that specific gravity was " neither where nor when. Please tell us what it is." Though one of the most consistent and really devout members of the church, Doctor Dascomb made it a condition of his accepting the professorship that he should not be called on to conduct Chapel exercises. His investigations were so accurate and thorough that when his conclusions were drawn he adhered to them with great tenacity. Among these was that lightning rods were a perfect protection to a building if properly put up, which of course we supposed his were. But the lightning struck his house more than once, I believe. Whereupon the Doctor simply remarked that he did not care so much for the house, but he did hate to have his theory proved untrue.   .

George N. Allen was Professor both of Sacred Music, and of Geology and Natural History. His musical taste was exquisite, and his love of natural history ardent. He did much to direct and develop the great attention to music that has characterized the whole life at Oberlin, though it should be said that both President Finney and Professor Morgan were very fond of music and no mean critics of it. Professor Allen was a good violinist. But when an organ was installed in the First Church, about the time when I made my first appearance in Oberlin, he found it difficult to get complete mastery of the pedals. He was compelled, however, to do the best he could until younger men were trained. It was not long till George Steele, Smith Penfield, and John Morgan became adepts at the organ, and electrified the audiences with their daring use of all the pedals. After some meeting in which Professor Allen had been compelled to play on the organ, and, naturally, had made blunders in his use of the pedals, a member of my class commented adversely on it in the presence of Professor Morgan. This aroused the Professor's wrath at such superficial criticism, and he said with much emphasis, " I don't care if Professor Allen does not always get his toe on the right pedal. When he does, he gets better music out of it than either of those young men does." Mrs. Allen was one of the first ladies to receive the degree of A.B. in course, and she kept up her knowledge of Greek sufficiently to read a Greek paper, which her son, Frederick D. Allen, who graduated at Oberlin, but became Professor of Greek in Harvard University, sent her regularly, while head of the American School in Athens.

Professor John Morgan was born in Cork, Ireland, but was brought to America in his infancy. He was a graduate of Williams College. His facility for learning languages was phenomenal, and his memory remarkable. During my college and theological courses he was Professor of Old Testament Literature, and was successful in inspiring his pupils to a high degree. At that time Hebrew was more in favor with theological students than it seems to be in these days when it is made " elective " in many of the seminaries. Our

class all elected Hebrew in the senior college year, and
were drilled in the elements of that language by Professor Penfield, whom Professor Morgan characterized as " a remarkable paradigm." Certainly we
were thoroughly drilled in the rudiments of that
Oriental tongue.   Professor Morgan also lectured to
his classes on the New Testament, with which he was
equally familiar.   President Finney used regularly to
call on him to offer prayer for him in the church services, and sometimes to preach in his stead.   His sermons were always full of thought, but rather lacking
in the eloquence which always characterized Finney's
logical discourses.

This was brought out in one of Finney's prayers
before the sermon when Morgan was to preach.
Among other things Finney asked the Lord to " help
Brother Morgan to speak so simply that we can all
understand him, and not have to stand on tiptoe to
see what he means."   Finney and Morgan were the
closest of friends, and supplemented each other so
completely that there was no jealousy between them,
and together they made a team that it would be hard
to duplicate.

Professor Morgan, like Finney, was very fond of
music, and they two had much to do in encouraging
that musical culture in Oberlin that led to the formation of the Oberlin Conservatory of Music, Professor

Morgan's son, John, being in fact, with George W.
Steele, the principal founder of it, having before this
attained such proficiency in his art that he was installed as organist in Trinity Church, New York
City.

Nor should I fail to mention the name of Professor
Henry Cowles, who was a graduate of Yale College,
and came to Oberlin early in its history and filled for
many years the chair of Old Testament Literature.
During the latter part of his long life in Oberlin he
devoted himself to editing the *Oberlin Evangelist,* a
biweekly paper devoted to spreading abroad the religious views advocated in the institution; and to preparing a series of Commentaries on the Old Testament,
which added much to the reputation of the Oberlin
faculty, and served an important purpose in promoting
rational as well as orthodox views relative to the Old
Testament. Especially was this true as related to
views concerning the second coming of Christ. In the
early history of Oberlin, Millerism had a great vogue
throughout the country, both east and west. As already remarked, 1843 was set as the year in which
Christ was to come, according to prophecy, and
destroy existing kingdoms, and set up his millennial
reign. Naturally the earnest advocates of this interpretation of prophecy came to Oberlin for a hearing.
According to the custom of the place, this was granted,

but on condition that there should be a public discussion. Professor Cowles entered the lists against Rev.
Mr. Fitch, a most exemplary, sincere, and able advocate of the startling doctrines of Millerism. In the
strong atmosphere of religious zeal which characterized the town everything was ready to sweep the
community into the vortex of this powerful delusion.
But it was met successfully by the calm reasoning of
Professor Cowles in his sound contention that " day "
did not always stand in prophecy for " year," and so
there was a fallacy in the reasoning of the Millerites.
Thus Oberlin was saved from what at one time appeared to be a very threatening delusion. This discussion by Professor Cowles prepared him for the
success which he attained in the sane and effective
interpretation of prophecy, set forth in his Commentaries on the Old Testament. His dignified and scholarly
presence was a most valuable asset among the influences at work in Oberlin during my student days.

Professor Timothy B. Hudson was another marked
character in the Oberlin faculty. He had come from
Hudson College to Oberlin at the time of the Lane
Seminary exodus, and for reasons similar to those
which actuated that movement. He finally became
Professor of Greek, of which language he was an
ardent student and a devoted lover. He was a man,
also, of wide interests, being through much of his

time an associate editor of an agricultural paper published in Cleveland. From his fluency of speech he was known as "the silver-tongued orator." In the midst of our course, however, he was killed on the railroad near Berea, where his body was found, horribly mangled by the train that ran over him. The circumstances attending his death were never known. Naturally the event made a powerful impression upon our class, as well as upon the community in general. How much this terrible event had to do in molding my own character, it is impossible to tell; but it was the more impressive because the victim generally exercised extreme caution in guarding against accidents and exhorted every one else to do so.

Professors Charles H. Churchill and John M. Ellis became members of the faculty so near the close of my college course that their influence upon me was not so great as that of the others, but it was by no means inconsiderable. Professor Churchill's varied accomplishments enabled him to touch my life in many respects. In addition to his scientific attainments he was an accomplished musician, and frequently led the great choir, of which I was a member, in preparation for the annual concerts. The dignified bearing of Professor Ellis, coupled with his kindly interest in the students and his wise management as an assistant to President

Fairchild in the general affairs of the college, fore-
shadowed his long career as college professor, which
made it natural that he should be looked upon by the
mass of the alumni, by a large part of the faculty, and
by President Fairchild as the logical successor of the
latter to the presidency. But it was ordered otherwise, and probably it was well that it was so, since
he died very suddenly soon after President Fairchild's
resignation.

The opening of the doors of the college to Negro
students brought to Oberlin a select number of that
race whose presence added much to the educational
interests of the place. Among these there was one
John M. Langston, a mulatto of rare gifts and eloquence, who used to thrill us on public occasions as
no one else could. Later he became prominent in
public affairs, and was for some years a member of
Congress.

On the whole I have no fault to find with the college course of study which was prescribed in the middle
of the nineteenth century. Ours was the same as that
of all the higher class of colleges in America which
gave the degree of Bachelor of Arts. Latin, Greek,
and mathematics formed the staple, including, of
course, the lessons of philosophy and politics and history connected with the study of the classics. But due

attention was also paid to political economy, mental
and moral philosophy, and a fair proportion of time
was given to botany, physiology, chemistry, and belles-
lettres. And as already remarked, I elected Hebrew
during the whole of the senior year, taking this in
place of more mathematics and Greek. But I have
been handicapped all my life for the lack of three
things which are generally provided in the curricula
of the present time, namely, conversational French and
German, and drawing. Photography, however, has
well supplied the lack of the latter, while it has been
possible to pick up a reading knowledge of modern
languages. Indeed, during the first ten years of my
country pastorate I wrote out translations of Kant's
" Critique of Pure Reason," and of the Bremen Lectures, exchanging translations with my brother, who
also pursued this course to enlarge the horizon of ·his
mental vision. I also wrote out a translation from
the Greek of several of the works of Plato. But as I
had no instruction in prose composition in Latin and
Greek, and no practice in conversation in those languages, when traveling in Siberia many years afterwards this lack was painfully borne home upon me,
in efforts to converse with various persons whom I
met, even in out-of-the-way places. At Minusinsk,
three hundred miles from the railroad, the anthro-
pologist in the celebrated museum there, wished to

converse in Latin, since I made such poor work in modern languages. I had the same experience, also, with the high-school superintendent at Semipalatinsk, four hundred miles from the railroad.

But from long experience and observation I am convinced, that my college course, by its concentration on fewer things, did as much for me as the wider and more superficial courses of study of the present time would have done. The specializations which have come in my later life, have been all the more fruitful for the thorough groundwork laid in the prescribed course of my college days.

I can truly say that I made the best of my time while in college. There were no exaggerated athletics to unduly absorb my attention. Oberlin did not allow secret societies, to induce undue waste in social festivities. Instead, we had open literary societies, which gave all the advantages for practice in debate and parliamentary law that were profitable. For exercise I did a fair amount of manual labor in sawing wood and making garden at eight cents an hour, earning in that way thirty dollars a year. For the most of the time I boarded in cultivated families, where I mingled with society in its normal condition. The fact that the men and the women were about equally represented in the class made very wholesome social conditions.

Antioch College at Yellow Springs had been founded as a co-educational institution a short time before I came to Oberlin, with Horace Mann as president. An English traveler who visited it, not knowing that co-education of the sexes had been established at Oberlin for twenty years before Antioch College was founded, was so impressed by the good manners of the young men at Antioch, that he wrote that "changing the Biblical passage but slightly, one might now say that 'At Antioch, college students were first called gentlemen '"; which he attributed to the influence of the young women in the classes. At Oberlin in that day we certainly had a class of women whose influence was most wholesome on the whole body of students. As I was the youngest member of the class, and bashful at that, I was not unduly influenced by the temptations to waste my time in the social engagements which are thought by many to be incident to the plan of co-education. Indeed, the whole life of the class was so much like that to which I had been accustomed in my home, and amid the large circle of cousins of which I have spoken, that there seemed nothing abnormal in the situation. The friendships formed with the ladies of the class were like that I felt for my sister, and have continued such through all the years which have elapsed since those halcyon school days. A noble lot of women they were and a noble work they have done in the world. In large numbers their children and grandchildren have come back to their Alma Mater for education, bringing with them the high moral standards of their parents.

Up to the middle of the nineteenth century, the college terms in most American colleges were so arranged that the students could teach school during the winter, and not lose their standing. Indeed, college commencements were then generally at the end of summer rather than at the beginning, as now. In most country districts they were content with a three months' term of school in the summer, and a corresponding term in the winter. The summer term was generally taught by a woman, and the winter term by a man, that being the time when the older scholars were free to attend. This arrangement gave a grand opportunity for the college men to earn something for their self-support, and at the same time furnished the colleges with a most effective advertising agency. At any rate this was so at Oberlin. At the close of the fall term five or six hundred students went out far and wide to obtain schools for the winter as they could. We might not know much about pedagogics but we were full of information and of zeal and good fellowship.

It was usual then for the teacher to board around,

so that he formed a rather intimate acquaintance with all the families, as well as with the children. The advent of the young college student was an event of great interest to all. It was the signal for the starting of a debating society, a singing school, a writing school, and perhaps a reading school for the older persons in the neighborhood. It was a rare thing if one or two pupils were not moved to follow the teacher back to the preparatory school that was then connected with the college. The influence thus exerted it is hard to overestimate. By this means the college was kept full of the most promising young men and women that the country contained. And the field from which they were drawn was a wide one. Not only did the teachers go into all parts of Ohio, but they swarmed over Michigan, Indiana, western Pennsylvania, and western New York, and many went as far as Illinois and Wisconsin. General Cox always maintained that it was the influence of these teachers for a generation, which, more than any other, saved the Middle West to the Union, for they went everywhere preaching the anti-slavery doctrines which gave victory to the Republican party and secured the election of Lincoln in 1860.

For the four successive years of my college course I was one of this great host that went out winter after winter to teach in the country schools of Ohio and

vicinity. When regarded from the outside, many of
the experiences through which I passed were such as
try men's, or rather " boys' souls," for I was not yet
eighteen years old. But as there were the courage and
strength of will of youth to meet them, hope always
prevailed over discouragement, and brought me
through with enlarged vision, and increased confidence
both in myself and in the Providence which cares for
us in our weakness and ignorance.

My first winter school while in college was obtained
for me by a Negro classmate who had procured one
for himself near by. This was done through a school
director who was noted for his anti-slavery views,
though the rest of the district for the most part cherished different opinions. But in the innocence of my
heart I went to my field in the central part of the
State, in the southwestern part of Delaware County,
and began my work. All went well for three weeks,
when I paid a visit to my colored friend's school and
staid with him at his very respectable boarding place
with a colored family. On a following day he visited my school, and as I had spoken to his scholars, he
was invited to speak to mine. I had no thought that
there was anything wrong in this, especially as Mr.
Greene was a fine-appearing, cultivated man in my
own college class. But the fountains of the great deep
were broken up, and my school was bedlam the next

Monday, and my anti-slavery patron told me that it was no use to try to go on. So I quit.

They honorably paid me the portion of my wages that was due, and I set out to find another school. But I was a thousand miles from home, and not much used to the ways of the world. A college mate (the late Rev. James H. Laird), however, with whom I was well acquainted, was teaching a few miles away, and I immediately reported to him. He received me with a warm welcome, and had an encouraging word. He knew of a school near by, at Hilliards, ten miles west of Columbus, where they had been disappointed in getting a teacher, and took me over there as soon as possible. The way was open, and they engaged me on Mr. Laird's recommendation, notwithstanding my youth and my unfortunate experience. The school was to begin the next Monday, and I was to have the same wages as at the former place.

My schoolhouse was of logs, but it was comfortable. Most of the houses where I was to board were also of logs, but they were filled with intelligent families and well-behaved children. I made my home with the head director, who kept the post office in a small store, and who was also an accredited Disciple preacher. With his family I spent the Sundays, and a more hospitable roof I was never under. The house was of logs, and the kitchen was separated from the living rooms by an open space which ran through the middle of the house from front to rear. Sometimes the water would freeze in the pail that sat by us as we ate our well-cooked meals, but we suffered no harm. The friendship formed with this family has continued to the present day. The oldest son followed me to Oberlin, as have his children and grandchildren to the third generation. One of these (Mr. Fletcher Dobyns) is now a lawyer of nation-wide eminence in Chicago, and several others, both men and women, are prominent in various spheres of influence.

Here it will be best to anticipate a little and tell of an incident that drew me very close in my feeling and regard for the mother of the family especially. Two years later I came down to the neighborhood to teach, thinking that I had a school engaged. But on reaching the place on Saturday afternoon I found that there had been a misunderstanding, and that the directors disagreed with one another so that I could not have the school, and must set out in quest of one, without any clue as to the best direction. In my distress I made my way over to Mr. Dobyns', ten miles away, and spent Monday night with this hospitable family. They thought of all the vacant schools they had heard of and laid out a route for me to follow on the next day. I was to walk nine miles east, and if that failed was to take another direction, and if that failed was to take the cars and look up a classmate who was teaching twenty miles south, and so on. Encouraged by their hospitality and good cheer I started out immediately after breakfast. But Mrs. Dobyns followed me, and having closed the door, said, " Here, take these, you may need them before you find a school," meanwhile slipping three silver dollars into my hand. She was right. I did need them, and have blessed God and her memory from that day to this for her motherly love and thoughtfulness. Presently I will tell of my tramping all through that week and finding a school fifty miles away on Saturday afternoon.

My second school was obtained for me by one of my pupils of the winter before, and not far away. One thing that recommended me was that the principal school director was anxious to have a teacher who could take his children along in algebra, for which they were fitted. This winter was most delightfully spent at a higher salary than I had had before, my home being in a cultivated family of Scotch Presbyterians who sang the Psalms of the old Scotch version. They were all good singers and had a cottage organ, which they used much on week days but would not open on the Sabbath. Like the annals of a peaceful age the story of this winter's experiences is short, and lacking in interest. But the remembrances of it are among the brightest in my possession. My host, Mr. Robinson, was a warm anti-slavery man, and called my attention to the remarkable speeches on the slavery question which my Professor, Monroe, was making in the State legislature. So, one Saturday I went to Columbus and had the privilege of sitting in the senate chamber with my beloved professor, in company with General Cox and President Garfield, who were then the trio that was swinging Ohio into line for the great contest that was impending.

The third winter was the one already referred to in which Mrs. Dobyns played the part of the good Samaritan so effectually to me. As already said, I tramped the whole week, following one clue after another, only to be disappointed, until the very end of the time. Thursday of that week was Thanksgiving, but in that part of the State little attention was paid to it. At noon that day I reached the school of a classmate, and my Thanksgiving dinner was such as he and his generous pupils shared with me from their well-stored baskets. The weather was brisk and cool, and the small streams, over which there were no bridges, were frozen, so that it was exhilarating to the nerves, if only hope had not been so long deferred as to make the heart sick. At noon on Friday, I turned in to a fine-looking farmhouse that stood far in from the

road, as most farmhouses did in that region, to see
if I could get something to eat. But I had met a boy
on horseback going out of the gate as I went in, and
he had a bag on the saddle under him. This looked
rather suspicious, for in my boyhood I had often been
sent with a grist to the mill in that fashion. And, sure
enough, when I reached the house and made my wants
known, I was told that they were all out of bread
and could get no more until the boy returned from the
mill. So I was compelled to tramp on till evening.
But then, at the very end of the week, light broke in
on my prospects. I came to the school district at
White Oak in Fayette County, where an Oberlin
student, Mr. E. W. Beckwith, was just closing a
fall term in a large district school, for the sake of accepting another near by which he preferred. He introduced me to the directors and I was immediately
engaged for the winter term, at a salary larger than
I had ever before had. But the school could not begin for a week. This, however, was not disappointing to me, as my trunk was left at Alton, near Columbus, where I had come expecting a school.

So I spent the week in walking back to Alton to
find and bring my trunk. The week brought ad-
ventures whose memory has been very fresh in my
mind ever since, and has served to intensify my sense
of dependence on Divine Providence whenever I have

been in circumstances of perplexity. When I came down, the streams were frozen over so that there was no difficulty in crossing them. But this week brought a thaw which broke up the ice everywhere. In walking across the lots to shorten the path, I came to Sugar Creek, which was clear of ice, and there was nothing to do but ford it. Rather than travel all day with wet clothes I removed my trousers, and crossed without difficulty, keeping my garments dry. But on reaching Clear Creek a more formidable task presented itself. It was too large and deep a stream to be forded when in flood stage as it then was. There were, however, the remnants of a footbridge which had once existed. This consisted of two upright posts on either side of the stream, with a transverse beam connecting them at a height of several feet above the raging current. But the approaches to it had been carried away. There were, however, rail fences built out on either side to reach the posts, or so it seemed. So I resolved to make use of these approaches to effect a crossing.

On reaching the end of the fence I found that there was one length missing. There was, however, a lot of driftwood between, which I thought was dense enough to hold me. So I ventured to trust to it and made a spring for the upright post. I was mistaken. The driftwood deceived me, and I plunged up to my arms in the icy current. But I reached the post, and climbing it like a squirrel, arrived safely at the top, threw up my feet to let the water run out of my boots, and proceeded to hitch myself across to the other side. There I descended without difficulty, in the midst of a herd of friendly cows, that were lying down and leisurely chewing their cuds amid the dry leaves in the fence corners. They all obligingly vacated their warm beds and gathered around me in a semicircle and looked wistfully on to see what I would do. What I did was to strip myself of my clothing and wring out of the various garments all the water that I could and then reclothe myself and start on as briskly as possible to keep from being chilled. This I succeeded fairly well in doing and in due time reached the boarding place of an Oberlin teacher whom I well knew. Here I was properly cared for over night and made ready to resume my tramp in the morning.

In due time I found my trunk and took an evening train for London, Madison County, from which a good pike led south, passing about five miles from my school. But how to get the trunk carried that distance was a problem, for the three dollars which Mrs. Dobyns had given me was nearly exhausted. Nothing daunted, however, I went to the principal hotel, where their rates were moderate, and took a room for the night. I was given a bed beside one already occupied by two full-grown men, and was told that another man would be assigned after a short time to the bed with me. Before this happened, however, I had fallen asleep, so that I knew nothing of my bedfellow until morning. Then I found that he was a prominent member of the United Brethren Church and a trustee of Otterbein University at Westerville. (I am sorry to have forgotten his name.) He told me that he had driven up from the south to bring some of his family to take the train, and was to return early in the day, and would be glad to carry me and my luggage along to the point where I would leave the pike. This relieved all my anxiety, and I was landed at " Hen Peck," the nearest settlement to my school.

The mud was so deep that it was impossible to get a team across, and so I took out a few necessary clothes from my trunk, did them up in a large silk handkerchief and trudged across lots to my boarding place. Open highways were scarce in that region, their place being largely taken by private roads, leading through gateways which had to be carefully opened and shut by each traveler. This, of course, was no trouble to one who was walking. But when, several weeks after, for it was impossible to go earlier, I went for my trunk on horseback, I experienced much trouble in getting through some of these gateways. All the fences were of rails and very high to keep horses from jumping them. As my trunk was balanced on the pommel of my saddle before me, I found it difficult to open and shut the large gates without getting off my horse, which I did not like to do as it was a difficult operation to keep the trunk in place while getting off and on. So for the most part I opened the gates according to custom without dismounting. At one gate, however, my trunk fell to the ground, forcing on me a task that was difficult to manage. To get it on again and be myself in the saddle was no easy matter. What I did was to first lift the trunk to the top of the fence, and then, mounting the saddle, try to pull it off so that it would strike the pommel before me and not scare the horse. After several trials I succeeded, and went joyfully on my way.

The school at White Oak was large, numbering more than eighty scholars; ranging in age from four to twenty years. But I succeeded in giving satisfaction, and at the same time made the winter more profitable to myself from the fact that I had a single boarding place, and so could continue my studies better than when boarding around. An event of much significance to me in shaping the work of my after life was, that by a singular combination of circumstances I here preached my first sermon. There was no church in the place or for several miles around. But about the middle of the winter a Methodist Protestant minister announced that he would hold a protracted meeting in the schoolhouse. At the appointed time he arrived, and came to my boarding place. But unfortunately he was taken temporarily ill so that it was impossible for him to attend the meeting. Under these conditions, he said the only thing to be done was for me to go and take charge of it. The schoolhouse was full, but there was no one but myself there to conduct any religious services. So I ventured to go ahead and do the best I could, and preached a sermon from Acts iii. 19, " Repent ye therefore, and be converted, that your sins may be blotted out, when the times of refreshing shall come from the presence of the Lord." In the sermon I tried to impress it upon them that they were not to wait for a revival to be converted, but that they were to produce a "time of refreshing " by-turning to the Lord and seeking the forgiveness of their sins. On the following day the minister was better, and afterwards conducted the meetings, relying constantly on me for support. The results were more than any one had anticipated. There was a large number who confessed conversion and a church was formed and soon after a meetinghouse erected, making it a permanent center of Christian influence.

My fourth winter was spent in teaching a school near Martins Ferry, in the southeastern part of the State, opposite Wheeling, Virginia. The conditions here were peculiarly pleasant. An older college mate had taught the school for three or four seasons, and recommended me as his successor. It was a country school in a district largely composed of Scotch Presbyterians, and I boarded in one place. It was of much significance also that I was now in the midst of the coal measures, where a new geological horizon opened up before me, just as I was in the midst of studying geology in college. Of the interest aroused in my mind by these telltale remnants of the distant past I have often been reminded when in later years I have met the men who were boys then and scoured the fields with me on Saturday afternoons to gather fossils.

THE ANTI-SLAVERY CONFLICT

To the friends of righteousness and justice in the United States the fifth decade of the nineteenth century was one of deep anxiety and gloom. Slavery was fastened upon the nation with a tightening grasp which foreboded evils to come from which the boldest heart shrank in terror. The Fugitive Slave Law made it a crime to help a panting fugitive who should call on you while escaping from the cruel bondage of a system that violated every human right and privilege of humanity. About the middle of my college course the opening up of the territory of Kansas to settlement, and the granting by Congress of the right of the settlers to determine whether it should be slave or free territory, convulsed the nation. It was a strife to see whether the Northern States could rush in settlers enough to outvote those from the South who favored making it a slave state. At one time Charles Finney, a son of President Finney, came home from a visit to Kansas and presented the situation in such a strong light that almost the whole sophomore class enlisted to arm themselves and go to Kansas to help the Free-state party repel the ruffians from the Southern States who were trying to dominate the policy of the territory and make of it a slave-holding state. It was only by the most strenuous efforts of the professors that the class was dissuaded from this rash undertaking.

The Oberlin-Wellington Rescue Case occurred in the autumn of 1858, and with its sequelæ was one of the most portentous presages of the Civil War, which followed three years later, while its influence on the student body at Oberlin was profound in the extreme. The circumstances were these. A negro boy named John appeared in Oberlin and remained for some time before anything was known of his origin or history. In the early autumn of 1858 two suspicious characters came to the town and put up at a hotel which was kept by a rabid pro-slavery landlord, and lingered around for several days without any ap-

parent object. But this was soon revealed in a
startling manner. A lad from out of town came in
one day and persuaded John to go with him a mile
or two to the east, ostensibly to dig potatoes. But
when half way to the place the two strangers referred to drove up, by arrangement, beside the buggy
and took John by main force into the carriage with
them and straightway started toward the nearest railroad station leading toward Kentucky, which was
Wellington, nine miles south of Oberlin. By good
fortune, a citizen of Oberlin met them on the way
and suspected what they were doing. He hastened
home and the news spread like wildfire throughout
the town that John was being kidnapped and carried
off to slavery. There was an immediate rush to get
teams to take the indignant citizens to Wellington in
time to intercept the party before the train should arrive. I was among those that found a place in a
team that started for the scene; but a taller and
stronger classmate intercepted us and persuaded me
that he could be of more service than I could be, and
so I gave him my place, and thus missed the scenes
which took place at Wellington. It was perhaps well,
since my substitute was J. L. Patton, one of the most
prominent actors in the actual rescue of the prisoner.
Suffice it to say that John was rescued, and brought
back to Oberlin, where he disappeared from sight, hav-

ing been secreted, as we learned later, in the garret of Professor James Fairchild, until he could be spirited off to Canada.

The sequelæ were that United States marshals came to Oberlin and arrested for violation of the Fugitive Slave Law, twenty-nine citizens and students, who were in due time taken to Cleveland, and on their refusal to give bail, incarcerated in the city jail until trial, and while the trial continued. Among those arrested were Professor H. E. Peck and several of my classmates. The principal evidence against Professor Peck was that he had been heard to pray in public " that justice might be done in this matter." He had not been present at the rescue. But as he was a man of prop-erty he was a conspicuous victim. In due time the trial proceeded, but slowly. The ablest lawyers of Cleveland volunteered their services for the defense of the prisoners. The law, however, was clear, and the first two who came to trial (Langston and Bushnell) were convicted. But, before proceeding to the other cases, the trial was stopped for a week to await the result of an attempt to enforce a writ of habeas corpus issued by State officials demanding that the prisoners be removed from the jurisdiction of the United States court and turned over to the State court. This case was immediately taken up to the Supreme Court of the State at Columbus and argued before them for a week.

While this was going on, a great mass meeting was held in Cleveland before the walls of the jail, and speeches of the most incendiary character were made by various prominent friends of the prisoners. At the same time a platform was erected inside the prison, so that some of the prisoners could address the crowd from the prison walls. Among those making addresses from the outside were Joshua R. Giddings, and Senator Benjamin Wade, both abolitionists, who urged active opposition to the enforcement of the law. But most significant of all was the address of Salmon P. Chase, then governor of the State. Referring to the writ of habeas corpus then being argued at Columbus, he assured the people that if it was sustained by the court, he would use all the power of the State to execute it.

Thus, only two and a half years before South Carolina set itself up in opposition to the general government, Ohio was on the point of bringing on the contest for states' rights, and plunging the country into a civil war with the advantages all in favor of the slave-holding states. But Providence interposed and prevented such a miscarriage. The court at Columbus consisted of five able judges, who, after considering all the arguments, were equally divided, two voting

to sustain the writ, and two against; so that Chief
Justice Swan had to give the casting vote. He had
been long in the service of the State, as judge in the
inferior courts and now for four years on the supreme
bench, and was well known as an ardent anti-slavery
advocate, so that the radical party fully expected that
he would sustain the writ. Moreover, his term was
about to expire, and the convention that was to nom-
inate his successor was to convene in a few days, and
such was the complexion of this convention that his
nomination would be impossible if he did not sustain
the writ. This, however, he failed to do, and in an
opinion that ranks among the most memorable ever
given by a United States judge, rejected the writ, in
this, disappointing the radical abolitionists, but saving
the country from a premature civil war, with all the
odds against the free states.

The closing words of his opinion are worthy of
permanent record: "As a citizen I would not deliberately violate the Constitution or the law by interference with fugitives from service. But if a weary,
frightened slave should appeal to me to protect him
from his pursuers, I might momentarily forget my
allegiance to the law and the Constitution and give
him a covert from those who were on his track. There
are, no doubt, many slave-holders who would thus
follow the instincts of human sympathy. And if I

did it, and was prosecuted, condemned, and imprisoned, and brought by my counsel before this tribunal on a habeas corpus, and was then permitted to pronounce judgment on my own case, I trust I should have the moral courage to say before God and my country, as I am now compelled to say, that under the solemn duties of a Judge, bound by the Constitution and the law *'the prisoner must be remanded.'*" The paragraph immediately preceding this, ran as follows:

"For myself as a member of the Court, I disclaim the judicial power of disturbing the settled construction of the Constitution of the United States as to the legislative authority of Congress upon this subject, and I must refuse the experiment of introducing disorder and governmental collision." It is a shame to the state of Ohio that Judge Swan was not only not renominated at the convention which met. soon after this decision; but that he was retired thereafter to private life, and the great service which he rendered the commonwealth, the nation, and the world, has never been properly recognized.

The end of the trial of the rescuers who were still in the Cleveland jail came soon in an unexpected way which sheds much light on the relation of the states to the general government. During the recess occasioned by the habeas corpus episode, the Kentucky slave catchers, who were needed to give witness in the cases, took occasion to go to their homes for the time that the court at Cleveland was not in session. When, however, on their return, they were passing through Wellington on the train, they were arrested by Lorain-county officials on charge of having violated a state law against kidnapping, for it was contended that they had not given evidence that John was a slave from Kentucky. Consequently they were incarcerated in the county jail at Elyria to await trial before a Lorain-county jury, for a most heinous offense. This brought them to terms, and they agreed that if they were let off further action against the Wellington rescuers would be discontinued. And so ended, for the time, the trial. But it had stirred the country to the depths, and had done much to prepare the public sentiment both of the North and of the South for the crisis that broke upon the world in 1861.

THE CIVIL WAR

After graduating from college in 1859, I began the theological course. But in 1861 there came the Civil War, and on April 15 the call of President Lincoln for 75,000 volunteers for a term of three months to put down the rebellion that had been started by South Carolina. Naturally this call came with peculiar force to the students of Oberlin. A mass meeting was called in the First Church, which was addressed by Professor Monroe, who came up from the legislature to urge on us the duty of showing our faith by our works. We at Oberlin had talked so much against slavery that it was now time for us to act and set an example to the rest of the nation. In fact, as it was said, " We must now put up or shut up." The roll for volunteers was opened on the spot, and I was among the first to sign my name. Professor Fairchild did not give us much encouragement, since he thought the South would be successful in setting up a rival government. But, he said, we must fight in order to obtain favorable terms of adjustment.

In a few days two full companies were formed and ready to offer themselves to the government. Only one of them, however, could be accepted. I was in the one which entered the service. The company consisted of students from all the classes, eight or ten being from the Theological Seminary, of which I was a member. The captain was G. W. Shurtleff, my roommate, who left the war a Brigadier General. The first lieutenant was J. N. Cross (severely wounded at Cross Lanes), the second lieutenant, E. H. Baker, from the class ahead of me. The whole town was active in making uniforms for us until we went into Camp Taylor, which we soon did at Cleveland, where we were made members of the Seventh Regiment of Ohio Volunteers. In due time we were ordered to

report at Camp Dennison in the southern part of the
State. It was a memorable scene when we marched
through the streets of Cleveland, with the accom-
paniments of music and banners, to the railroad train
that was to convey us to our new quarters. The tears
of our friends and loved ones were strangely mingled
with the encouraging hurrahs of the crowd, who were
moved by nothing but their patriotic feelings. We
reached Camp Dennison in a soaking rain which had
transformed our grounds into a mudhole, only to find
that our barracks were only partially erected, and that
we had but a half blanket apiece with which to protect
ourselves from the inclement weather. In fact it appeared that we had been hurried into camp in order
to circumvent a crafty contractor who was defrauding
the government by his dilatory and dishonest work.
But we all made the best of the situation, some of us
even courting hardships in order to show ourselves
good soldiers. Everything was in confusion and disorder for some time.

It was not long, under these conditions, before a
crisis came in my career. In fact I was not of a robust
constitution to begin with, and had contracted a severe
cold immediately on arriving in the camp. But nothing daunted I did not object to being put out on
picket duty one night about nine o'clock to guard the
headquarters of General Cox, who had been appointed

to command the brigade. This was before we had been provided with arms, and I had nothing but a stick burnt black at one end with which to shoot, as I was commanded, anyone who could not give the password, and refused to halt at my order. Unfortunately I was forgotten by the sergeants that should have brought me relief in proper time, and was left on my beat all night, not being relieved till nine the next morning. The exposure was too much for my reduced system, and before noon I was prostrated with a severe pneumonia, accompanied with racking pleuritic pains. As no hospital had been provided I was taken by my comrades into a large barn standing near and laid on a haymow to spend the afternoon and night. Mr. Austin, who afterwards became a successful physician, and was even then a noted nurse, devoted himself to me and did all that could be done to make me comfortable under the circumstances. On the next day an adjoining shed was cleared and transformed into a temporary hospital, and a large number of cots brought up from Cincinnati with accompanying bedding. Against the rules and in violation of the red tape, Mr. Austin broke open a box and got me on a cot the first one. But before night there were more than fifty brought into the shed in much the same condition as that I was in. The first night the patient who lay on the cot next me died. My fever

was high, and my life was despaired of. In a short
time, however, I was convalescent and taken into a
private family in Cincinnati to stay until able to go
back to Oberlin on a sick-leave furlough. This was
as far as I ever got toward actual warfare. But it
was far enough to prepare me to take an interest in
the contest such as to make a permanent influence on
my whole subsequent views of life and of religious,
social, and political duties.

While I was in the hospital the order was given for
the re-enlistment for three years of such members of
the company as were willing to do so. I gave my
name for re-enlistment, but when the time arrived my
health was not sufficiently recovered for me to be accepted, and in fact it was not till the war was nearly
over that I was again physically fit for military service. But harder to bear than the hazards of the battle
field itself was the anxious waiting to hear the news
from the front in which so many of my comrades
were exposing their lives for the common weal. The
Company to which I belonged began its career in the
field in West Virginia, where after arduous and trying marching and counter-marching they were surrounded on the 24th of August, 1861, at Cross Lanes,
near Gauley Bridge, by an overwhelming force of
Confederates, and a disastrous engagement followed.
Six were left seriously wounded on the field, two of

whom (Collins and Jeakins) died, while the other four were maimed for life. Twenty-nine were captured, and languished in Southern prisons for a year or more, two of them (Parmenter and Biggs) dying in New Orleans. The rest, after untold hardships in making their way through the trackless forest surrounding them in a mountainous region, reached the main army, under General Cox, and resumed their military duties. Other recruits joined them, and the regiment was transferred to the eastern side of the mountains, and entered on a long career of most trying campaigns. Through two long winters they camped and did picket duty amid mountains deeply covered with snow, alternately advancing and retreating in endeavors to defeat the plans of the enemy under Stonewall Jackson. During it all they maintained their regular religious services. Professor Ellis visiting them in their camp near Romney in the middle of the winter wrote as follows of their courage and devotion: "When their ranks had been thinned by capture and death, and they had passed through all the corrupting tendencies and temptations of their new life for nearly a year, I saw them in their tents in the heart of Virginia, and nightly from the six tents went up the voice of song and prayer as they bowed before their family altars."

At the battle of Winchester, March 22, 1862, Dan-

forth, Sackett, Palmer, Coburn, Worcester, and Cyrus
W. Hamilton were killed and six others seriously
wounded.   At the battle of Port Republic, June 9,
Romaine, J. Kingsbury, Hamilton, Judson, Gates, and
Magary, were either killed or mortally wounded.   At
the battle of Cedar Mountain, August 8, Ross, Bowler,
Evers, Shepard, Rappleye, and Richmond were killed
and seven others were wounded.   Seventy-five per
cent of all the members of the regiment were either
killed or wounded on that fatal day.   Later they were
at the battles of Antietam, Chancellorsville, and Get-
tysburg, when they were transferred to join the army
of the Tennessee.   Here the regiment took part in
the battles of Lookout Mountain and Mission Ridge,
and then were rushed on to the most disastrous day
of all, the battle of Ringgold, which General Grant, in
his " Memoirs," passes over with the simple remark
that " it was a mistake."   They were ordered to
charge an impregnable position on Taylor's Ridge.
There was nothing for them to do but obey, so on
they pressed through a narrow defile amid the roar of
" cannon to right of them, cannon to left of them, and
cannon in front of them."   Every commissioned officer of the regiment but one was killed.   " Of the
twenty men in Co. C, who entered the action, six
[Jones, Fish, Wall, Wood, King, and Sweet] were
killed and eight, wounded," one of whom (Gardner)

died on the next day. The touching summary reads, "The Company marched 2,400 miles, and traveled by rail and steamers 4,800 miles. It encamped 194 times. Thirty-one men lost their lives by battle, seven by disease, and one was drowned."

But this is only a specimen of what occurred to thousands of other companies from all over the land. A still larger number of Oberlin students than those in Co. C joined other regiments and suffered fatalities in equal proportions. General Shurtleff organized the first Negro regiment that went from Ohio. This was in the slaughter pen at Petersburg, Virginia, when an advance was ordered into a gap in the fortress in which a mine had been exploded. But the order came too late, and the enemy had time to rally and concentrate artillery fire upon them; when, as the General told me, more of his men were killed in ten minutes than were killed in the whole Spanish war in 1898. Altogether 3,000,000 men enlisted in the war, 350,000 of whom never returned. Two cases from the parish in Vermont which I was serving during the last years of the war, specially impressed me, and they were but specimens that could be duplicated in almost every hamlet of the land. One was that of a prisoner taken to Andersonville whose emaciated form was last seen as he was trying to escape from the horrors of that charnel house. The other was that of a half-witted

boy who was forcibly carried off to the war just before the battles of the Wilderness. In them he disappeared, and never could we learn the circumstances
of his death. No one can pass through such experiences and not be a changed man. Since then life has
never looked the same to me.

The experiences of the last winter vacation while
in the Seminary are worthy of note in shaping my
career. My most intimate companion during the last
years of my course of study was Henry S. Bennett, of
Brownsville, Pennsylvania, later for many years professor in Fisk University. His parents were Quakers
of considerable prominence in the place, but he early
became a member of a Cumberland Presbyterian
church in his native town. More than once I visited
him at his home in the picturesque and thriving valley
of the Monongahela River. In the winter of 1861-62
he went to spend the vacation with his parents. The
church to which he belonged was in a very depressed
condition, so that the pastor had resigned and was
teaching school in a neighboring district. In the
emergency my friend began to supply the pulpit, and
soon there was manifest a marked increase of interest.
The work which was opening being more than he felt
prepared to undertake alone, he sent for me to come
to his assistance, as he knew that I had not thought it

best to undertake full work anywhere on account of my health. Very soon the interest so deepened that meetings were held every evening with preaching alternately by him and myself. We were spoken of as the " boy preachers." But we made no effort at sensation, simply presenting the gospel as we understood it and the church believed it. The results were re-markable. There were more than a hundred substantial additions to the church, putting it into a condition which has made it a power ever since. This experience gave a turn to the preaching of both of us during our later years. But the conditions were never repeated, and we had to adjust our efforts to the needs of the several fields which opened before us. What these were in my own case will presently appear.

CHAPTER III

TEN YEARS IN A COUNTRY PARISH

THE choice of a field of labor at the close of my
theological course was made from such a variety of
motives that it is difficult for me to understand what
they were and what were the predominating ones. In
making it, Providence took advantage of my ignorance both of the world into which I was to be ushered,
and of my own capacities. Realizing this, and seeing
the outcome, I have been slow to give advice to young
men about their choice of fields of labor. Several
years later, Hastings H. Hart, when about to graduate from Andover Seminary, asked my advice about
accepting one out of several openings that were before
him, and all that I could say was that he should think
the matter through as well as he could, and pray over
it, and then shut his eyes and take a leap in the dark,
and that he would not know till well along in eternity
how fortunate a choice he had made. But in his case
he did not have to wait so long as I expected. He
decided to go to a small church in southwestern Minnesota. There I found him two or three years later,
just after a terrific tornado had desolated the region
and opened to him the career for which he was spe-

cially fitted. He plunged into the relief work with
such zeal and success that he became a marked man,
and was soon called to take charge of general relief
work throughout the State, and later was promoted
to a prominence which has made him a leader in guid-
ing the work of the National Conference of Charities
and Correction. He is now at the head of the Child
Helping Department of the Russell Sage Foundation
in New York City.

Several churches were ready to call me when I
graduated in 1862. For some reason or other, I
scarcely know what, I chose the field which offered
the smallest salary and about which I knew the least.
This was in Bakersfield, near St. Albans, in the northwestern part of Vermont.

Before going, I married Huldah Maria Day, who
for almost forty years afforded me just the companion-
ship and sympathetic support I needed in my work.
She was the daughter of Judge William Day of Shef-
field, Ohio, and had been educated not in Oberlin but
at the girls' school at Willoughby, taught by Miss
Roxana Tenney, a very eminent teacher of the time.
Upon the burning of the building at Willoughby the
parties interested in the school founded Lake Erie Seminary, now Lake Erie College, at Painesville, and the
Willoughby graduates were counted as alumnæ of that
institution. Four children were born to us—two in

Vermont, Mary Augusta, now the wife of Dr. A. A. Berle of Cambridge, Massachusetts, and Etta Maria, ever my faithful assistant in literary work; two in Andover, namely, Frederick Bennett, for twelve years editor of *Records of the Past* in Washington, District of Columbia, and Helen Marcia, who has devoted herself to settlement work. All these graduated from Oberlin College. Mrs. Wright died in July, 1899.

Immediately after our marriage we set out into the great unknown. But President Lincoln had just ordered a draft of 500,000 soldiers to fill the depleted and hard-pushed ranks of the Union army, and I was held up in Cleveland until I could secure some one to sign a bond of $1,000 that I would come back to the State and enter the army if the lot should fall on me. This having been procured without difficulty, I proceeded on my way, and in due time reached what was to be my field of labor for the next ten years.

Bakersfield was a small village at the foot of the Green Mountains, fifteen miles from the railroad. It was surrounded by a large, sparsely settled farming region, with much woodland which could not be cultivated. The village was very pleasantly situated, and had been the seat of one of the most flourishing academies of the State. Indeed, there were two academies, which had ruined each other by their fierce competition. One of these was favored by the Con-

gregational constituency and the other by the Methodist.   The one adjoining my own church had become
famous the country over under the administration of
Mr. Jacob Spaulding, and had sent out a number of
students who had made great names for themselves.
But Mr. Spaulding had been drawn away to another
town (Barre) in the State, and after the competition
subsided, both academies were practically suspended.
Still the village was divided into jealous cliques, occupying the different ends of it, who could not forget
the conflicts of the past.   The town, however, still
had a goodly proportion of educated and cultivated
residents, but mostly of limited means.   Besides, the
church to which I came had suffered the former pastor
to be starved out, and he was still living in the place,
and justly claimed the warm attachment of many of
my parishioners.   He was in fact an accomplished
scholar, whose sermons were of a high literary character.   Had I known the whole situation I should
doubtless have declined to accept the invitation which
I had received.   But having once put my hand to the
plow, it was not best to look back, so I plunged into
the work before me.

The salary was small, four hundred dollars a year,
without a parsonage, and the parish so scattered that
it was necessary to keep a horse.   Happily situated in
my domestic affairs, we began to keep house in three

small rooms upstairs in a building which was occupied
by one of my most active, officious, and ill-balanced
parishioners. But his intentions were good, and he had
inherited so many of his peculiarities that I could
never blame him much for his inconsiderate conduct.
But one of his actions, the first winter, I could never
wholly forget. When snow fell it was necessary for
me to get some kind of a sleigh. So as befitted my
financial standing I purchased a plain " pung," which
was stronger and more comfortable than it was elegant. Naturally the people were somewhat piqued
to see their pastor riding about in such a primitive
mode of conveyance, especially as one of the outspoken
deacons in a neighboring church said, " Your minister
ought to ride in a pung if you pay him only four hundred dollars a year in war time." Whereupon my
friend started a subscription to get his pastor an up-to-
date " cutter " of which no one need be ashamed. It
is needless to say that he was successful, and thereafter we appeared as well as the best of our parishioners whenever we drove through the street or on the
country roads. But the name of one of the wealthiest
parishioners (if anyone could be called wealthy where
all were compelled to practice the strictest economy)
was conspicuous for its absence from the subscription
paper. As, however, he was one of my warmest
friends and admirers an explanation was necessary to

satisfy the people in general. The explanation was that my officious friend had scrupulously avoided showing the subscription paper to Captain Barnes, in order to cast odium upon him.

This brother was guilty of many other things of the same character during the ten years of my stay in the parish. For instance, he enticed me to draw up a lease between him and an elderly lady for the cultivation of a garden spot. To save lawyers' fees I did so to the best of my ability, though the amount involved was only the increase from half an acre. I thought of everything I could at the time; but I did not specifically define what was to be done with the currants, and included them under "small fruit." Before the season was over, the church and town were thrown into convulsions over an arbitration to settle the right of the owner to allow a friend a pick two quarts of currants from the bushes in the garden. Only on one other occasion did I attempt to usurp the functions of an attorney. One other illustration of the weakness of my friend's good resolutions is too characteristic to be omitted. Toward the close of my ministry he came to me one morning as I was starting across the common to church services, with a written confession which he wished me to read, after the custom of former days, to the whole church. It read, " In a controversy with Freeman Farnsworth yesterday

I called him 'a miserable mean old hunks,' and I
ought not to have done it." But he added to me with
a significant gesture, "He was all that, but I should
not have called him that." Fortunately, a poor memory which has afflicted me from my youth up, served
me a good purpose that morning and the confession
was not read. Meeting me as I came down from the
pulpit my friend remarked that he presumed it was
best to leave it so.

I mention these facts which served to lighten up
my ministry, partly in order to say that through them
I learned to recognize goodness in very untoward dis-
guises. I had no more sincere and faithful friend in
all the years of labor in the parish than he. If he
was weak in his resolutions he was ever ready to con-
fess his sins, and he loved much because he had much
forgiven. As one of my parishioners who was not a
member of the church used to say, "It takes more to
make some persons decent than it does to make others
saints of the first water." Again, speaking of a numerous family descended from one of· the first settlers
who lived on the outskirts of the town five miles
from church, but who was always present with his
children at the Sunday services, he said, "It is as
natural for a Perkins to be religious as it is for a
chicken to eat dough." I always doubted whether
this goodness of the Perkins family was due more to

heredity than to the good example of the parents, and their inheritance of the Divine promise to the fathers and their children and children's children. But certainly my friend had a good deal to contend against on the score of inheritance. This appears from a story which was current relating to his father.

Near the beginning of the century the Congrega- tional churches of that region were served by a num- ber of remarkable men, who were imbued with the old idea that when a pastor is settled over a church it is for life, the relation being about as permanent as that of marriage. Several of these old pastors were living when I came to my field, having been in their places for fifty years. Among them are the names of Parmelee, French, Ranslow, and Wooster, though the latter had past away some years before. But remem- brances of "Father Wooster" were very numerous and vivid. He was specially noted for the part he took in leading a company of his parishioners to rein- force our army in the battle of Plattsburgh, in 1814. The church had gathered on Friday for their service preparatory to communion on the following Sabbath, when news came of the impending battle. Whereupon Father Wooster told his people that it was no time now to pray, it was a time to put on their armor and fight. Coming down from the pulpit he forthwith invited volunteers to follow him to the scene of con-

flict. All but one present enlisted. The one whose
name did not appear on the roll was the father of my
friend. When the meeting closed and Father Wooster
went out to the shed to get his horse, this one followed
him and said, " I doubt if this is right." Whereupon
Father Wooster turned and said, " He that doubteth
is damned," and went on his way. The company led
by· this doughty pastor won plaudits from the whole
nation, and the legislature of the State presented him
with an elegantly bound Bible in recognition of his
services. But notice had to be taken of his curt remark to his dissenting parishioner. So after the war
was over the pastor was brought before the church for
profanity. He was charged with having substituted
" be " for " is " in the Biblical quotation given. But
the church sustained the pastor.

The conditions made by the decline of the two
academies, to which reference has been made, were
accentuated by the disbandment of several churches of
different denominations which had flourished for a
season, thus leaving a considerable number of families
scattered over the town who were not affiliated with
either of the remaining churches, and the most of whom
regarded the village people as aristocratic, and lacking in cordiality. The result was that it was difficult
to persuade them to join with us. It was on the

outskirts of the town that President Arthur was born, his father being pastor of a Baptist church that became extinct not long before my advent on the scene. I soon learned that the evangelistic methods which had been so effective and successful in Brownsville, here must be joined to more systematic and prolonged efforts in a variety of directions in order to produce the desired results. Still, I wish to bear witness that my main dependence for producing the results for which the church exists, was the preaching of the gospel; and in order to do this satisfactorily I was compelled to begin anew the study of the Bible, with all the helps that I could lay hold of.

Hence, at the outset, I began to devote my forenoons sacredly to study. I read the Bible through in Hebrew and Greek, consulting the most scholarly commentaries at my command. The result was that I found that subjects for sermons never thronged into my mind so plentifully as when working over the Hebrew and the Greek with the lexicons at my elbow. But my studies were not limited to the Bible. I systematically reviewed all those I had been over in college, and enlarged greatly the circle of my investigations. I partially made up for not having taken German in college by studying it by myself, and, as already said, I wrote out a translation of Kant's " Critique of Pure Reason," and the Bremen Lectures, and, likewise, translations from the Greek of several of Plato's dialogues. The works in philosophy occupying attention at that time were those of Sir William Hamilton, John Stuart Mill, and President Noah Porter. Careful study of these works, together with the scientific discussions aroused by Darwin's "Origin of Species" and Lyell's "Antiquity of Man," led me, toward the close of my pastorate in Bakersfield, to prepare an article on the "Ground of Confidence in Inductive Reasoning," which was published in the *New Englander* for October, 1871. This, as I afterwards learned from him, was approved for publication by President Porter. It received high commendation from one of the Scotch philosophical periodicals, and was the means of attracting to me the attention of Professor Asa Gray, with whom an acquaintance was formed which ripened into a lifelong friendship, indeed, I may say partnership, in which he assisted me in the preparation of the first book which I published, in which I was asked to discuss the relations of theology to current speculations concerning the origin of species. He, in turn, sought my aid in the preparation of various of his publications having the same end in view, especially in the last chapter of his "Darwiniana."

But I can confidently say that I did not neglect my pastoral work, or any of the natural responsibilities

of my position. I carefully wrote out about thirty
sermons each year. I held meetings in the school-
houses in all the outskirts of the town, and cultivated
the acquaintance of all the unconnected families that
might properly be reckoned as belonging to my parish.
I sunk tons of enthusiasm in helping to keep the temperance sentiment of the County up to such a pitch as
to secure the enforcement of the State prohibitory law.
I joined heartily in promoting the musical conventions
which were held in different parts of the County, to
which we drew the best talent for conductors, and for
soloists to sing the parts too difficult for our local
talent, which, by the way, was by no means of a low
order. I was for several years town superintendent
of schools. I organized a farmers' club, and taught
them the use of superphosphates, and the advantages
of soiling their stock. I organized a band of hope
among the young people. How successful all these
endeavors were it is not for me to say, but I shall
certainly be rewarded if the will is taken for the deed.
I fear my success in stock breeding was not of the
first order, since the highest praise I got was from
the Irish boy who drove my cow to pasture. One
night he forgot to bring her home, but he came up
smiling the next day with the exclamation that my
cow "was bully. She was the best in the pasture.
She could 'lick' every one of the lot." Among other

things I secured the building of a parsonage, hauling much of the lumber myself. I started to do the inside painting, having obtained the paint as a special contribution. But I was making such a botch of it that two of my elderly parishioners who were used to painting woodwork came in and forcibly took the brush from my hands, and finished the job in good style.

After years of patient effort I had the satisfaction of seeing the social prejudice entertained by many families in the outskirts of the town break down, and them come to be among the most efficient helpers in the church. So far as I can sum up results they were greater in that small parish than they have been in the larger, and apparently more important, fields which I have since occupied. F. B. Denio, who has long filled with credit the chair of Old Testament Literature in Bangor Theological Seminary, was the first fruits of my ministry, and I was responsible for getting him ready for college. Several others became ministers either in the Congregational or the Methodist churches. Among them was Fernando C. Willett, one of the most brilliant young men I ever knew, but who, on graduating from Lane Seminary, developed tendencies to tuberculosis, which led him in search of health to go to Mexico as private secretary of the eminent diplomat, John W. Foster, at that time minister to the Mexican Republic. Another was George W. Scott, who, after many years' successful service, died in his pulpit as he was beginning the service, several years ago. Waldo Worthing became a Methodist minister, as did George Frederick Wells, so prominent at the present time in promoting the union of small churches in country parishes. Though born soon after my leaving Bakersfield, he was named after me by his parents in grateful remembrance of my instrumentality in leading them into the Christian life and into the church. Among other indications of the latent cultivation of my parishioners was, that among the various clubs which the women organized there was one for the study of Plato, which they did to good effect through Jowett's translation, which I purchased for them.

Shortly before I left, and partly through my influence, the Academy was revived, and soon after largely endowed by members of the Brigham family. Brigham Academy is now one of the principal preparatory schools of the State.

I cannot say that it was smooth sailing all those ten years. I made some phenomenal mistakes. But they were in days of ignorance at which the Lord evidently winked. On one occasion I innocently offended a number of large and influential families in the church and town by choosing an unfortunate text for a funeral sermon. An aged member of the church who was reputed to be one of the most wealthy, suddenly died while I was absent, but I returned just in time to preach the sermon at his funeral. It was known that he had recently asked me to write his will; but I had no suspicion that this had aroused any special interest. It appeared, however, that there were strong suspicions that he had not made such a will as his large number of relatives would approve; and they were all gathered with a determination to break it. The deceased was a warm friend of mine, but he was very severely and, as I believed, unjustly criticised by outside parties for some of his business transactions. I therefore conceived the idea of making my sermon an indirect defense of his real character, and tried to show that few of us accomplished the good which we really aimed to do; that none of us came up to the ideal which as followers of Christ we attempted to attain; but that the Lord, who sees the heart, takes cognizance only of the aims which we cherish, and will reward us solely for our faithfulness. Unhappily I chose for my text a part of the eighteenth verse of the seventh chapter of Romans which reads, " For to will is present with me; but how to perform that which is good I find not." The relatives heard nothing beyond the text, and as soon as the burial was over proceeded to raise such a commotion that it almost seemed that it would be necessary for me to leave town at once. But time gradually softened their feelings and in after years I had no firmer friends than they were. Months afterwards, however, I had to spend considerable time and skill in convincing one of the most prominent of them that I did not mean to " hit them in the text."

It is proper that I should say a word about my associates in the ministry. Nearly all the Congregational churches of the county were small, but they all paid larger salaries than that which I received. These churches were served by a noble and highly educated ministry with which it was a great privilege to be associated. We assisted each other in many ways, in the winter season holding what were called "circular conferences," in which we went in considerable numbers to each other's parishes and held meetings for two or three days during the middle of the week. Thus we all became well acquainted with each other and with our various parishes. Sometimes I would drive off through the snow forty miles in the winter to attend such meetings. The ministers were nearly all graduates of college and of a theological seminary, and made Hebrew and Greek the basis of their interpretation of Scripture. Their society was a constant stimulus. I could not but be somewhat flattered when at one time with Mrs. Wright I was compelled by a snowstorm on a forty-mile drive in the winter to turn in to the hospitable parsonage of Father Dougherty (on whom Vermont University conferred the degree of D. D.) and seek shelter, to have him give thanks, saying that the best culture his family received was by contact with the clergymen and their families whom he was permitted to entertain.

In the end the smallness of my salary proved a blessing to me, and I hope to the world. We lived comfortably, notwithstanding war prices. Gold went up to 285 premium, and calico cloth accordingly, plain prints selling at fifty cents a yard. But we commenced housekeeping with a good supply of sheets and clothing, which lasted until prices began to come down. Besides, I made one speculative venture that netted me something. I bought a kitchen stove for seven and a half dollars when we began housekeeping. Three years later when I wanted to get a "Stewart stove" at the discount which the inventor offered to ministers, I sold the kitchen stove which had been in constant use all the time since it was purchased, and received eleven dollars and a half for it. This was the only profitable speculative venture I ever made. Besides, my salary was raised at last to five hundred and fifty dollars, but was never fully collected. I was like one of my neighboring pastors who begged his people not to raise his salary again, he had so much trouble in collecting the smaller amount.

The real advantage of my smaller salary was that I had to make a virtue of necessity and dispense with expensive vacations, and get my recreation in studying the topography and geology of the interesting region in the vicinity. With my horse I drove extensively over the Green Mountains and into the French settlements in the broad plain of the lower St. Lawrence River in Quebec. I also toured afoot with companions the region of the Adirondacks, on the western side of Lake Champlain. The result was that I became something of a local authority on the glacial deposits of a most interesting region. If I had only known as much about the subject then as later study has brought to light it would have, added immensely to the joy of those years. But that was impossible at that time. It is in place here, however, to anticipate and tell what I see there now in light of later investigations.

Bakersfield village is built on a beautiful level-topped sand deposit six hundred feet above the sea, covering about a square mile. This breaks off abruptly on both sides, and wells a hundred feet deep do not reach the bottom of the deposit. (Similar plains I had been familiar with in my boyhood near the south

end of Lake Champlain in Castleton, Fairhaven, and
Westhaven, on the east side of the Lake.)   There was
also an adjoining area about as large which was dotted
over with " kettle holes," and running into it from the
north a well-defined "esker" a mile or more in
length.   All this was a mystery to me and to all
geologists at that time, but as interpreted by investigations which I afterwards set in motion in my next
parish,[1] had significance as follows:

The glacial ice which came down from Labrador,
on crossing the St. Lawrence Valley, was for a time
obstructed by the mountains of northern Vermont and
by the Adirondacks in New York, and pressed down
through the valley of Lake Champlain in a great glacial
tongue, fifty or sixty miles wide.   Finally, however,
it overflowed, and extended as far south as New York
City, having a depth of more than one mile over the
northern part of New England, thus covering the
highest mountains of that region.   But so far all this
had nothing to do with the gravel terraces at Bakersfield, which belong to the closing stages of the period.

In the light of our present knowledge of the progress of events during the recession of the continental
glacier, we interpret the facts as follows.   The retreat of the ice was accompanied both by the with-
drawal of the southern front, and by the lowering of
the surface by melting.   Thus the mountain tops

would at length reappear above the glacial tongue
which filled the Champlain Valley. One result of
this would be that the reflected heat of the sunshine
from the mountain sides would make the ice lower
at the margins than in the middle, so that there would
be established lines of drainage along the sides, with
the ice maintaining the level on one side of the stream
and the mountain on the other. Marginal lakes would
likewise be formed at these levels on the serrated flanks
of the mountains. And such are found on the flanks
of the Green Mountains up to a level of one thousand
feet or more. At the time when I became familiar
with these gravel terraces it was generally supposed
that they indicated a former submergence to that extent below the ocean, and hence were called "marine
terraces." If I had only known their proper explanation during those first ten years of my ministerial
labor it would have lent a wonderful charm to the
recreation of vacations and blue Mondays, and would
have afforded me abundant material to interest the
members of my parish both young and old.

It is thought of this, largely, that moves me to
write these simple annals of my life. The mental
picture which now comes up to my mind of the slow
but majestic advance of this mighty engine of erosion
as it filled the St. Lawrence Valley, projected itself
southward between .the Green Mountains and the

Adirondacks, and finally overwhelmed their summits (leaving bowlders on the top of Mt. Washington more than a mile above sea level), until it reached Staten Island beyond New York City, piling up immense moraines there and on Long Island out of the débris which it had gathered in its course—this picture is equalled only by that of the glacial lakes, streams, and deltas which marked its retreat and decline. The sandy plain about Saratoga where Burgoyne struggled amid innumerable ravines which small streams had worn in it, similar plains about my early home in Fairhaven, Castleton, and Rutland, and innumerable others with which I became familiar, all along the western flank of the Green Mountains, and which so often served for beautiful village sites, are all now seen to be the products of this slow-moving, complicated, but most majestic cause. The interpretation of such natural phenomena by teachers and pastors to their pupils and parishioners should be regarded as a bounden duty.

CHAPTER IV

TEN YE.ARS AT ANDOVER

PROVIDENCE played a principal part in my removal to another field of labor. Friends had often spoken to me of vacant parishes which seemed to offer wider opportunities than those in Bakersfield, together with a larger salary. And now as I was entering on the tenth year of my ministry I began to consider such openings. In the spring of 1872 an invitation came from a parish in Michigan which I had conditionally promised to accept. But meanwhile I was invited by one of my warmest personal friends (Rev. Edwin S. Williams) to preach one Sunday for him in his pulpit in Andover, Massachusetts. On responding to his request I found, when on the ground, that my friend was soon to leave the parish for another field and wished to get me before them as a candidate to succeed him, so that there might not be any interregnum. The result was that a call came from the church almost immediately. Delay in the mails caused by a terrible snowstorm prevented the. Michigan call from reaching me till after I had accepted that from Andover. On this hung all my future career. I went to Andover instead of to Michigan, and was at once plunged into the midst of theological and scientific discussions that have given character to all my subsequent labors and investigations.

The Free Church in Andover to which I came was in most respects an ideal field. It had in it the rich manufacturing families of the town who were as devoted to the welfare of the church and society as they were to their business. Some members of these families were Harvard College graduates, among them a young retired Congregational clergyman, Rev. Francis Howe Johnson, one of the profoundest thinkers on the ultimate facts of Theism, and author of two volumes ("What is Reality?" and "God in Evolution: A Pragmatic Study of Theology"), deserving of the attention of all scholars. His friendship and advice played a very important part in furthering and directing my investigations and study during my eventful years in Andover. Nearly half of the congregation were Scotch workmen skilled in the manufacture of flax threads; while a third were from old-time New England families living both in the village and on the farms surrounding it. The inmates of the poorhouse also belonged to the parish and always formed a part of the congregation. For nearly ten years the gospel as I preached it seemed to satisfy all these classes equally well, and the church continued to thrive and increase, and ever since has been a growing power in the community, thus demonstrating that the gospel is addressed to the "common man" and not to the classes into which society is divided.

My wealthy parishioners consisted of members of the Smith & Dove Manufacturing Company. The success of this company and the relation of its members to their working people and to the community in general, have served to form, to a large degree, my views concerning the relations of capital to labor. Mr. John Smith, the senior partner, came from Scotland in 1816, getting employment as a journeyman machinist in Medway, Massachusetts. In 1824 he came to Andover and in company with one or two others set up a manufactory for cotton machinery. Meantime his brother Peter had joined him in 1822, and in 1833 they persuaded a young countryman of inventive genius, who had just come to America, to join them in their work. This was John Dove. The three directed their energies to the manufacture of flax yarns, including shoe thread, then coming more and more into demand. Gradually their products attained such a reputation that they could dispense with selling agents, since orders came to them direct from those who had learned to trust their honor and skill in producing goods that were in demand. Thus it was difficult for them to avoid becoming rich, as new com-

peting firms could with difficulty earn the confidence
that belonged to the good name of the Smith & Dove
Manufacturing Company.   During my pastorate the
company annually consumed 2,000,000 pounds of flax
and flax tow, importing much of it from Archangel,
the freight from there to Boston being somewhat less
than from Buffalo to Boston.   They employed about
three hundred operatives, with whom their relations
were most cordial.   Especially do I remember the
genial cordiality of Mr. Joseph W. Smith, who succeeded his father, and who, though not born in Scotland, preserved the flavor of Scotch humor even better
than those who were native born.   The members of
these families were always present at the church services and identified themselves with all the interests of
the town.   Now for seventy-five years this firm has
continued business through all the fluctuations of the
market without failure, or interruption, giving continuous employment to a large number of workmen,
from whose families have gone forth most worthy
and successful members into all ranks of society.   It
is difficult to see how any better results could have
been produced through any system of communism that
interfered with the rights of private property and
chilled the ardor of private enterprise.

At that time the Andover Theological Seminary
still maintained its preëminence among the theological

forces that had dominated the country for three-quarters of a century. Edwards A. Park, the prince of American theologians and preachers, was then in his prime. Austin Phelps, the prince of homiletical teachers, was at his post, and his daughter, Elizabeth Stuart Phelps, was just beginning her remarkable literary career, injecting her keen criticisms of the current theology into the popular literature of the time. John Henry Thayer was hard at work on his grammar and lexicon of the New Testament. Charles M. Mead was concentrating his metaphysical mind upon the problems of the Old Testament, and preparing himself to answer the destructive critics of the Old Testament by issuing, in both English and German under the pseudonym of MacRealsham, a documentary theory of the origin of the book of Romans which was as convincing as the theory of the higher critics that the Pentateuch was a combination of unconnected documents, put together by skillful editors long after the occurrence of the events. Wesley Churchill was charming the world with his dramatic readings, and Selah Merrill was well along in his preparation for his work in Assyriology and Biblical Archæology. In the Andover Association of Congregational ministers, as in that of Franklin County, Vermont, I enjoyed the privilege of consorting with a highly educated body of men. The study of the Hebrew Bible was carried on continuously,

esulting among other things in a valuable commentary
in the book of Esther. The names of Street, Baker,
Greene, Coit, Charles Smith, W. E. Park, Haley,
I. H. Barrows, Munger, and J. H. Merrill are among
hose whose stimulus to study was inspiring. The
Bibliotheca Sacra, under the editorship of Professor
Park had for thirty years been the main scholarly
expounder of the New England theology, and was the
representative of the two thousand living Andover
graduates scattered all over the world. But the influence of Darwinism, and of the so-called liberalizing
tendencies of the time, was pressing for attention, and
naturally I was soon drawn into the vortex of discussion, a vortex from which I have not yet emerged.

Before going to Andover my glacial studies had attracted the attention of Professor Charles Hitchcock,
then of Dartmouth College, and he had been in correspondence with me concerning the glacial phenomena
of northern Vermont. Knowledge of my interest in
geological matters had preceded me. But I was
commiserated by one of the older ministers on having
come to a region which had nothing in it of general
geological interest. It soon developed, however, that
I had been put down where one of the most important
and interesting problems in glacial geology presented
itself at the very back door of the Free Church par-

sonage. This problem pertained to the remarkable congeries of gravel ridges locally known as Indian Ridge. A paper on this ridge had been presented by President Hitchcock, father of Professor Charles Hitchcock, to the American Association of Geologists and Naturalists in 1842. This paper was substantially reproduced in the Geology published by President Hitchcock and studied by our class in college. It turned out that this was the only geological problem of importance that I could have attacked with any probability of finding a satisfactory original solution. On writing to Professor Hitchcock about it, he expressed gratification that it was being studied anew; but he believed the ridge to be of marine origin, as his father and more lately James Geikie, writing of similar ridges in Scotland and Ireland, had supposed. Observations carried on chiefly on " blue Mondays," soon showed that this explanation did not cover all the facts. So I kept on for three years until a new theory was established to my own satisfaction, and I was ready to bring it before the public. In all this I had the backing of my highly educated parishioners, especially of Mr. George W. W. Dove, who contributed his skill as a draughtsman in putting my paper into more intelligible form than I could have done myself.

The theory, which has since been universally ac-

cepted, connects the ridges with the closing stages of
the great Ice age, when the surface of the continental
ice sheet had been lowered, by melting, to near the
land surface, leaving much stagnant ice in the hol-
lows and depressions, partially to determine the course
of the superabundant drainage waters flowing off toward the sea.   In the process of this long-continued
melting of the ice surface, the gravel incorporated into
the moving mass accumulated in large quantities on
the surface, and was consequently swept into the channels in the ice and under it by the floods which were
seeking egress.   Thus the ridges would be somewhat
independent of the lines of drainage as determined by
the land surface alone, and might undulate over small
elevations and depressions.   After having traced this
ridge over the undulating country from Boston up
into New Hampshire for a total distance of thirty or
forty miles, I was ready to present my theory to the
scientific public.   This was first done before the Essex Institute of Salem, Massachusetts, one of the most
venerable and cultivated scientific associations of the
country.   This was in 1875, and the report may be
found in the minutes of the Association for that year.
My theory received almost immediate confirmation in
what is thought to be the best proof of a supposition
dealing with physical forces.   For on that occasion I
ventured to prophesy by it.   I said that if it was

true there should be a parallel line of gravel ridges presenting corresponding phenomena, running northward from the vicinity of Salem into New Hampshire, and asked for information of such ridges. Within two weeks such a parallel line of ridges was established for a distance of fifty or sixty miles, and I was able at once to examine it at various points.

Thus encouraged, I was invited to present a more formal paper on the subject before the Boston Society of Natural History, which was composed of the most eminent scientific authorities of Boston and Cambridge. The paper was at once accepted for publication in the proceedings of the Society, under the title " Some Remarkable Gravel Ridges in the Merrimack Valley." This appeared in the volume for 1876.

My paper was brought to the attention of scientific men in an unexpected and interesting way, by a chance meeting with Clarence King, just back from his geological survey of the fortieth parallel. I was on the way with Mr. George Dove to visit in South Carolina the phosphate mines of the company to which he belonged, and when passing through New York City dropped into their office there, just as Mr. King came in, and was introduced to him. The proof of my paper had been given me as I was leaving home, so that I had it with me. On speaking to Mr. King about it he requested to see it, and on looking it over said at once that my explanation was correct, and that as soon as he returned to his room he would write out for me, to incorporate in the paper, observations which he had recently made in the Cascade Mountains of California, which completely confirmed my theory. At the same time he told me of his discovery but a short time before of the great terminal moraine south of the Massachusetts coast, which Dana and Lesley had recently said did not exist. But he said there could be no doubt that the Elizabeth Islands southwest of Woods Holl were part of a genuine terminal moraine; and in the communication which he wrote out for me to incorporate in my paper all these facts were stated, thus giving me an initial endorsement which at once brought my work to the notice of glacial geologists the world over. But for this there is no knowing whether my paper would have attracted much attention.

Very early in my stay in Andover Professor Park associated me with him in the preparation of articles for the *Bibliotheca Sacra*. The first work he requested me to undertake was to show how Infant Baptism could be made in practice to consist with the Congregational principle of a " regenerate church membership." This discussion was made incumbent by various challenges of distinguished Baptists, calling attention to the apparent inconsistency of applying a rite to persons in anticipation of their having the character which the rite assumed them to have. The task was a difficult one, and I fear my efforts were not productive in changing the opinion of our opponents. But I have the satisfaction of knowing that in the two articles which I prepared the discussion was carried on in a courteous spirit, and that I did not belittle the arguments by which the Baptists defend their practice of close communion, and their neglect of infant baptism. For the ordinances are but means to an end, and where the end is of transcendent importance we may be allowed to differ with respect to the means which contribute to that end.

Then Professor Park wished me to prepare a series of articles stating the arguments for and against Darwinism, and showing the bearing of that theory upon the doctrine of design in nature, and upon theological opinions in general. Fortunately my readiness to undertake this work was greatly facilitated by the friendship, to which I have already referred, of Professor Asa Gray, who in addition to his regular work in botany had been foremost in contending that the doctrine of design in nature was not at all endangered by Darwinism, and who, as already remarked, after reading my article in the *New Englander*, on the " Ground of Confidence in Inductive Reasoning," had requested my acquaintance. This I cheerfully granted, and he became from that time like a father to me in the work in which I was engaged. It was enough for me that these articles on Darwinism in the *Bibliotheca Sacra* met his approval, and were indebted to him for much of their form of statement. It was gratifying, also, to have a letter from Darwin, written in his own hand, in which he said that the statement of his theory "was powerfully written and most clear," and requested me to send him the following article in which objections were to be presented.

These articles maintained what has been more and more evident as attention has been given to the subject, that the observed variations in both plants and animals are much greater than Darwin had supposed, and that so many correlated variations had to take place at once to make any one variation an advantage, that nothing less than design either wrought into the original plan, or added by way of increment, could account for the facts. From the theological side it was maintained that Calvinism and Darwinism had so many points in common that theologians could not consistently cast stones at the men of science favoring a scheme in which "predestination and foreordination" were salient features. In fact, from a philosophical point of view, Darwinism has all the unlovely characteristics of hyper-Calvinism without any of the

redeeming remedial features inherent in the Calvin-
istic system. Pure Darwinism leaves no place for the
gospel. These essays were subsequently republished
in a volume, together with the essay on the " Ground
of Confidence in Inductive Reasoning," and an essay
on " The Antiquity of Man," dealing especially with
the evidence of glacial man in America, also an essay
on " The Relation of the Bible to Science." From a
copy owned by Henry Ward Beecher, which has fallen into my hands, I have found from his annotations
that he had read the book carefully, and been duly
influenced by it.[1]

My scientific associations during all the period of
my stay in Andover were of the greatest value to me.
The leading men of science in the vicinity of Boston
were connected with the Boston Society of Natural
History, and I was honored by being made for some
years one of its directors. Among the distinguished
men of science with whom I was associated in the
Boston Society of Natural History, and who gave me
aid and inspiration, were the following: Alexander
Agassiz, J. A. Allen, G. H. Barton, T. T. Bouvé,
L. S. Burbank, E. Burgess, W. O. Crosby, W. M.
Davis, W. G. Farlow, J. W. Fewkes, A. W. Gra-
bau, Asa Gray, H. W. Haynes, Alpheus Hyatt, J. E.
Jeffries, J. Marcou, C. S. Minot, E. S. Morse, W.
H. Niles, T. B. Perry, F. W. Putnam, W. B. Rogers,

S. H. Scudder, N. S. Shaler, M. E. Wadsworth, J. D. Whitney, J. B. Woodworth, and J. Wyman.

In glacial studies, my chief coadjutors were Mr. Warren Upham, of the New Hampshire Geological Survey, and Professor George H. Stone, of Kent's Hill, Maine. Taking up my clue, Professor Stone soon mapped a series of fifteen or twenty eskers, or "kames" as they were then called, parallel to mine in eastern Massachusetts, extending to the New Brunswick line. Later he published a Monograph on the glacial deposits of Maine, for the United States Geological Survey. Mr. Upham, not only published elaborately on the eskers of New Hampshire, but, taking up the clue to the great terminal moraine furnished me by Clarence King, located in a marvellously short time the whole moraine [1] along the south shore of New England, and through Long Island. It is interesting to note, however, that at this time there was considerable hesitation about accepting the reality both of eskers and of terminal moraines. Professor Dana had another explanation for the gravel ridges which Mr. Upham had described in the Connecticut Valley, and had it already in print in the *American Journal of Science,* but before the number was issued, he came to Andover to look over the field with me. That satisfied him, and he added an appendix of a few lines to his destructive article, saying that my gravel ridges were eskers without doubt.

About this time Dr. C. C. Abbott, of Trenton, New Jersey, was reporting the discovery of palæolithic implements in the gravel terrace on which the city of Trenton is built. From all reports it seemed that his discoveries were similar in significance to those made in France by Boucher de Perthes and others, in the valley of the Somme. Professor F. W. Putnam and Professor Gray suggested to me that I should go to Trenton to see what light my knowledge of glacial gravels might shed on the question of the age of Abbott's implements. Accordingly I went to Trenton in company with Professor Boyd Dawkins, one of the most prominent of the authorities on the prehistoric antiquities of Great Britain, and with Professor Henry W. Haynes, one of the best qualified authorities on the subject in America. We were joined in Trenton by Henry Carvill Lewis of Philadelphia, whom I had interested in the subject a short time before. This visit to Trenton under the direction of Dr. Abbott, brought evidence of the clearest character of the existence of man on this continent, as well as in Europe, before the close of the Glacial epoch, and so gave new zest to my investigations, since now glacial studies touched on the theological and Biblical questions in which I was primarily interested. I will say more

on this point later.   But here it is proper to remark
that scarcely a year has passed since, that I have not
·visited Dr. Abbott, and his coadjutor, Mr. Ernest
Volk, to see for myself the discoveries which they
were making, and twice I have spent a week at a
time in Trenton, conducting independent investigations there with a committee of the American Associa·
tion for the Advancement of Science.

During the later part of my stay in Andover it was
suggested to me both by Professor Asa Gray and by
the Andover professors that my familiarity with
science and the Bible gave me an opportunity to write
a book on the evidences of Christianity which would
meet a deeply felt want.   The result was "The
Logic of Christian Evidences," in which I endeavored
to apply the principles of inductive logic to the evidences of Christianity in the same rigorous manner in
which they were being applied to the more indefinite
of the natural sciences, such as geology and biology.
The first part of the book was devoted to illustrations
of what constitutes proof in the various sciences; the
second part, to the consideration of Theism and
Christianity, in which my studies of Darwinism were
used to advantage in discussing the doctrine of design; the third part, to the specific evidences of the
genuineness and authority of the New Testament.
Professor John Henry Thayer offered to take the

manuscript, when it was finished, to the Appletons, and give to them his endorsement as to its value. But they declined to publish, saying that although it was an ably written book, they did not think it would be profitable to the publishers; for, they wrote, " those who believe in Christianity do not need it, and those who do not believe in Christianity will not read it." Whereupon it was given to Warren F. Draper, the Andover publisher, who issued it in 1880. Suffice it to say that the book met with a large immediate sale, and has continued to sell up to the present time, six editions having been issued. Professor Otto Zöckler of Germany spoke of it as deserving " to be conspicuously mentioned." Dr. Thomas Hill, one-time President of Harvard University, pronounced it " a remarkable and remarkably successful attempt to condense a library into a small volume." Mr. Draper advertised that President Hill said it was a "success-ful attempt," etc. But I called his attention to this as another illustration of the fact that strong adjectives often weakened the positive statements to which they were prefixed. He did not say a " successful attempt," but only a " remarkably successful attempt."

In the spring of 1881 Professor J. P. Lesley, direc-tor of the Second Geological Survey of Pennsylvania, asked Mr. Henry Carvill Lewis and me to trace the

terminal moraine of the great Ice age across that State.
He said that he did not believe there was any well-
marked moraine, but. he wanted the facts known and
put on record among the results of his survey. We
were to have our expenses paid, but were to offer our
services gratuitously. Accordingly we set about the
work as soon as my summer vacation began, which
was generously extended somewhat by my church.
Taking up the line on the Delaware River a little
above Easton, where Professor George H. Cook, of
the Geological Survey of New Jersey had left it, we
prosecuted our investigations continuously throughout
the summer until the work was nearly completed.
Finding where the southern limits of northern bowlders, scratched stones and . surfaces, and unstratified
transported material ended, we proceeded to drive in
and out over every road, marking the limit as we
went along. We thus surveyed a belt of territory
across the State about twenty miles in width, and
much to Professor Lesley's delight, made our report
fixing the line that is shown on all maps of glacial
phenomena covering that State. Our report, prepared by Mr. Lewis, constitutes volume Z of the
elaborate report of the Second Geological Survey of the
State, and was entitled " The Terminal Moraine in
Pennsylvania and Western New York," to which is
appended " The Terminal Moraine in Ohio and

Kentucky, by G. F. Wright," thus including some of my later work which was done before the Pennsylvania report was published.

Professor Lesley was partly right and partly wrong in his surmises. The terminal moraine which we traced did not mark the extreme limit of the ice sheet in Pennsylvania. It was, however, a genuine moraine of the latter part of the Glacial epoch, now spoken of as the Wisconsin episode. Before we had finished our survey we perceived that there was a border covered with scattered glacial marks extending an indefinite distance farther south than our moraine. This we denominated " the fringe." Later authorities (we never could see why) objected to that word so strongly that we have adopted their word, " attenuated border." But in my subsequent explorations west of Pennsylvania (of which I will speak later) I delineated the limit of this attenuated border, while Professor E. H. Williams has prepared an elaborate report, begun at my suggestion, on the attenuated border of glacial action in the State. One of the most striking things revealed by our survey was that the glacial border is very irregular. In the eastern part of the State it is as far south as the latitude of New York City, while south of Buffalo it has swung as far north as Salamanca in New York State; whence it runs southwest as far as Cincinnati.

CHAPTER V.

TRANSFER TO OBERLIN

ANOTHER of the great turning points in my life occurred at this time. I had been invited a year before to take the chair of New Testament Language and Literature, to succeed my old and beloved Professor Morgan, in Oberlin Theological Seminary. At that time, for various reasons, I declined the invitation. But now, partly in view of the approaching theological convulsion which I dimly discerned as rising above the horizon in Andover, I wrote to President Fairchild that if the chair was not yet filled I would reconsider my decision. An immediate repetition of the call came. I am not much given to following vague impressions that come unbidden into the mind; but in this case such an impression, of which I have never before spoken, came upon me at a definite time and place as I was one day, in the early spring of that year, walking past the Memorial Library toward home. The impression was so strong, that, without being able to give any adequate reason for it, I wrote as I did to President Fairchild.

And hereby hangs a tale. Professor Dana expostulated with me for leaving the East, where I had made my scientific reputation, and going so far away from the leading centers of scientific investigation. But it soon developed, that the only place in the world where I could have carried on my glacial investigations successfully was again unexpectedly opened to me. The Western Reserve Historical Society of Cleveland had for its presiding genius Judge C. C. Baldwin, a man of remarkable breadth of view, and deeply devoted to the propagation of the higher interests of his city and state. Professor Charles Fairchild was the financial agent of Oberlin College, and was on the lookout for fields of labor in which the various professors might distinguish themselves. Rev. Charles Collins was pastor of the Plymouth Congregational Church, of Cleveland, and was thoroughly interested in scientific investigations affecting theological views. When it was brought to the notice of these men that remains of glacial man had been discovered, as we have related, at Trenton, New Jersey, and that I had traced the glacial boundary across Pennsylvania to the Ohio line, they said, " Here is work for the Western Reserve Historical Society. If man was in America during the Glacial epoch, then everything bearing on that epoch has historical significance, and opens a proper field for us to enter." No sooner said than done. Funds were raised to pay my expenses in extending my explorations of the glacial boundary across Ohio and the states farther west. In those days railroad presidents were permitted to give passes to their friends, and my cousin, Jarvis Adams, then President of the New York, Pennsylvania and Ohio R. R., secured passes for me and an assistant over every road from Pittsburgh to St. Louis. My services were gratuitous.

Space will not permit me to go into details concerning the prosecution of the work that now opened so auspiciously. Suffice it to say that for three years it occupied the long vacations, of about four months each. The work was continued as in Pennsylvania, and like the investigations in that State was beset with many difficulties, because of the irregularity of the line. For days at a time the line would be found to run in a southwesterly direction, as in western Pennsylvania and southern Ohio, then it would turn directly westward, or, as in eastern Indiana, directly to the north to make a great unexpected loop. Thus prophecy of the direction the line would take often led us astray, and sent us forward to waste days either in or out of the line before we found the real margin. The vagaries of our wanderings often greatly mystified the people. At one time we were gone so long with the livery rig, and our whereabouts was so unknown, that advertisements were out for us as horse thieves. At another time it was supposed that we were advance agents of a circus, going ahead to put up advertisements. As such we were favored by the livery men, as belonging to a class that liberally patronized their business and paid well for the services rendered. At another time we were taken for lightning rod agents, in a region where the buildings were provided with gilt-top rods projecting from each end of the roof gables without any ground connection — the theory being that the lightning would run down one end and go off into the sky at the other end. We lived with the people, and were well taken care of, so that the work was a real and profitable vacation. Thus I obtained a knowledge, incidentally, of the general geology, the topography, the botany, and the social conditions characterizing a belt of territory, twenty miles wide, extending from the Atlantic Ocean to the Mississippi River. The livery horses were all faithful, the people all obliging so that my respect for both human nature and horse nature was raised to a high degree. The nearest to real danger which I ever came was at a small settlement in Indiana called "Lick Skillet," in the region made celebrated by Eggleston's "Hoosier Schoolmaster." On reaching that place I was ill and needed to consult a physician. But the only sign to be found was "Sam Jones, Physician and Undertaker." I gave him a wide berth, and drove on to the next settlement.

As my explorations proceeded, great interest was shown in Cleveland, where large audiences gathered to hear my annual reports. Professor Dana published articles with maps in the *American Journal of Science,* and the Boston Society of Natural History received the reports which I personally made to them as being a continuation of the work which they had had the honor of first recognizing and endorsing. Some said it was work that anybody could have done and required only that a person keep right on to a finish. And that was what I did. Some said that there was no more interest attaching to the marginal deposits than to any portion of the glaciated region above the border. This I did not dispute. The fact remains, however, that the establishing of the actual limit of the advance of the continental glacier has furnished a basis for all subsequent investigations, besides bringing to light a great variety of facts which are obscured above the line by the complicated movements of the ice during various episodes of advance and retreat. The irregularity of the line traced can be studied on any of the maps showing the limits of glaciation in America.

CHAPTER VI

SIGNIFICANCE OF GLACIAL PHENOMENA

THE work of determining the glacial boundary west of the Mississippi has been carried on by a number of field workers; but I have familiarized myself with the greater part of the ground, so that I have personal knowledge of the field nearly everywhere across the continent. Since the determination of the southern boundary of the entire glaciated area in North America, an immense amount of expert work has been done by a large number of investigators in all the region between the boundary and the North Pole. No other scientific subject has so continued to occupy investigators, and to interest the public, as this has done.

Especially productive have been the investigations of Robert Bell, G. Bownocker, A. P. Brigham, Samuel Calvin, R. Chalmers, T. C. Chamberlin, A. T. Coleman, W. O. Crosby, W. M. Davis, G. M. Dawson, B. K. Emerson, H. L. Fairchild, Gerard Fowke, G. K. Gilbert, A. W. Grabau, O. H. Hershey, C. H. Hitchcock, J. F. Kemp, Joseph LeConte, Frank Leverett, E. H. Mudge, Miss Luella A. Owen, Harry

F. Reid, I. C. Russell, R. D. Salisbury, J. W. Spencer, G. H. Stone, R. S. Tarr, F. B. Taylor, W. G. Tight, J. E. Todd, J. B. Tyrrell, Warren Upham, E. H. Williams, N. H. Winchell, and J. B. Woodworth.

The expectations of the Western Reserve Historical Society in promoting the interests to which they were devoted, were amply met. The determination of the limits of ice extension across the Mississippi Valley brought to light a large number of localities in which the conditions were similar to those in northern France and in Trenton, New Jersey, where palæolithic implements had been found, so that local observers were induced to be on the lookout for similar discoveries here. These localities were on those streams through which the enormous floods accompanying the final melting of the ice poured forth, depositing gravel terraces far above the reach of any present floods. In almost every instance these terraces are nearly one hundred feet above the present flood plains of the streams. In due time implements were found in these undisturbed gravels, by Mr. Sam Houston at Brilliant, near Steubenville, in the gravel terrace on the Ohio River; by Mr. W. C. Mills, the present accomplished Curator of the Ohio State Archæological and Historical Society, at New Comerstown, on the Tuscarawas River; and by Dr. C. L. Metz, Professor Putnam's colaborer, at Loveland and

Madisonville on the Little Miami River, a short distance above Cincinnati. Later, similar discoveries were made by Miss Babbitt on the Mississippi River at Little Falls, Minnesota; while human bones, in similar deposits, have been found on the Missouri River at Lansing, Kansas, and at Florence, a little above Omaha, Nebraska.

One of my discoveries, which attracted most attention, was, that the ice crossed the Ohio River at Cincinnati and formed a dam five hundred feet high, sufficient to raise the water enough to submerge Pittsburgh three hundred feet, though several hundred miles distant. This discovery was first presented at the meeting of the American Association for the Advancement of Science at Minneapolis in 1883, where Professor I. C. White furnished facts concerning the horizontal clay terraces extending for a hundred miles up the Monongahela River south of Pittsburgh, indicating standing water there at the height supposed. When this evidence was presented it brought Professor Lesley to his feet to express his delight that at last evidence had been produced to establish such an obstruction to the drainage of the Ohio Valley. He said that several years before he had observed high-level terraces in the streams west of the Alleghany Mountains and had attributed them to a general subsidence of the whole region, permitting ocean waters

to form shore lines at that elevation on the flanks of
the mountains. But later, on finding that there were
no such high-level terraces on the eastern flanks of the
Alleghanies, he had been compelled to abandon his
theory, and to cancel all that he had written about
them. Since then he had been looking for some explanation, and "now," said he, "Providence has provided it and Wright's dam will explain everything."
This endorsement gave the Cincinnati dam a notoriety
that has been somewhat embarrassing, since it raised
extravagant expectations of finding its shore lines all
along up the Ohio Valley. As these did not everywhere appear, there was a tendency to discredit the
dam altogether. But such negative testimony was not
of much value, since the dam was obviously of rather
short continuance.

But most important of all were the modifications of
the original theory, arising from facts which came to
light concerning the formation of the channel of the
present Ohio River. It appeared that the original
drainage of the upper Ohio, and its tributaries above
Pittsburgh, was into the St. Lawrence Valley to the
north; so that when the glacial ice in its southern
progress reached the highlands of Pennsylvania and
Ohio, the drainage was reversed,—temporary dams
raising the water high enough to run over the cols
between the ramifying tributaries, and, after wear-

ing them down, to produce the present tortuous channel of the Ohio. Thus it became apparent that the clay terraces on the Monongahela described by I. C. White were the result of the damming up of the outlets of the original Allegheny and the Monongahela River, causing the water to stand at the level of those terraces until the cols separating their valleys from those farther down were lowered sufficiently to constitute a continuous channel. This, however, does not do away with the Cincinnati dam. For when at last the ice reached Cincinnati and crossed over into Kentucky, as all agree that it did, there was a dam there, though of shorter duration than that in the upper portions of the valley. The ice dam at Cincinnati still remains one of the most spectacular of the phenomena of the great Ice age in North America.

My report to the Western Reserve Historical Society, on " The Glacial Boundary in Ohio, Indiana and Kentucky " was published in 1884. After that, 1 was commissioned by the United States Geological Survey to complete the survey to the Mississippi River, to revise as much of my previous work as was necessary, and to publish the whole results as a Government document. This appeared in 1890 as Bulletin No. 58, and was entitled " The Glacial Boundary in Western Pennsylvania, Ohio, Kentucky, Indiana, and Illinois."

In 1886, through the advice of Mr. Elisha Gray, of electrical fame, who partly bore the expense of the expedition, I went to Alaska and spent a month at the foot of the great Muir Glacier. I had as companions my classmate Rev. J. L. Patton and S. Prentiss Baldwin, a youth of seventeen years, in rather delicate health. With Mr. Baldwin this was the beginning of a lifelong friendship and coöperation in geological studies. The Muir Glacier had been discovered a few years before by Mr. John Muir in company with Rev. Mr. Young, a Presbyterian missionary. At the time of our visit, tourist steamers had for two or three years been going up to the glacier to remain a few hours and then return. We were the first to spend any length of time in studying it. It was four years later that any one else visited it (or any other Alaskan glacier) to give it scientific attention, so that we had a monopoly of knowledge on the subject for that time, which proved of great advantage to me.

Two incidents having no bearing on our scientific investigations, nevertheless made such an impression on me that I cannot forbear mentioning them. Mr. Baldwin was a member of the Agassiz Club, and so was averse to killing any birds except for scientific purposes. But he thought it proper to collect specimens of birds to stuff for a museum. One morning

I saw him trying to shoot some of the small birds that flitted about our tent; but was surprised to see the birds abandon their resting place and light on the gun that was aimed at them, so little did they know of the cruel nature of the beings that were for the first time visiting the region. This was too much for Mr. Baldwin. He let the confiding little creatures live, and put up his gun without any further attempts to stock a museum.

The other incident related to a Creed, which we drew out of our uneducated Indian helper named Jake. We had two Indians to help us, one, named Jackson, who could speak English indifferently, and so could interpret Jake's language for us. We endeavored to rest on Sunday, and went through the formality of some sort of a religious service each week. On one of these occasions we drew from Jake his religious creed, which, as interpreted by Jackson, was as follows:—

1. I believe that God is the Boss of us fellers, and every man all.

2. I believe that God loves us fellers and every man all.

3. I feel in my heart that I love God. I love my brother, my sister, every man all.

4. I wish every man loved Jesus, then he good, no bad, no fight.

Jake had made no profession of religion, but this much he had absorbed from the godly life of a missionary (Rev. Mr. Corleis, of Philadelphia), who had spent a single winter with his tribe in southeastern Alaska. We have recommended this creed for incorporation in future revisions of the Presbyterian Confession.

The facts which we collected concerning the Muir Glacier proved to be of the greatest interest and importance, for the light which they shed on theories concerning the Glacial epoch. At that time this was the largest glacier, outside of Greenland, which had been carefully observed, and at once threw into the shade all that had been inferred from the diminutive Alpine glaciers. The Muir Glacier presented a front more than a mile in width where it entered the head of Muir Inlet, and this was perpendicular in height, more than 300 feet above the water, while the depth of the water, as near the front as the captain dared to sound, was 700 feet, thus presenting a face 1,000 feet high and a mile in width, which was being pushed forward to break off in icebergs of immense size. The calving of each iceberg was accompanied by a tremendous detonation, which reverberated from the lofty mountain side with majestic effect. The noise of these reports was almost continuous. Our measurements established a rate of motion in the center of the glacier, which exceeded anything found elsewhere outside of Greenland. Moreover, we collected evidence that the front of the glacier had withdrawn more than twenty miles in the hundred years which had elapsed since Vancouver visited the region in the latter part of the eighteenth century. My inferences on this point were amply sustained by Professor H. F. Reid, who studied the glacier and the region round about, four years after my visit. Moreover, from surveys made twenty-five years later, it appeared that the recession of the front has continued at about the same rate which we had inferred for the previous century. In 1909 the front was seven miles and a half farther back than it was in 1886 when my photographs were made, while the surface had been lowered, by melting, 700 feet. These facts, as they become known and appreciated, cannot help having great influence in modifying current theories about the time which has elapsed since the ice retired from the glaciated area in the United States and Canada.

CHAPTER VII

RECEPTION OF MY GLACIAL VIEWS

On my return from the Muir Glacier I was invited to give a course of eight lectures before the Lowell Institute in Boston, the subject being " The Ice Age in North America." This at once gave me opportunity to collect all the material which had accumulated during the fifteen years that I had been pursuing the subject, and the liberal honorarium (one thousand dollars) given, furnished me means to go on with further investigations. The lectures met with a very warm reception, being attended by large audiences throughout. Soon after, Mr. Warren Upham, with whom I had been associated so long and intimately in glacial studies, wrote me that for some time he had cherished the plan of writing a book on the Glacial epoch in America. "But now," he said, " it is evident that your observations have covered a so much wider field, that you are the one to write the book, and I will coöperate with you to the extent of my ability." This most generous proposition could but be highly appreciated, especially as at that time Mr. (now Doctor) Upham had been for several years studying the glacial phenomena in Minnesota and adjoining territory, while a member of the geological survey of that State, so that he had a more detailed knowledge of a large section of the glaciated area than anyone else had. It was thus a great advantage that I could associate him with me in the volume which I set out to prepare, by revising and enlarging my Lowell Institute lectures.

"The Ice Age in North America and its Bearings on the Antiquity of Man" was published by D. Appleton and Company in 1889. It formed a book of nearly 700 octavo pages, and was put on the market at five dollars a volume. It met with a large sale at once, and successive editions were called for from time to time, permitting the incorporation of such new material as seemed important. The fifth edition was issued in 1911. This was thoroughly revised and considerably enlarged, among the additions being a bibliography giving the titles of articles that had been published on the subject in the scientific journals since the first edition appeared. Thirty closely printed pages are required for this bibliography. The book aimed to meet both the scientific and popular want, and many things indicate that it has done this fairly well. This the very sale itself would indicate. But two instances of the use of the book furnish interesting confirmation of the fact.

A friend of mine was riding from Buffalo to Albany with a Chicago drummer, and got into conversation with him about the scenery through which they were passing. The drummer had a good many remarks to make that showed knowledge of the country, but he said he was sorry he did not have his guidebook with him, which it appeared was Wright's "Ice Age in North America," which he ordinarily carried for the interesting light it shed on the scenery of all the northern part of the United States.

In 1901, when my son and I had reached Petrograd in our trip across Siberia and Central Asia, we were told by the geologists there that it was important for us to visit Kiev, to see the human relics which Professor Armaschevsky had recently found deeply buried beneath the glacial deposits. We therefore turned aside on our way to Odessa, and visited Kiev without any notice of our intentions having been sent to the Professor. On reaching the city we found our way to the university, where several thousand students were gathered, and, on inquiring for Professor Armaschevsky, were shown to the museum, where, after the door was opened, we were directed to a tall man at work among fossils behind a counter. On approaching him and giving him my card with simply my name and address on it, he, after scanning it closely, without a word, turned around and took down "The

Ice Age in North America," and laid it before me. This was his introduction; for, though he could read English, he could not speak it. Suffice it to say that he immediately secured an interpreter, and put himself at our service for the remainder of the day.

My travels have been somewhat extensive since my exploration of the Muir Glacier; and, it is needless to say, have all been arranged to gather facts bearing on the Glacial epoch, though the incidental opportunities to enlarge the general horizon of my mental vision have been about as great as if that had been the sole object of travel in foreign lands. The college authorities soon after so arranged my teaching term that I had five or six months at my disposal for outside work. This time I scrupulously devoted to the field of investigation which had opened itself before me, and which, I may say, was not merely scientific, but the harmony of science and the Bible, my avocation having attained such manifest importance that in 1892 a special chair was provided for me under the title of the Harmony of Science and Revelation.

The summer of 1890 was spent in the Rocky Mountains and on the Pacific Coast in company with Mr. Prentiss Baldwin. I was induced to take this trip at the suggestion of Charles Francis Adams, who was then president of the Union Pacific railroad. He had been on a visit to the Muir Glacier, and took

with him my "Ice Age in North America." On his
return he stopped off with his staff at Nampa on the
Oregon Short Line, near Boise City. The party arrived there a few days after a remarkable discovery
of a small, well-shaped, though imperfect, clay figurine, had been made by Mr. M. A. Kurtz while driving a well through a thin coating of lava, and about
three hundred feet of sand, clay, and quicksand. This
object was taken with his own hands from the bailer
as it came from the bottom of the six-inch hole which
had been driven. Suffice it to say that Mr. Adams
and several officers of the road who were with him,
who from their training constituted the best jury that
could be obtained by any process of selection, and who
knew all the parties engaged and made all possible
inquiries at the time, were sure that there could be no
mistake about the reported facts. Their interest in
the discovery was such that Mr. Adams wrote to me
about it and told me that if I would go out there and
prosecute further investigations he would give me a
pass for myself and an assistant over the entire railroad system of which he was president. Accordingly
Mr. Baldwin and I set out on a most interesting and
enlightening expedition. We entered Yellowstone
Park from the west, and camped out with the aid of
a single guide while making the tour of the park.
After passing south to the then unfrequented Jack-

son's Hole, where the Snake River takes its rise, and over the Teton Mountains, we followed leisurely down the lava-covered plains of the Snake River Valley, past Shoshone Falls (where we stayed several days), till we reached Nampa. There we found everything to confirm the conclusions of Mr. Adams concerning the Nampa figurine and its significance.

During the remaining part of the season we visited the lower Columbia River, and, going down to California, drove through to the Yosemite from Sonora. At Sonora we had unusual opportunities to verify the reports which Professor J. D. Whitney had brought back concerning the discoveries of human relics beneath the lava deposits under Table Mountain. We also secured there, on the best of evidence, facts about the discovery of a small lava mortar for the grinding of grain and nuts, which has played quite a part in subsequent discussions. This was finally given to us, and is now the property of the Western Reserve Historical Society in Cleveland, Ohio. The genuineness of the Nampa figurine was amply supported by the examination to which it was submitted after it was brought to the notice of Professor F. W. Putnam and others at the East.

The determination of its antiquity, and that of the discoveries under Table Mountain in California, depends on theories concerning the date of the great lava flows which cover vast areas over the Pacific slope. Every investigator of note who has visited the region has been compelled to assign to these deposits a very recent date, geologically speaking. Indeed, it is evident that very extensive lava flows have poured over the Snake River plains within a few hundred years, while extensive volcanic outbursts of Lassen Peak in California, in 1890 and again in 1914, have confirmed Professor J. S. Diller's inference that within two hundred years at least there had been other extensive lava flows in that region, though there had been no tradition of it among the inhabitants. Indeed, such a high authority as the late Alexander Winchell has maintained that there was some causal connection between these great lava flows on the Pacific Coast and the Glacial epoch. Hundreds of thousands of square miles there are covered with recent lava, in some places thousands of feet in thickness. To account for these vast eruptions, Winchell surmised that the weight of the glacial ice over the eastern part of the continent by its pressure squeezed the lava out of great vents, which were opened by it over the Rocky Mountain region, and so brought the latter part, at least, of the lava flows within the Glacial epoch. But, however this may be, the facts indicate a very recent date both for the glacial conditions in the Rocky Mountain region and for the volcanic activity of which there is so much evidence. The specific evidence of the recent date of the deposits in which the Nampa figurine was found is so interesting that I cannot forbear summarizing it here.

The efforts to discredit the genuineness of the Nampa figurine have been wholly based on unverified theoretical considerations. The direct evidence is such as to satisfy any one who is accustomed, as Mr. Adams and his companions were, to weighing direct human testimony. This they considered unassailable. But to those who are not familiar with all the evidence it seems impossible that such a human relic should be found in such a place and in such a way. I have been compelled, therefore, to repeat that the diameter of the sand pump was ample, that other things larger than the figurine were brought up, and that so much material was sucked up from the bottom of the hole that it was not the mere problem of hitting a mark at a venture three hundred feet below the surface, but of gathering material in from considerable distance all round the bottom of the hole. Adequate additional light to remove *a priori* objections was not slow in coming. It came in one of the most instructive and spectacular discoveries which have ever been made in glacial geology, namely, that concerning the past history of Great Salt Lake in Utah, made by

Dr. G. K. Gilbert of the United States Geological Survey.

Mr. Baldwin and I had found inklings of the discovery during our trip down the Snake River, while at Pocatello. This town lies at the junction of the Port Neuf, a very small stream, with the Snake River. South from this point, towards Great Salt Lake, the land rapidly rises into a mountainous region, but to the north the wide lava-covered plain of the Snake River Valley spreads out for many miles. What we discovered was that Pocatello was built on an immense bowlder bed, such as would be brought down the Port Neuf if there were a powerful stream of water flowing through it; while towards the mountains the bed of the stream had been swept clear of the bowlders for a half mile or more. The facts presented a puzzle, which we were unable to solve. So we laid them aside in our minds and notebooks for future light.

Such light was not long in coming. Mr. Gilbert soon after published his Monograph on Lake Bonneville, which is the name given to the enlargement of Great Salt Lake during the Glacial epoch. From this it appeared that during that period of greater precipitation and smaller evaporation over the region, the basin in which Great Salt Lake is situated had filled up till the water in it was 1,000 feet higher than it is now, and that it had enlarged its surface till it covered 20,000 square miles instead of the 2,000 of its present surface. It further appeared that when the water in this basin had reached the 1,000-foot level it began to run over a dirt dam into the Port Neuf towards the Snake River at Pocatello. This dam consisted of débris that had been brought by mountain streams into the lowest pass separating the two valleys, and was 375 feet in thickness, resting on a rock shelf 625 feet above the present level of the lake. Evidently this dirt dam permitted the water, when it overflowed, to open a wide channel so that it poured into the Port Neuf in a tremendous torrent. Mr. Gilbert calculated that it would require twenty-five years for a stream the size of Niagara to draw off the upper 375 feet of water in Lake Bonneville, that poured through the Port Neuf into the Snake River Valley at Pocatello. That is enough. Here was the explanation of our bowlder delta at Port Neuf, and likewise of the deposits of quicksand and clay at Nampa, 250 miles to the west, and at a level several hundred feet lower. By these discoveries all reasonable theoretical objections were removed.

Subsequent investigations have raised no new objections to the genuineness of the Nampa figurine; on the contrary the discovery of a figurine, in a prehistoric cave in southern France, of almost exactly the same type as this, must do much to reconcile even the most skeptical to a just recognition of the claims of the discovery by Mr. Kurtz in Idaho. As to the reported discoveries in California, no doubt has fairly been cast on any of them except the Calaveras skull, respecting which it appears that in the interval of some months during which it lay neglected with others outside of Dr. Jones's office it was not identified by him, and the wrong skull was sent to Dr. Wyman of Harvard University for examination. But that a skull was found by Mr. Mattison is still among well-established facts. Mr. Baldwin and I had opportunity to go over the evidence with Mr. Scribner, the most important witness, in the course of which incidental evidence came out which easily accounts for the mistake. This I have recounted in the fifth edition of my " Ice Age," and elsewhere. So the whole question of the antiquity of man as affected by the discoveries in California and Idaho is still open, and evidence is accumulating that extensive outflows of lava on the Pacific slope have occurred at a very recent date, while Dr. G. F. Becker, one of the most capable members of the United States Geological Survey, accounts for the long survival of the prehistoric animals which were cotemporary with man on the Pacific coast, on the theory that it was then a health resort for animals, now for human invalids.

CHAPTER VIII

FIRST VISIT TO EUROPE

THE summer and part of the autumn of 1892 was spent in a visit to the most interesting glaciers and glacial fields of Europe, again accompanied by Mr. Prentiss Baldwin. The visit was instigated by an invitation from the Northwest of England Boulder Committee, who had their interest aroused by my former colaborer, Mr. Henry Carvill Lewis. After finishing our joint exploration of the terminal moraine in Pennsylvania, Mr. Lewis and his accomplished wife went to England to do for Great Britain what we had done for Pennsylvania, namely, determine the exact limit of the country which had been overrun by glacial ice,—a proposition which had been freely talked over by us during our joint labors. Mr. Lewis succeeded in arousing great interest in the subject, and among other things became an ardent advocate of the theory that the molluscan remains found on Moel Tryfaen in Wales, at Macclesfield, near Birmingham in England, and in other places, were evidence not of a submergence of the land allowing the oceanic waters to cover those heights, but rather of an extension of glacial ice which pushed up before it masses of the clay deposits at the bottom of the Irish Sea, carrying with them the molluscan remains to be redeposited in stratified gravel as the ice melted. The height at which these shell beds were found in Wales was about 1,400 feet above sea level, and at Macclesfield 1,200.

The occurrence of these shell beds had been interpreted by all the older geologists as indicative of a postglacial submergence. But before Mr. Lewis's visit it had been suggested by Mr. Clement Reid that their explanation was that given above. This the investigations of Mr. Lewis made a certainty, at least to those who properly considered the new evidence. The Northwest of England Boulder Committee was organized at the suggestion of Mr. Lewis, in order to carry on the investigations till the most sceptical should be convinced. The invitation to me to visit them was a part of their program; for unfortunately Mr. Lewis died of typhoid fever when on his way back to England to resume his investigations. My familiarity with the fields which Lewis had investigated in America, and my personal knowledge of his way of looking at things, made it seem important that I should go over with the Committee some of the typical fields in which the best evidence of Lewis's explanation was to be found. This was certainly a privilege which I could but highly appreciate and I availed myself of it with great pleasure. Among the prominent members of the Committee were Percy F. Kendall, C. E. DeRance, Clement Reid, George W. Lamplugh, John E. Marr, and Rev. Dr. H. W. Crosskey. Professor Kendall was then editing a periodical devoted to the discussion of the glacial phenomena of Great Britain.

After visiting various typical places which displayed the evidence of the theory, and making a trip to the glacial boundary in Holland and to the fields of most archæological interest in France, Belgium, and southern England, and traversing the most important glacial fields in Switzerland and northern Italy, we returned to attend the meeting of the British Association which met at Cardiff, Wales. Here I read a paper on the relation of the Glacial epoch to the question of man's antiquity, and the subject was discussed in other papers by members of the Committee. Subsequently I published two papers on the glaciation of Great Britain, one in the *Bulletin* of the Geological Society of America, the other in the *American Journal of Science*. Altogether this summer's trip to Europe was of the greatest value to me.

This was especially evident in the fact that I thereby secured the coöperation of Professor Kendall in the preparation of the volume on " Man and the Glacial Period," which the Appletons published for me

late in that year. I had previously been asked to give
a second course of Lowell Institute lectures in Boston,
on the " Origin and Antiquity of Man." This volume
was based on the portion of those lectures which treated
of glacial man. The chapter in the book which
treated of the glaciers of Great Britain was generously
prepared for me by Professor Kendall. His contribution extends from page 137 to page 181, and is accompanied by a colored map showing in more detail
than had been done before, or has been done since, the
complicated movements of the glaciers of Great Britain. An eminent English man of science soon after
paid me the compliment of using, in a book of his own
having only twenty-four illustrations, this map together with sixteen of my photographic illustrations,
without the least acknowledgment of the source from
which they came. The contribution of Mr. Kendall's
was fifteen years ahead of time, but its conclusions are
now almost universally accepted. " Man and the Glacial Period " was incorporated into the International
Scientific Series, and has had a large circulation, something like fifteen thousand copies having been sold, and
it is still having a steady sale. A second edition was issued in 1894, with a chapter answering numerous
criticisms which had appeared.

CHAPTER IX

SHIPWRECKED IN GREENLAND

IN 1894 I had the privilege of spending a summer in Greenland. This was with a party gotten up by Dr. Frederick A. Cook, who had won considerable reputation for his report on the anthropology of the Eskimos as a member of Mr. Peary's first extensive expedition to the northern shores of that continent. Our party included several men of note, making it very instructive and enjoyable. Among the members were Mayor George W. Gardner, of Cleveland; Professor William H. Brewer, of Yale University; Professor L. L. Dyche, of Kansas University; Mr. James D. Dewell, afterwards Lieutenant Governor of Connecticut; Mr. G. W. W. Dove, of my Andover parish; Mr. (now Professor) Samuel P. Orth; my son Frederick, and others. The expedition met with many reverses, but still gave large opportunity for study both of the Greenland ice fields, and of the social conditions which prevail in that little-known land.

Our ship, the Miranda, was not fitted for contending with ice fields, being simply a tramp steamer covered with a thin shell of iron. Our first disaster was to run straight into an iceberg about ten miles off the Labrador coast. There was a dense fog so that nothing could be seen ahead, and the vessel was going slowly, but with sufficient force to smash in the iron plates of our ship, and bring us to a sudden halt. Fortunately, the sea was calm, and the injury to the ship was above the water line. This was remarkable, since icebergs, such as the one encountered by us, usually project forward below the water. This one, however, did not do so and the whole force of the impact was felt above the water line. Great masses of ice fell upon the deck of the ship, and marks where the paint was rubbed off from our prow were clearly seen in the berg as we slowly backed off from it. As we were only ten or twelve miles from St. Charles Harbor on the southeast coast of Labrador, we put in safely there and stayed until temporary repairs could be made.

This gave us opportunity to explore the adjoining coast, and to visit Battle Harbor, the capital of Labrador. Nothing could be more uninviting than this whole region in summer. What then must it be in winter? But it is inhabited by a courageous and law-abiding class of settlers, who are ready to welcome the throngs of fishermen who come up from Newfoundland, in the summer, as the ice permits. The great business is to capture the crowds of seal which float down on the ice from the far north. We saw, also, the skin of a magnificent white bear which had come thus far south with his companions of the seal tribe. The bear had come on shore and was trying to make his way back to the polar regions from which he came, when the deep snows interfered with his progress, and he was easily captured, his skin being kept as a souvenir. Battle Harbor was merely a forlorn village on an exposed shore, nevertheless it was beginning to be made famous by the missionary labors of Dr. Grenfell. Our experience in subsequently coasting along the shore gave us a good idea of the character of his philanthropic work, especially in the rôle of physician. Everywhere we were met by fishermen who had been disabled and were in need of medical assistance which their associates were unable to give.

After making temporary repairs it was necessary to return to St. John's, Newfoundland, to make such further repairs as were necessary if we continued our voyage to the north. This done, we worked our way slowly through the magnificent icebergs, which glistened in the sunshine from every side, and which rose up from the water in every fantastic shape. In variety of form and beauty of color the cathedrals of Europe could not bear a comparison. The shallow ice flocs interfered with our reaching the coast of Greenland, until we were opposite the picturesque bay on which Sukkertoppen is situated. This we entered, passing the innumerable islands, with which it is dotted, although to enter was contrary to law; for, in order to protect the natives from the corrupting influences of visitors from civilized nations, the Danish government has been compelled to prohibit all intercourse with the outside world except as under their official supervision. But, as we were in need of assistance and repairs, we were allowed to steam in and tie up to a huge iron ring, which was fastened to the rocky precipice guarding the settlement.

The two or three days of our stay gave opportunity for a portion of our party to make a trip up the South Isortok Fiord, which penetrates the coast about fifty miles, and is bordered by extensive moss-covered areas which furnish pasture for herds of reindeer. In the summer these fields are very attractive to the Eskimo, and they resort to them to spend a month or two in fishing and hunting, bringing with them on their return supplies for winter consumption. This expedition gave us our first view of the " ice blink " occasioned by the reflection of the sunshine from the continental ice sheet, which covers the interior over an area of 500,000 square miles. Our expedition did not take us quite up to the ice margin, but we had abundant evidence of its proximity, by the extent to which the water was discolored by the " glacial milk " which issued from the streams at the foot of the projecting tongues of ice coming into the inlet from every side, as well as at its head. In front of one of these glacier tongues we debarked after spending one night sleeping on the luxurious bed of moss which formed our resting place. The scene was far from being desolate. Birds in innumerable numbers flew over us. Mosquitoes in dense swarms fell down on us and made life unendurable. But the scenery was so entrancing that it was with a pang of regret that we started back for our boat.

On reaching Sukkertoppen again, we found the steamer all ready for a fresh start for the far north. But, alas, in trying to find our way through the maze of islands and reefs, which fill the bay at low tide and are but partially revealed at high tide, we ran on one of the reefs and severely injured the bottom of our boat! How seriously we were damaged no one could tell. So there was nothing for us to do but get back to the harbor if that were possible. Fortunately we succeeded, and tied the Miranda again to the stout iron ring which hung from the rocky precipice at the entrance of the harbor. On examination it was decided that it was not safe to venture out to sea with her, and that we must seek some other way of getting home. In short we were shipwrecked on the inhos-

pitable Greenland coast. Dr. Cook, however, was
equal to the occasion, and the versatility and courage
which he showed in rescuing us, has ever since made
us have confidence in his statements concerning his accomplishments in seeking the North Pole and in
climbing Mt. McKinley. On learning that there was
a Gloucester fishing schooner near Holstenberg, one
hundred miles, or more, north of us, Dr. Cook at once
called for a few volunteers and started off in an open
boat to wend his way along the coast in search of the
help which this might afford us. It was estimated
that he could not return for about two weeks. This
gave me opportunity to organize an expedition for the
survey of Ikamiut Fiord, twenty miles to the north,
into which a tongue of the inland ice projected. But,
before starting, we all wrote letters home telling our
friends of our catastrophe, and that we were comfortably situated and if we did not get home this year we
could be expected next year. These letters we dis-
patched by kayaks to Ivigtut, three hundred miles distant, at the southern extremity of Greenland, where
we hoped they would arrive in time for the last vessel
that would sail for Denmark. These letters arrived at
their destination about two months after we did.

Our expedition to Ikamiut Fiord met all my expectations in every way. We saw southern Greenland at its best, and worst. We clambered over the

tongue of the glacier that projected into the head of the fiord. We saw where it pushed up upon the point of the promontory which separated Ikamiut Fiord from Sermilik Fiord (which leads directly down to Sukker-toppen), the ice behaving exactly as a flood of water would do when meeting a similar obstacle only as modified by the diminished fluidity of ice. We studied with interest the difference between the appearance of the northern slope of the mountain range which shut the fiord in on the south, and that of the southern slope of the opposite range, from which the glaciers had entirely disappeared. We saw the millions on millions of birds which nested in the clefts of the rocks bordering either side of the fiord, and saw native hunters go out in kayaks and scare the birds up from their feeding places and with primitive weapons bring them down in sufficient quantities for their needs. I cannot conceal my delight on learning that my exploration of this region was thought of sufficient importance to lead the Danish map makers who followed soon after, to give my name to the nunatak (mountain peak) projecting above the glacial ice which comes down to the head of the fiord. So I am in doubt whether to choose Wright Mountain in Alaska or Wright Nunatak in Greenland for my burial place, since either of them would be the noblest and most enduring monument one could desire for his last resting place.

The insight which this visit to Greenland gave me into the political, social, and religious conditions which prevail there, was among the most valuable of all the results of the trip. At Sukkertoppen we found in the Danish officials and their families one of the most cultivated companies of Europeans that it has ever been my fortune to meet. The company consisted of Mr. Bistrup, the governor, and his wife; Mr. Bauman, the assistant governor, and his wife; three children of the Bistrups; and Miss Fausböll, the daughter of the Professor of Sanscrit in the University of Copenhagen, who was the governess of the children. These had charge of four hundred or more natives who lived in small settlements along the shore, and gathered, in larger numbers, about the residence of the officials. The natives lived largely on the products of the land, namely, fish, birds, eggs, the blubber of seal, and the half-digested contents of the seals' stomachs. The officials had all their food except the meat brought from Denmark, and they were compelled to keep two years' stores on hand, to provide against an occasional interruption of communication for a season. A small garden, made rich with soil brought from Denmark, enabled them to raise a few radishes and some other such vegetables, to a limited extent. But the warmly protected house was a center of European culture such as only highly educated women can make. There was a piano, there were violins and other musical instruments, all of which could be played upon with skill and effect. There were books and magazines in several languages, among them many in English. Hence the long season of nearly eight months, when there was no communication with the outside world, was filled with congenial cultivation of the higher tastes with which nature has endowed mankind.

In every year but one since our visit I have exchanged letters with some member of this interesting colony. The exception was when ice prevented the incoming ship from home to return before the next year. The children that Miss Fausböll was tutoring and two other members of the family, who were away when we were there, have become members of the Danish service in Greenland, or have entered and risen to high position in the Danish Navy. The Governor and his wife, after thirty years of devoted service to the interests of their Eskimo wards, returned to Copenhagen on a pension to spend their declining years in enjoyment of the rich opportunities for gratifying their cultivated tastes, which the capital of Denmark affords. The *Century Magazine* published, in September, 1911, a most interesting article from Mrs. Bistrup, on the Eskimo Women.

The native Eskimos have nearly all been converted to Christianity, partly through Moravian missionaries,

but more extensively through the efforts of Lutheran
clergymen who have accompanied the Danish officials.
But now the Moravians have retired from the field
and left the whole work to the Danes. The results of
the efforts to civilize and Christianize the natives are
very interesting. It has been impossible to make much
change in the general manner of life among the people; for the problem of how to meet the trying conditions under which life can be maintained in that in-
hospitable land had been pretty well solved by the
natives before the whites took charge of them. They ·
are still most comfortable in their sod-covered " igloos."
They are still kept warm by clothing of sealskin and
by vests of eider down worn next to the skin, and their
igloos are warmed and lighted by lamps fed with the
blubber of the seal. They still have community of
ownership in many of the necessities of life, the most
conspicuous exception being the pieces of wood which
are thrown upon the shore by the waves of the sea.
When such a prize has been found and placed in safety
above the reach of the tide, it is regarded as the most
sacred piece of private property. No greater crime can
be committed than to steal such a piece of wood. And
well may this be so; for all the wood they have for
making the frames of their boats, and for handles to
their spears and harpoons, is obtained from this supply
thrown up by the waves; and this has floated all the

way from Siberia, past the North Pole, and around the northern shores of the continent itself.

A Sunday service at Ikamiut told volumes as to the influence of the Christian missionaries over the natives. It was a rainy morning, so that we could scarcely venture out of our tent, thus enforcing on my party a stricter observance of the Sabbath than could have been secured if the weather had been propitious. While we were eating our frugal breakfast of griddle cakes, slowly and imperfectly cooked on a recalcitrant oil stove, a lean, short man, clothed in skins, came to the door of the tent and pointed to a book which he had in his hand, and after making various signs as if something was going on near the boat landing, went away and we could see no more of him. A little later, on going down to the boats to look after them, I heard the sound of voices proceeding from one of the mounds of earth which we were told were the houses in which the colony lived. Following the direction of the sound, I got down upon my hands and knees and, pushing my head against a small wooden door, found myself in an outer room, which was protecting the main room to the right. Turning in that direction and pushing my head against another small door, I discovered the whole colony, of about twenty persons, gathered for a Sunday-morning religious service. On crawling through the door, a place was made for me to sit on the foot of the low sleeping shelf, by turning up the furs which served for bedding. Meanwhile the services proceeded without interruption. They were singing an Eskimo hymn to a slow German choral, the words of which, of course, I could not understand. But the tune was one which, a few years before, I had heard sung by the vast congregation which weekly gathers in the Cologne Cathedral.

After the hymn, the wizen-faced little man who had vainly summoned us to worship as we were eating breakfast, read what I suppose was a prayer, the phrases "Christ's sake" and "amen" being the only familiar words. Then followed what I suppose was a sermon, the only indication to my mind being the strict attention which the audience gave to the reader. Then followed another hymn, sung to another German choral that had a very familiar sound. Thus ended the morning service in that dismal igloo on that dismal Sunday. How it would have cheered the heart of Hans Egede, if he could have foreseen the influence here exhibited of his devoted but disappointing efforts to win the Eskimos to Christianity two hundred years before!

But now they are all nominally Christian, observing all the Christian ordinances, and sharing with the most enlightened and prosperous nations the last consolations of the Christian faith, the road to heaven being as short from Greenland as from the most cultivated centers of civilization. The Eskimos have a literature of their own, and publish a paper, which has general circulation. All this is certainly to the credit of the Danish officials who protect them from the demoralizing influence of the offscouring of civilized nations if they were permitted free access to their shores. Here, certainly, is a lesson in " home rule," or rather one to show the limitations of that much vaunted principle of many reformers. Races as well as individuals have their infancy.

Soon after returning to our ship from our ten-day expedition to Ikamiut Fiord, a small fishing schooner, of about one hundred tons' capacity, hove in sight, with Dr. Cook and his party on board. This was the " Rigel," under command of Captain George W. Dixon, of Gloucester, Massachusetts. He had been out all summer, fishing: first, off the coast of Iceland; and later, where he was found one hundred miles north of us, on the Greenland coast. His success had been rather indifferent, and he was about to start for home when hailed by Dr. Cook. With the generous instincts of a sailor, he did not hesitate a moment in coming to our relief. On reaching the Miranda and seeing the situation, he threw overboard all his fishing tackle, and every article of furniture, leveled the fish

in the hold and, after covering them with the salt in
the ship, spread canvas over all to provide a place in
which our party could sleep.

There were about forty of us tourists, so that we
were pretty well crowded when all were transferred
to the Rigel. But it was decided that it was not safe
for the Miranda to attempt to cross Baffin Bay alone.
However, it ventured to take the Rigel in tow with
all of us on board. Everything proceeded well until
midnight of the second day, when we were about three
hundred miles from harbor. Then a signal of distress
was sounded from the Miranda, and Captain Dixon's
voice was heard ordering all passengers to keep below,
and all hands to come on deck. I disregarded the
order to stay below, and so was permitted to witness
a scene such as can never be blotted out of memory.
The Miranda was rolling heavily in the trough of a
rough sea, showing by turns the red color with which
her bottom was painted. Meanwhile the captains were
exchanging signals. Captain Farrell, on the Miranda,
asked our captain to come up close and take off his
crew. Captain Dixon replied, " I won't do it. I am
near enough now. If you go down you will draw us
with you. Put off your boats and come alongside."

Meanwhile we were bound to the Miranda by a
stout hawser eight hundred feet long. But our captain had a man stand ready with an axe to cut this if

the Miranda should sink. It seemed an age before the first boatload of the Miranda's crew reached us, and then another age before we could get them safely on board our vessel; for their boat would come on the crest of a great wave, as if to plunge down upon us, and then move off again on top of another wave. The futility of securing safety to travelers on the ocean by compelling vessels to carry enough small boats to hold all the passengers and crew became painfully apparent when we saw the difficulty of transferring even thirty experienced sailors from one ship to another during a storm. But, at length, after three hours of anxious effort, all were safe on board the Rigel. The hawser was cut, and the Miranda drifted away in the mist and darkness with its lights still burning and the steam still pouring out of its chimneys. What became of it we never knew. We learned two years afterwards that the insurance company declined to pay the loss, because they had had no official notice that it had sunk.

None of us saved any of our belongings which were left upon it, and we made our way towards home with only the clothes we had on our backs. There were now ninety of us on board the Rigel, and we filled the schooner from stem to stern when we were all on deck. Nor did we have an abundant supply of water or food. This was the less important to me and some others who were desperately seasick all the while.

How the cook managed to do his part is something I
have never been able to comprehend; for he had room
in the forecastle for only fifteen to eat at a time, making it necessary to have six rotations of hungry men
for each meal. The whole situation tested the character of all; and brought out the weak points of some,
as well as the admirable qualities of others. The Captain and his crew showed to the best advantage. The
crew were to be sharers in the profits of the fishing
trip, and two of them were brothers of the Captain.
It was noticeable that he never gave an absolute command to his crew, but would say, "Hadn't you better
haul down the topsail? Hadn't you better haul up
the mainsail?" and the topsail came down and the
mainsail went up, as promptly as if he had given a
positive order. But the crew of the Miranda had not
been used to such mild language; and when he said to
them at one time when they were smoking in the hold,
and thus endangering the vessel, "Hadn't you better
put your pipes away? It isn't safe to smoke here,"
and they kept on smoking, a thunderstorm was nothing to what followed. He told them that if they did
not stop smoking, or were seen to do it again, he would
throw the whole of them overboard. And they believed that he would, and made no more trouble.

After putting in at two or three ports in Labrador
for safety during storms, and to get water, we at

length, after two weeks, reached Sydney, in Nova Scotia, from which place we could communicate with the folks at home, and where the accommodating merchants showed no hesitancy in trusting us for new suits of clothing to replace the dilapidated garments we had on. We all reached home safe, as I have already said, two months before the letters sent from Sukkertoppen came. The expedition, though unfortunate in many respects, was by no means a failure. It enabled me with more confidence to form conclusions concerning many problems connected with the Glacial epoch. We had opportunity to observe that, vast as is the present ice sheet, it was once much larger. The grooves and scratches on the mountainous border of the continent showed clearly that the ice sheet had formerly covered all the border which is now inhabitable in southern Greenland. Much was also learned about the way in which moraines, eskers, and kames were formed. One of the great mysteries, however, remains unsolved. This is connected with the existence of reindeer in southern Greenland. How did the species get there? It would seem impossible for them to traverse the vast ice fields in northern Greenland, which now separate them from any known original habitation. This we leave for future light.

About a year after returning from Greenland, the

Appletons published " Greenland Icefields and Life in the North Atlantic, with a New Discussion of the Causes of the Ice Age." In the preparation of this volume Dr. Upham again coöperated with me, he writing the chapters dealing with the theoretical problems connected with the distribution of plants and animals over the continent, and with the stages of the glaciation of North America, and the causes of the epoch. I still regard his discussion of these topics as of the greatest value, and would refer all students of the subject to the chapters written by him, for light which they can get from no other quarter. Unfortunately the plates of this book were early destroyed by fire, so that the volume has not had the circulation and the influence which it deserves. But it can be found in a wide range of libraries.

CHAPTER X

THEOLOGICAL STUDIES

MEANWHILE religious and theological problems were being thrust continually on my attention. In 1890, Houghton, Mifflin and Company asked me to prepare a life of President Charles G. Finney for their American Religious Leaders series. This was published in 1891, and has had a fairly wide sale down to the present time. In its preparation I was led to review thoroughly the literature of the so-called New England theology, of which Jonathan Edwards was the most noted representative in the early stages of its development; and Professors Edwards A. Park, of Andover, and N. W. Taylor, of New Haven, President Mark Hopkins, of Williams College, and Lyman Beecher and President Finney among the great preachers, were the later representatives. As this theology has so much to recommend it to thoughtful minds, and has been so buried out of sight by the vague and jaunty speculations of the last few years, it will be profitable to give a brief abstract of it, showing how completely it satisfies the demands of our reasoning faculties. Finney's presentation of this system has the advantage of proceeding from one who had had a thorough legal training, and so had command of the lines of argument which satisfy men as they are immersed in the ordinary task of drawing conclusions from such evidence as is at hand. As Gladstone has pointed out, such a mind is much more likely to reach reasonable conclusions than is one whose investigations are in some narrow line out of the ordinary region of human experience. The demands of the " moral law," as revealed in conscience, and the accordance of these demands with the revelation in the Bible, was a favorite theme with Finney in his preaching. At one time as he was passing through Rochester, New York, and stopping over night with a friend, the lawyers of the city sent a delegation to him asking that he would give them a course of lectures on the moral law. This he did with such effect that the whole body of lawyers in the city were not only persuaded of the truth of the Biblical plan of salvation, but became active participants in the church work of the city.

As nearly as I can state it in brief, Finney's system is as follows: The fundamental virtue both on the part of God and man is love. But this love is not mere affection, but an active choice of the " good of being " and the devotion of all our activities to its promotion. This proposition is arrived at not by reasoning, but by intuition. It is a fundamental affirma-

tion of the human mind. The ultimate " good of being " consists in the pleasurable feelings and emotions
connected with sensations of every sort, from those of
the worm, which we should not needlessly crush beneath our feet, to those of the Divine Being in the
eternal communings of his nature, and in contempla-
tion of the creation which he pronounces " good." Between these extremes man occupies an intermediate
place, in the good which he is capable of experiencing.

The human race is endowed with freedom of will.
Man has a moral nature. He makes his own character. He is to be governed according to his nature.
His choices cannot be compelled, they must be secured
by persuasion, if they are to have any character at all.
To such a kind of government of man, God has
pledged himself in the very act of creation.

But it is evident to all that the human race has departed from its high prerogatives of virtue and plunged
into a warfare with its higher nature, and is following
a line of self-indulgence, in disregard of the general
welfare. The extent of this rebellion against the law
of right is seen in every man's conscience, which tells
him that he has in ways without number fallen short
of his high prerogatives, and done many things which
he ought not to have done, and left undone many
things which he ought to have done. There is no man
but has reason to be ashamed of the mean things both

in thought and deed which he has done. Furthermore, the extent of this departure from the law of love
on the part of all men appears in the universal distrust
which men, and especially nations, cherish regarding
each other. The whole machinery of human govern-
ments illustrates the lack of confidence which we have
in our fellow men. The courts of law, the police, the
jails, the prisons, the armies and navies of the world,
and the incalculable miseries of mankind caused by
"man's inhumanity to man," all show that the whole
human race is in rebellion against the law of love
written on every man's heart.

The remedial system revealed in the Bible is so perfectly adapted to the wants of man, that it bears on its
very face evidence of its truth. As ruler of mankind
God is not at liberty to be indifferent to the sin of his
creatures. In their very creation God has bound himself to restrain them from evil and to promote their
choices of good so far as he can. This he is doing by
brandishing a flaming sword to warn them against evil
(whatsoever a man soweth that shall he reap) and by
the love displayed in the atoning work of Christ to win
them back to virtue's path. So clearly were these
truths pressed home in Finney's preaching, that they
never failed to produce conviction in the hearts of all
but the most hardened of his congregations.

But Finney did not, as many modern apologists are

wont to do, rest wholly on this direct evidence of adaptation. His legal mind took in all kinds of evidence. The intellect must be satisfied by the presentation of all the arguments for the existence, omnipotence, omnipresence, and perfect goodness of God; as well as the evidences on which the Bible is shown to be a revelation from God. He was especially successful in removing the superficial objections which are put forward by critics both to the evidence of the divine power and goodness in natural theology and to the historical character of both the Old and the New Testament. Here his legal training showed to great advantage.

It cannot be shown that death in the animal creation diminishes the sum of good experienced by them. A succession of fresh lives may be better than a prolongation of those already existing. The existence of sin is incidental to the possession by his creatures of moral freedom. The joy connected with redemption doubtless far exceeds the misery which sinners bring on themselves. Sin furnishes the occasion for a display of divine love which would have been impossible without such an occasion to draw it forth.

The " New School Calvinism," which lay at the bottom of all Finney's preaching and writing, is shorn of the objections urged against that system in its ultra forms. There may be certainty without necessity. It may be certain that a man will commit murder, though he acts as a free agent, and is impelled by no necessity. It may be certain that motives will prevail to·induce a benevolent or a sinful choice without involving any necessity. Thus the divine mind may foresee all things in the moral world where necessity is excluded, as well as in the physical world where it is involved in every step. It is greatly to be desired that all preachers and theologians would go through the whole question of Christian Evidences as Finney taught his pupils and hearers to do.

Nor did he rest with these generalities of natural theology. His defense of the divine authority of the Bible was powerful and most convincing. Like Judge Greenleaf, he was able to marshal the facts as only a lawyer can, and show that according to all the rules of evidence which govern us in practical affairs, the Bible is an authoritative and genuine revelation from God, and its credibility is established by abundant evidence, both external and internal. After marshaling this evidence ("Skeletons of a Course of Theological Lectures," Oberlin, 1840, pp. 39-51), he concludes:

"1. If this testimony does not establish the truth and divine authority of the Bible, there is an end of attempting to establish anything by evidence.

"2. If all this testimony can exist and yet the

Bible fail to be true, it is the greatest miracle in the universe.

"3. If the Bible be true, everything is plain, and the whole mystery of our existence and circumstances is explained. If the Bible is untrue we are all afloat. The existence of the universe, the existence, and character, and destiny of man, are highly enigmatical, and we are left in the most distressing darkness and uncertainty, in regard to everything which we need to know."

In 1896 I was invited to give a third course of Lowell Institute Lectures, this time on " The Scientific Aspects of Christian Evidences." These, as rewritten and enlarged, were published the next year by the Appletons, this time without such misgivings about lack of interest in the subject as determined their decision with reference to " The Logic of Christian Evidences " offered to them sixteen years before. The book has had a large and continuous sale up to the present time, and like the other was republished in England, and has been used more or less as a textbook. As preliminary to a brief presentation of the historical evidences on which we accept the New Testament, giving special prominence to the new evidences which had been brought to light during the preceding decade, successive chapters discuss the Limits of

Scientific Thought; The Paradoxes of Science; God
and Nature; Darwinism and Design; Mediate Miracles; and what constitutes proof "Beyond Reasonable
Doubt." In these preliminary discussions the reader
is made to see that Christian evidence is as really
scientific as is that of any of the physical sciences, and
that proof in one case is no more certain than in the
other. The mysteries underlying the Christian system
are no greater than those which underlie every system
of knowledge. If Darwinism be a true representation
of the manner in which species have come into existence, it only increases the evidence of design; while
study of the miraculous accounts in the Old Testament
indorsed by Christ shows that most of them are plain
historical accounts of phenomena brought about by
physical forces which could not have been understood
or their action foreknown by the men of that time;
and so the events were really miracles of foreknowledge, or prophecy. This subject was more fully
treated in a subsequent book to which I will refer
later, entitled "Scientific Confirmations of Old Testament History."

CHAPTER XI

ACROSS ASIA

Soon after the death of my wife in 1899, my friend Mr. S. Prentiss Baldwin, who was so situated that he could no longer accompany me on extended excursions, came to me and asked what further expedition I most wished to take to enlarge my knowledge of the Glacial epoch and its archæological connections. I outlined to him one across Asia, substantially as it was made in 1900. He at once said to me that I might plan for it and take my son, Frederick Bennett, along for protection and assistance. Furnishing us with abundant letters of credit, he bade us Godspeed in the winter, and we started by way of New Orleans, over the Southern Pacific railroad to California, and thence went westward across the Pacific Ocean and Siberia, and came home across the Atlantic. The college generously gave me a year's leave of absence, which was extended to fourteen months, with my salary continued. The specific object in view was to determine the extent of glaciation in central and northern Asia. It had been reported that Siberia, like northern Alaska, had never been covered with glacial ice. But the new edition of Geikie's " Great Ice Age " contained maps showing supposed glaciated regions in eastern Mongolia and over the Vitim plateau, east of Lake Baikal. My expedition was not therefore, as some said, needless; for, although what I found out had been commonly believed before, it had been merely surmised, not known. But aside from settling this mooted point, the expedition accomplished much more in several directions, which will appear as an account of it is briefly told.

To see with one's own eyes the wonders of the lower Mississippi, and the deserts traversed by the Southern Pacific railroad; to clamber over the highest mountains of southern California, and to sail out of the Golden Horn, were experiences worth while in themselves, but were only introductions to rarer and more wonderful things awaiting us. We had expected to spend a month in the Hawaiian Islands, my friends there having planned various excursions, and made arrangements for a series of lectures on the Glacial epoch. But the bubonic plague was raging when our steamer reached Honolulu, and no one was permitted to land. Therefore we were compelled to lie still in the harbor all day and satisfy ourselves with looking out on the enchanting scenery which surrounds that lovely spot. Some of our friends rowed around in sight of the steamer and waved their welcome, but that was all they were permitted to do, and we sailed on to the Asiatic coast.

In due time we landed at Yokohama, to find that the missionaries had planned an extensive . lecturing tour for us throughout Japan. The arrangements, however, were left to the Japanese themselves, and invitations came in from societies extending from Sendai to Okayama. I was to give illustrated lectures on the Ice Age in North America. The Japanese furnished lanterns and operators, and an interpreter. At Maebashi, in the interior, where I began, the women were for the first time permitted to attend a public lecture. This was given in the high-school assembly room, and there were one thousand in the audience, as shown by the number of wooden shoes piled up at the entrance of the hall. A banquet was given to us on the following evening, and my son and I were placed in the seats of honor. Sixty of the prominent citizens paid a dollar a plate to share in the festivities. All were seated crosslegged on the floor, while beautiful girls brought in the endless round of dishes for our refreshment and set them down before us one after another. The dishes were mostly soups with strong fishy flavors. The guests in general had only chopsticks with which to get the soup into their mouths, but spoons were very considerately

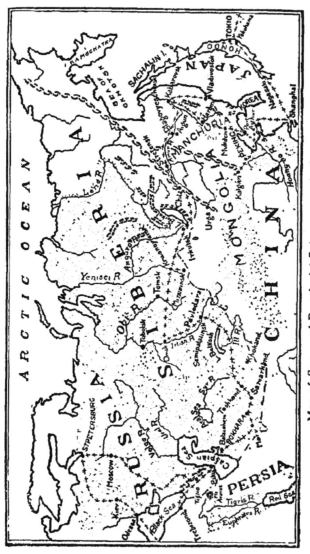

Map of Supposed Postglacial Submergence in Asia
Zigzag Line, our Itinerary in 1900

brought to us, and cushions to relieve our weary limbs. On following days we went with the professors of geology and natural history to visit the crater of an extinct volcano, a few miles away, and during the whole stay had before us in full sight an active volcano, which was showering dust so thickly as to cover the whole land with a thin film. But this was commonplace to the Japanese.

At Sendai three or four lectures were arranged in the University hall, and the mayor of the city presided, introducing me, so I was told, by saying that he considered it a greater honor to preside at such a meeting than to be mayor of the city. At the close of my lectures there, the papers contained articles in high praise of me and my work, remarking that it was a wonderful display of public spirit for a man over sixty years of age to circle the globe for the purpose of gathering and imparting stores of scientific knowledge. But, true to their own principles, they added that it was even more wonderful and praiseworthy on the part of my son to accompany his father for his protection and care. All these lectures in Japan were given without charge on my part, or admission fees at the door. But in every case presents of rare value were bestowed on me. At Sendai it was a painting, of priceless value, by one of their old masters, who died before contact with the outside world had corrupted their taste, and cheapened their art. This painting reveals more and more of suggestive beauty to the eye the longer it is studied.

At Tokyo the lectures were before the National Education Society, and were attended by a high class of citizens and scholars. Here I had the rather annoying, or I should say amusing, experience of having my lecture, as given in English, understood by a considerable portion of the audience, so that the jokes with which the lecture was sparingly interspersed would produce two ripples of laughter a short distance apart. At Tokyo, I was asked to give a special lecture to the ladies of high rank. This introduced me to the interior of one of the most elegant Japanese houses, where the lecture was held. The audience was as distinguished and elegant as the house, the daughter of the late Tycoon being one of the auditors. I could not see but the ladies appreciated the lecture as well as the members of the University did.

Other lectures were given in Yokohama, Kyoto, Kobe, Osaka, and Okayama. In every place they were received with enthusiasm. The genuineness of their appreciation was witnessed by the fact that I am one of the three or four foreigners elected to membership in the Imperial Education Society of Japan. Altogether I had unusual opportunities to get an insight into the

Japanese efforts to assimilate Western civilization. The professors of natural science with whom I came in contact, and with whom I made scientific excursions, were remarkably well-informed respecting the geology and natural history of foreign countries as well as of their own. They knew the literature of European and American science as fully as the average professors in those countries know it. This wealth of knowledge was associated with a childlike simplicity of character that was charming.

After taking an extended trip with one of the teachers of geology in Maebashi, I accompanied him in his ride on the railroad to his home for a vacation. We were much of the time alone together in the car, and our ingenuity was taxed to keep up the conversation with our imperfect knowledge of each other's language. At length my friend took out from his traveling bag a carefully wrapped package, which I supposed at first to be cigarettes, but instead it was a mouth organ, on which he proceeded to play a number of familiar Sunday-school airs. Among them was the old tune that I had learned in my childhood, "There is a happy land." When he found that I knew the tune, he was very anxious to get the words. So I racked my brain to recall them. This I did to the extent of at least two stanzas, which I carefully wrote out for him. He said he wanted to teach them to his brothers and sisters whom he was to see on his vacation.

Speaking of cigarettes reminds me that we were there when a vigorous effort was being made to prohibit their use by the school children. The move began a short time before, among the teachers, who organized total abstinence societies among the pupils, pledging them not to smoke as long as they were in school. The inconsistency of urging this reform while the teachers themselves were freely indulging the habit, was so apparent that the most of them also took the pledge with their pupils. This led to the promulgation of a law prohibiting the use of cigarettes by school children. But tobacco was widely used by the people in general, and was advertised most profusely in every available way. I was impressed by one incident, showing how the best intentions of reformers sometimes miss the mark. The head of the Japanese-American tobacco trust was induced to go into the business on this wise. When a young man he was taken ill, and while convalescing in a missionary hospital, was supplied with tracts of various kinds intended to promote good morals and habits, as well as to impart the knowledge of Christianity. Among them were a number detailing the evil effects of the use of tobacco, of which not the least was its expensiveness. Figures were freely given showing the enormous amount annually spent on the noxious weed. These figures impressed him very deeply, and his conclusion was that where there was such a great demand there must be an attractive opening for business. Into this, therefore, he entered and became immensely prosperous. But he never could forget the favor which the tract distributors had bestowed upon him, and so was ever afterwards a generous contributor to the missionary society that had unintentionally directed him to a lucrative occupation.

While in Japan, Baron Rosen, the Russian ambassador, on learning of our intention to traverse Siberia for scientific purposes, requested, through our ambassador, Mr. Buck, an interview with us. On meeting him we found him much interested in America, he having been at different times connected with legations both of Mexico and of the United States. His main object in wishing to see us was to induce us to go through Manchuria on our way to Siberia. The Chinese Eastern railroad, leading from Port Arthur to Harbin, was then only partially built, but the whole was under construction, and engineers with their corps of assistants were scattered all along the line, so that we could safely traverse the country under their protection and guidance. He offered to facilitate our investigation of the line by giving us letters of introduction and recommendation to Admiral Alexieff, stationed at Port Arthur; and then the ranking admiral in the foreign fleets in Asiatic waters; and to Colonel of Staff Samoieoff, stationed then at Khabarovsk. Furnished with these letters (of which more anon) we set out for China.

We had intended to sail on a Japanese steamer which went by way of Korea, but as this vessel was sunk during a storm, we took one from Nagasaki, by way of Shanghai. Nothing could be more entrancing than the preliminary sail, from Kobe, through the eastern channel, among its countless islands, with the snow-covered cone of Fujiyama rising above the extended mountain chain which constitutes the backbone of the larger islands forming the western skyline. We passed by the mouths of the coal mines at which the steamers take their supply of fuel, and had opportunity to see the contrast between Japanese methods and our own. In Japan the coal is all carried aboard in baskets passed along a line from hand to hand, women with babes in their arms taking their turns indiscriminately with the men. So cheap is labor in Japan, that this is the most economical way of loading. Besides, they say it is better distributed by this method than by machinery.

After a brief stay in Shanghai, our vessel went along as near the shore as the depth of the water permitted, to Chefoo. A striking feature of this part of the journey is the evidence of the immense amount of sediment that is brought into these seas by the great rivers which traverse northern China. The Hwangho and the Yang-tze-Kiang come down to the sea loaded with silt as dense as that in the Missouri or the lower Jordan. This silt discolors the water out to a distance of many miles, and as it settles is producing shallows, which eventually become tidal beaches and finally dry land. Thus a wide belt of productive soil has been added to China since the historical period. Tientsin, now twenty miles from the sea, was originally a seaport. All this is connected with the problem of the "loess," the study of which was our principal reason for going to China. But the sharp line of demarcation separating the silt-laden water brought down by the Chinese rivers from that of the open ocean cannot fail to attract the attention of even the most unobservant traveler..

Chefoo, at the time of our visit, was a center of great activity, both native and foreign. But from reports, the effects of the use of opium on the native merchants, many of whom had acquired great wealth, only to spend it in the use and abuse of this noxious drug, were deplorable. Missionary enterprise was everywhere evident here. The China Inland Mission had a large and excellent school where the children of missionaries were receiving their education. The ingenuity of the Presbyterian missionaries in getting the attention of the Chinese was impressive. As the Chinese were very anxious to learn about Western ways of accomplishing work by labor-saving machinery, an enterprising missionary had gathered together in a museum models of every sort of machinery used in the Western world, together with natural history specimens, and the Chinese were invited to inspect the objects to their hearts' content; the only condition being that, to reach the museum, they pass through a chapel, where they were detained a half hour or so to hear a gospel sermon. In this way the gospel was preached to multitudes who could have been induced in no other way to give attention to it.

From Chefoo we steamed to Taku, at the mouth of the Pei-ho, where we anchored some distance from the shore on account of the shallow water occasioned by the rapid silting-up of the bay already referred to. From here we were transferred to Tientsin on a railroad which had recently been built. Previous to its building, all transportation to and from the gulf had been through the tortuous stream. Huge piles of salt, made from sea water by government agents, were conspicuous evidence of the government's plan of collecting revenue through monopoly of this necessary article of consumption. Tientsin itself has its permanent

future insured by its being both the terminus of the
great Chinese canal, which brings to market the rich
products of the Hwangho Valley, and the point from
which supplies are transported to Peking up the Pei-
ho, *via* Tung-chau. At the time of our reaching the
place, everything was running smoothly, and the city
was bustling with all sorts of commercial activities. I
was specially interested in a technological school which
had been established by Li Hung Chang, and put under the direction of Mr. Charles D. Tenney. This
was filled with students picked from different parts of
the Empire, all of whom were fitting themselves to
take part in the material development of China, which
every one thought was to take place in a short time.
I was invited to address them on geological subjects,
and found a most responsive audience, the most of
whom could understand English. A single incident
speaks volumes concerning the social conditions of
China. Mrs. Tenney asked if she could not attend
the lecture, but was told that on no condition could
she do it without practically breaking up the school,
so fixed was the prejudice at that time against having
women attend public places with men.

From Tientsin we went to Peking by the railroad
which had been recently opened—a distance of about
eighty miles, through a barren, sandy country. But

the railroad was not then permitted to approach nearer than a mile of the city. Here we were transferred to an electric road, which took us to the city wall, but no farther. The city would have been desecrated by its entrance into the sacred precincts. But all this is now changed. On our way we met a gorgeous funeral procession; but we did not make the mistake made by Secretary Seward when he met such a procession on his approach to the city. He thought it must be designed to show honor to him, and so stood still and with uncovered head continued to bow his recognition until it was past—much to the astonishment of the Chinese. Once within the walls, we were taken by jinrikishas to the compound occupied by Rev. W. S. Ament, one of the missionaries, who was to entertain us and help us to prepare for a journey into the interior.

The streets of Peking at that time were the most filthy and dismal thoroughfares imaginable. There were no closed sewers, and often the sewage flowed through the street itself. But the "compounds," as they were called, where the better class of the citizens resided, were separately surrounded with walls, which shut out all disagreeable sights, and inclosed flower gardens, making them very attractive places for residence. Thus the city was made to cover an immense area, in order to accommodate its vast population of official and well-to-do classes. As time was rapidly passing we were anxious to get into the interior as soon as possible, so as not to be too much delayed in beginning our journey across Siberia. Our missionary friends joined in the effort to help on our plans, by making for us in very short order the mattresses and quilts which we would need, both in a caravan journey into China, and on the Siberian trip. Meanwhile, Mr. Pokateloff, the accommodating and courtly Russian agent of the Chinese Eastern Bank (who died shortly afterwards as Russian Ambassador), supplied us with money on our letters of credit, and we went to a Chinese banker and transformed what was necessary into "cash" and silver bars. The "cash" were copper coins with a square hole in the middle, and of such small value that a silver dollar was worth fifteen hundred of them. Hence their very bulk prevented taking a sufficient supply to last long. So, when we reached a city of size enough to have a bank, we would find the banker and have him chop off a piece of silver, which he would weigh and then give its value in fresh cash. These pieces of cash had also much of historic and antiquarian interest, since it was unlawful to destroy a coin with the imperial stamp on it. Some of the cash which came into our possession were fifteen hundred years old.

Another preliminary that must not be forgotten was to get our passports "viséed." Our ambassador, Mr.

Conger, obligingly took them over to the Chinese officials, and after due time they were returned, covered all over with Chinese characters, which we were told gave us the freedom of all northeastern China, and of Mongolia and Manchuria. These have been framed and preserved as curiosities to ornament our library shelves.

Here I must pause to relate another of the many providential deliverances which intervened to make our trip a success, or rather to save it from disastrous failure. Our special object was to study the vast deposits of loess which cover portions of northeastern China. There were two localities within reach where this could be done with prospects of success, one was in the province of Shansi, the other in the vicinity of Kalgan. Shansi really offered the better field; and, besides, ten or twelve of my pupils were located there in the mission which had been organized by Oberlin students. The pressure was very strong to induce us to go there, and both study the loess, which covers the whole region in unequaled quantities, and renew my acquaintance with my pupils and perhaps cheer them in their lonely situation. But, if we went in that direction, the time required would be about two weeks longer than if we went to Kalgan, and that would interfere with the latter part of our trip, so we turned a deaf ear to the entreaties to visit Shansi. As it turned

out, all our missionaries in Shansi were massacred during the Boxer revolution, and we would have been of
the number if we had gone there.

It is one hundred and sixty miles from Peking to
Kalgan. To make the trip then, there was no way to
do but to organize a caravan. Ours consisted of four
mules and two donkeys with two drivers, and a half-
educated Chinese from the mission to act as cook and
interpreter. Our bedding, food, and other luggage
were piled upon the mules, and we surmounted all
and rode there as comfortably as we could, when not
astride of one of the donkeys, which were so small
that our feet almost touched the ground.

When night came we sought the shelter of Chinese
inns, which were usually kept by Mohammedans—indeed the Mohammedans controlled all the caravans
and caravansaries in this part of China, and it was well
for travelers that they did, for they were more cleanly
in their habits than were the other Chinese. The inns
were simply large inclosures, around two sides of
which were small rooms for guests, with a large
kitchen where our cook could prepare food for us.
The sleeping places were what are called " kangs," i. e.,
brick platforms, two or three feet high, under which
ran the flue which carried off the smoke and surplus
heat from the kitchen fire. This added to the comfort

in cool weather, but had the disadvantage of keeping
the insects which infested the quarters alive and active.
Sometimes, also, there were no divisions between the
sleeping quarters, and we had to content ourselves with
marking off space for ourselves on the long platform,
which was open to all comers, and was one with the
kitchen.   There were no glass windows, but in their
place glazed paper, through which the Chinese women
were accustomed to punch holes with their fingers, so
that their children, held in arms, might look in and see
the " foreign devils," as we were called.

The poverty that met us all along was heart-rend-
ing.   The country is entirely stripped of its forests,
and the chief fuel to be had was the roots of last year's
millet and sorghum, which were carefully grubbed up
and collected, and the droppings of animals that passed
along the road.   Men and boys would often follow
us for miles to collect this material.   Stalks of millet and
sorghum were also used by the well-to-do classes.   We
saw brick kilns where this was the only fuel for the
fires which were required.   In other places, however,
the mountain sides were scoured by the poor peasants
in search of seedlings of trees of two or three years'
growth, which were to be found in protected crannies.
Numbers of these peasants could be seen towards night-
fall returning with a small bunch upon their shoulders,
for which they would receive a few cents.   At Shi-

wantse we saw an immense pile of such material ready to feed the fires of a brick kiln.

Our first bill at a Chinese inn was 1,350 cash, which paid for the lodging of four persons, and a portion of their food, and for the feed of the animals. In gold currency this was about sixty cents, or fifteen cents apiece. At every inn where we stopped there would be a noisy altercation between our interpreter and the innkeeper just as we were mounted and ready to start. It would be claimed that some item amounting to twenty or twenty-five cash had been overlooked, and this sum would be demanded. Usually a compromise was made, and we were permitted to go on by paying an additional ten or twelve cash.

Characteristics of the Chinese are well illustrated by an incident which occurred at one of these inns the year before, when Rev. Mark Williams, one of the missionaries accompanying us from Kalgan, was passing over the route. Just as their party were emerging from the inn into the highway they encountered a Chinaman driving a donkey, loaded with a pannier of some kind of grain on each side. A frisky mule of Mr. Williams' party suddenly threw up his heels and knocked the grain into the dusty road. Thereupon the owner of the grain vigorously protested and demanded recompense. But while the altercation, which was accompanied by threatening attitudes on the part of both

the owner of the donkey and the guide of the party,
was going on, friendly bystanders scooped up the grain
with their hands and returned it to the panniers,
mingled with so much dust that they were fuller than
before. On seeing this the owner ceased to demand
indemnity but contented himself with asking for an
apology. This was refused on the ground that it was
the nature of a mule to kick, and consequently it was
to be expected that he would do so. While the altercation was continuing, the mule himself got free and
lay down and rolled in the dust. This was satisfactory. The aggrieved one said, "The mule has apologized, the mule has apologized, it is enough," and,
shaking hands with the guide, wished the party a safe
journey.

Between the plain on which Peking is built and the
borders of Mongolia there are three parallel chains of
mountains running northeast by southwest. When we
set out on our journey on the ninth of May this mountain range, which had the appearance of the walls of
a vast amphitheater, rising from 4,000 to 7,000 feet
in height, was covered with freshly fallen snow. As
the peaks, about fifteen miles distant, were glistening
in the sunshine of a clear day, they presented a scene
which I had never seen equaled except in northern
Italy. But alas, at the time we were gazing with

rapture upon the scene, we knew that hundreds of pilgrims who had gone in holiday attire to these mountain heights to worship on a festal day were perishing from the effects of the storm!

The pass across the first range of mountains out from Peking begins at Nankao, about twenty miles from the city, and extends fifteen miles to Shadou, rising there to a plain which is 2,500 feet above the sea. The gorge is exceedingly picturesque, not only by reason of its natural scenery but still more because there is crowded into it the traffic of all Mongolia on the way to Peking. The procession of pack animals did not seem to cease day or night. We made the passage after sunset by moonlight. We counted 960 camels which we either met or passed on the road, while there were numerous inns where uncounted numbers of pack animals were recuperating for an early start in the morning.

The reason for our night journey through the pass was, that during the day we had made a detour to visit the Ming Tombs, which are situated at the base of the mountains, fifteen or twenty miles northeast of Nankao. These tombs are justly celebrated for the situation chosen for them, and for the grandeur of the scale on which everything related to them is constructed. Considered from any point of view, they contradict the prevalent impression that the æsthetic

element is largely lacking in Chinese nature. The
tombs are situated in a vast amphitheater in the snow-
clad mountains towards which we had been riding for
the greater part of the day. The access to this is
through an opening about three miles wide, partially
closed by hills of upturned rocky strata several hundred feet in height. Across the entrance was a high
wall, now mostly in ruins, running far up on the
mountain sides. At this entrance there begins a
grand succession of gateways, arches, bridges, built
of marble, and avenues of gigantic statues of animals
and men, each carved from a single piece of stone
which must have been brought from a distance.
Among the animal sculptures, of which there were two
on each side, were horses, camels, elephants, and grif-
fins, followed by heroic statues first of soldiers and
then, most honorable of all, scholars with their scho-
lastic robes upon them. An immense mausoleum
closes up the avenue at the foot of the mountain.
This is where the first Ming emperor was buried more
than five hundred years ago. Everything about the
building is on a gigantic scale, while the details of the
work invite the closest inspection. The principal
room of the Confucian temple within the inclosure is
220 feet long, 100 feet wide, and fully 50 feet high.
In rear of, and surmounting all, is a forest-covered
mound about two hundred feet in height where it is

presumed the mortal remains of the first emperor are deposited. There are thirteen similar monumental tombs in different portions of the amphitheater. Altogether nature and art have here conspired to make this one of the most impressive burial places in all the world. It is noteworthy that the revolutionary Manchu dynasty which succeeded the Ming emperors continued to keep these tombs in repair and to maintain the ancestral worship at their shrines.

The inherent love of the Chinese for the beautiful is touchingly shown in the regard which the common people have for birds. The plains of northeastern China and of Mongolia are rendered jubilant in the spring by innumerable meadow larks, which soar and sing even better than their relatives do in England. Everywhere, also, on the road to Kalgan, we found these beautiful birds confined in cages and most tenderly cared for by their owners. Outside the walled cities, men and boys were seen bringing their pet birds to enjoy the air and sunshine. Peasants hoeing in the field had these pets with them, to beguile the weary hours of labor while shifting from one row to the other, and little naked boys had their birds so trained that they could carry them around the streets perched on their fingers. It was also a frequent occurrence to meet a foot peddler balancing upon the pole over his shoulders a lot of bird cages at one end and of flowering plants at the other. A Chinese flower garden, if only one gets admission to it, is an object of beauty ever to be remembered. It is only the hard conditions of life in a country overcrowded with population which make the Chinese seem lacking in æsthetic inclinations.

Beyond the Nankao pass the road crosses diagonally the Gui-ho Valley and ascends the Yang-ho to the second range of mountains at Shiming, the distance being about forty miles. In this valley loess appears in increasing quantities, especially in the vicinity of the mountains, where the travel had often worn paths twenty-five or thirty feet deep in the loess, with perpendicular inclosing walls on either side. Across the Shiming Mountains the Yang-ho has forced its way through a picturesque gorge, which the road follows in many places along a narrow pathway cut in the face of precipitous rocks. Everywhere the procession of pack animals continued, being increased beyond the Shiming range by long trains of mules and donkeys carrying coal on their backs to regions beyond. Donkeys were often seen carrying panniers of coal destined for Kalgan, sixty miles away. At last, on the fifth day out from Peking, in the midst of a blinding dust storm lasting many hours, the terrors of which baffle description, we reached Kalgan, the gateway to Mongolia and all Central Asia, and were warmly greeted by the missionaries, Rev. Mark Williams and Rev. Mr. and Mrs. Sprague. (Since that time a railroad has been built to Kalgan and the journey from Peking can be made in a single day, without discomfort.) After a Sunday's rest at the compound of the mission, and another day spent in visiting the interesting localities in the vicinity, and in forming the acquaintance of the Russian officials, we were ready for an excursion beyond the outer Chinese wall and the high border of the vast plateau which occupies the interior of the continent. It was gratifying to find the most cordial relations existing between the Russian officials and our missionaries. Indeed, the Russians had paid half the salary of the lady missionary physician, who had been some years at the station. On her departure from Kalgan much regret was expressed, and the Russian ambassador at Peking wrote her a most cordial letter of thanks.

Kalgan, a city of about one hundred thousand, is literally the gateway to Mongolia. The outer Chinese wall, built more than two thousand years ago, constitutes the upper wall of the town. Here a number of converging streams, coming down with rapid descent from the lofty mountain chain beyond, narrow to a single channel, which is effectually guarded by the city. All the commerce between China and Central

Asia, and, until recently, with Siberia and Russia, passes through the single gate at the end of the principal street. Until two or three years before our visit this gate was so narrow that two loaded animals could not pass in it; but now it was so enlarged that the processions could be continuous both ways.

Strange as it may seem, the completion of the Suez Canal seriously affected the interests of Kalgan and of a large surrounding population. Immediately upon that event a considerable portion of the commodities which had been shipped to Russia and western Siberia across Mongolia found an easier route by way of the canal, and great temporary suffering was wrought upon the northern provinces. The cause of this was not evident to the secluded sufferers and it was still among the disturbing mysteries of the region. The tea trade, however, was preserved to this route for a time, by maintaining the belief that the quality of the tea was injuriously affected by an ocean voyage. But, now that the Siberian railroad was approaching completion, there was another struggle impending to retain the tea traffic of Russia in its old channels. Even at that time, the Russian merchants assured me that the traffic was largely diverted by way of Vladivostok.

Still, Kalgan will never cease to be an important center of business; for there are two million Mongo-

lians who will find this their natural commercial outlet to the world. In addition to this, Chinese farmers
are rapidly spreading over the eastern border of the
Mongolian plateau, and are transforming the thinly
populated grazing land of the Mongols into more
thickly populated agricultural colonies. One of the
great national products of Mongolia must certainly
find its way out through the present gateway. This
is the crude soda of the desiccated lakes of the region.
In ascending the narrow gorge leading from Kalgan
to Hanoor, on the summit of the plateau, 2,500 feet
above the city, we met thousands of oxcarts loaded
with this native soda, found one hundred and fifty
miles farther inland. This is all owned by the Chinese government and is refined at Kalgan and distributed from that point. Another rather curious
sight that met our eyes during this part of our trip
was large droves of black swine which had been driven
long distances on their way to market. But it was not
the swine themselves which attracted our curiosity so
much as their feet, which were all shod with felt shoes
to protect them from the stony paths over which they
were compelled to travel.

The eastern edge of the Mongolian plateau is 5,400
feet above sea level, and what is most surprising is that
the surface begins at once to slope away to the west.

Indeed, in less than a mile from the edge of the escarpment the streams are running towards the great Gobi
desert, which is only 2,500 feet above sea level. The
view from the towers of the Chinese outer wall, which
runs along the front of the escarpment, is extremely
impressive and suggestive. To the west and north
stretch, as far as the eye can reach, the undulating plain
which occupies the interior of the great continent and
which is largely rendered barren from lack of rain.
But here in the month of May innumerable camels,
oxen, and mules are spread abroad to recuperate for a
short time from the arduous tasks which have been
laid upon them in their long journeys to and from the
interior. To the east and south are endless stretches
of mountain peaks, along the central line of which the
great wall is conspicuous as far as the angle of vision
permits the eye to take cognizance of it. Later we
learned that this is by no means a barren country.
Between these mountain ranges there is a succession
of fertile valleys, where irrigation partly counteracts
the prevailing droughts, and the teeming population is
able to procure a comfortable livelihood.

After following for two days the great caravan
route from Kalgan to Siberia, we left the high plateau
and struck eastward across the upper portion of the
streams which center at the pass at Kalgan. This took
us into an unfrequented country and revealed to us

the inner life of the Chinese people, for though we were still in Mongolia, the Chinese were the main occupants of the soil. On reaching the little village of mud houses named San-ha-pa; on the very edge of the escarpment, we found it necessary to seek shelter for the night. But as there was no inn this was a matter of no small difficulty. We were the wonder of the whole community, attracting so much attention that we actually broke up a funeral procession which was passing by. At length, however, an elderly couple consented to vacate all their house but the kitchen, and even that was given up to our attendants. The curiosity of the people was insatiable. Till late in the evening an unmanageable throng crowded into the vacant space of the room, and pressed against the paper windows until they had broken them through, to see us eat and drink, and to inspect our clothes. Even the women ventured into conspicuous places, and stood on the housetops all around to gaze at us whenever we ventured out. But it was a harm-less, good-natured crowd. It is true that they called us " devils,"—the mothers, as usual, holding up their children to the windows of our inn and rebuking them for being afraid of the " devils." This, however, meant nothing more than " foreigners." So, as far as we could learn, they did not in that village, as they did near Tientsin, call us " long-haired devils."

Going on farther east·from this point, we descended
1,500 feet into a broad longitudinal valley, lined on
all the southeastern slopes with hills of loess, on which
the villages were built, many of the houses being mere
excavations in this remarkable formation.   Passing
again over another north and south ridge which carried us up to the level of the plateau, we sought
shelter the third night in an inn which had no private
room.   The " kang " adjoined the kitchen range,
which was heated by dry manure of the various animals cared for in the inclosure or passing by on the
road.   As most of the smoke was left to find its way
without proper guidance to a solitary hole in the roof,
the scene must be left to the reader's imagination.
Without any partition walls we shared the sleeping
place with an unknown number of Chinese.   No
harm, however, ensued, and we had excellent opportunities to observe the conditions under which this
industrious and patient people spend their lives.

The poverty of the great mass of the people had
been forced upon our attention in many ways, but in
none more than in the matter of dress.   Peking is in
the latitude of Philadelphia, yet in the ride from that
city to Tung-chau on the first of May, when snow had
fallen to a depth of several inches, we saw many children from six to ten years of age who had already
donned their summer apparel, consisting simply of a

little colored cord braided into their long hair. On the way to Kalgan naked children became too frequent to attract attention. In the inn at one of the villages a little boy about five or six years old, without even a cord in his hair, walked in with great dignity carrying carefully in his hand a single egg which he wished to barter for thread. The innkeeper, who was as well a storekeeper, attended to the wants of the child with as much obsequiousness as he would have shown to a grown-up patron, and the boy departed with perfect satisfaction. On asking Mr. Williams if there was not danger that the boy would be imposed upon, he answered, "No: for his mother has a tongue." Thus the Chinese women secure their rights without the ballot, about as they do in other countries.

On inquiry we ascertained that in this section of China, carpenters get what in America would amount to eight cents a day. A boss mason receives eight and a half cents, and his attendant six and a half. Ordinary workmen and sewing women get five cents. But this low scale of wages is offset by the low cost of living. Oatmeal, which is the staple here as rice is in the south, ordinarily sells for less than a cent a pound. When it rises to a cent and a half, a famine is produced and multitudes die from lack of nutriment. The food for an ordinary workman costs a cent and a half per day. A large part of the unrest culminating

in the Boxer revolution, which was beginning to con-
vulse China at that time, was occasioned by the wide-
spread pressure for food, caused by the partial failure
of crops in the northeastern provinces. A hungry people are not amenable to reason.

The fourth day carried us over another mountain
ridge level with the plateau, and brought us at night
to the noted Catholic mission of Shiwantse, maintained
by a society in Belgium. It was surprising to find in
this remote locality so many indications of Christian
civilization. Here was a boarding school for Chinese
girls with an attendance of four hundred, and another
for boys with two hundred. In the village eighteen
hundred Christian Chinese are living with every sign
of contentment, in houses excavated in the extensive
loess deposit which has collected at the southern base
of the encircling mountains. The bishop and a half
dozen associates hospitably welcomed us, and showed
us with just pride through their new building, more
than three hundred feet long and two stories high,
which they were constructing for the enlargement of
their work. Altogether they reported 30,000 converts
in Mongolia, and 780,000 in China. All the fifth
day we slowly worked our way down the ever-deepen-
ing valley towards Kalgan, only reaching there on the
sixth day from starting.

The objects of our trip were accomplished. As Kal-

gan is in the latitude of New York City, where the
marks of the Glacial epoch are abundant, and as the
general conditions of eastern Asia are so like those of
eastern North America, it was necessary, in fixing the
limits to glacial action in Asia, to explore thoroughly
this region. Our trip demonstrated that glaciers
never have extended as far south as that, on the Mongolian plateau. To find glacial phenomena we must
now go to Mukden (north of Korea) and make a section of the country thence to the Sungari River.

We left Kalgan for Peking on the 21st of May,
and arrived on the 26th, having been absent, without
news from the outside world, for three weeks. We
found the city in a state of great excitement on account of the menacing attitude of the " Boxers." On
two or three occasions we had come in contact, more or
less directly, with these malcontents. At one time
we encountered a large crowd that was gathered
around a company of them as they were going through
their contortions. They seemed to embody in one the
fury of religious bigotry and that of political enthusiasm, fanned into flame by the manifest rapid progress
of foreign enterprises and the wide-spread failure of
crops already referred to. For many months companies of them had been gathering in increasing numbers, and by practices familiar to religious enthusiasts

had worked themselves up into an hypnotic state, in
which they made themselves believe that they were in-
vulnerable to bullets. Two Chinese army officers
were overheard one day in a railroad train discussing
this claim of the Boxers. One of them thought there
was really something in it, and that they were invul-
nerable. The other called attention to the fact that
in a recent engagement some of them had been killed
by bullets, to which the other replied, that probably
they had not passed through all the degrees.

. We left Peking for Tientsin on the 26th of May.
We were none too soon; for, on the following day, the
Boxers, with arms and munitions of war obtained from
the sympathetic soldiery, attacked the railroad south of
Peking, burnt the stations, and advanced to within a
few miles of the city, where they destroyed the main
railroad and cut Peking off from connection with the
outside world. The foreign powers were taken completely by surprise. On the 29th, about midnight, a
company of marines from the United States gunboat
Newark reached Tientsin and were welcomed with
noisy demonstrations. But they could get no farther.
On the 30th we were glad to escape from the confusion, and take a train for the harbor, where we could
get a boat for Chefoo. Already there were fourteen
men-of-war of all nationalities hovering about Taku,
eight of them being Russian. Five hundred Russian

soldiers, who had attempted to follow the United States marines up to Tientsin, had been turned back. No one knew what to expect.

On reaching Chefoo we soon found a small Russian steamer bound for Port Arthur, which at this time was little else than a military post, where active operations were going on to complete the fortifications. We found shelter in a miserable inn, partly dug out from the side of the hill on the west side of the town, and set ourselves at work to procure an interview with Admiral Alexieff, who was still there, though the ranking admiral among the fleets assembled to protect foreign interests in China. That afternoon there was to be a reception given by the Admiral, so we attended, expecting to hand him there our letter of introduction from Baron Rosen. But the extra duties thrust upon him by the Boxer revolution kept him from being present, and so we failed to secure an interview. And here comes in an incident in my experience, such as has often occurred, when ignorance was bliss.

The next morning we went over to the Admiral's office and presented to the guards both the letter to the Admiral, and the one to Colonel Samoieoff. But, if we could at that time have read the address on the letter to Samoieoff, we would have learned that his station was not at Port Arthur, but at Khabarovsk, several hundred miles away. In our ignorance, however,

we handed both letters to the guards. After waiting
an hour or more, we were put in charge of a Cossack
and marched off through the streets, we knew not
where, or what for. We were taken to military headquarters, and, to our great joy, ushered into the presence of Colonel Samoieoff, who the day before had
reached Port Arthur, having been transferred there
on the breaking out of the Boxer difficulties. Good
fortune had again attended us. Colonel Samoieoff
spoke English fluently, and was greatly interested in
our plans, and said he would secure an interview with
the Admiral in a short time. He took our letter and
sent it to the Admiral's residence and told us to return
to our inn, where we would be called for soon. In due
time an orderly came to us with an invitation for a
private interview the next morning. Meanwhile the
Colonel took us in charge and showed us everything
about the place which it was lawful for us to see, and
aided us in selecting and purchasing photographs.

Our interview with the Admiral was very satisfactory. We found that he, too, had been in America,
and was interested in the objects of our investigations.
Next morning he put us on a construction train, which
was to go leisurely up as far as the rails were laid on
this end of the Chinese Eastern railroad, to Teling,
thirty miles beyond Mukden. It was interesting to
notice that we were drawn by a Baldwin locomotive,

built in Philadelphia, over rails made in Baltimore and laid on ties from Oregon. We were crowded into the caboose with officers, and engineers of the road, together with a number of the higher class of the workmen. The train stopped everywhere to put off supplies, or to transport timbers which had served their purpose in one place and were needed farther along, so that, so far as observation was concerned, it was next thing to making the distance in a Chinese cart. The superintendent of the stations to be erected along the road was going the whole distance to Teling, and had with him a tow-headed Scandinavian servant, who had been in New York and could speak English indifferently. The superintendent was very helpful to us in every way. So the journey passed off as pleasantly and profitably as could have been wished if we had planned everything ourselves.

Port Arthur is the " nose " of the Liao-tung peninsula, which is essentially a mountainous range, bordered by fertile lands on either side. For the most part the road runs so near the south side of the peninsula that the ocean is in view. Near Te-lien-wan, however, the water is for some distance visible on both sides. Altogether the ride much resembles that from Florence to Genoa in Italy. From Niu-chuang to Mukden the road follows up the middle of the rich Liao-tung Valley, which is fifty miles or more wide,

with every acre under cultivation. At the time we
passed through it, squads of Chinese were cultivating
the vast fields of sorghum, millet, and beans, which
form the staple crops. Not a weed was to be seen. We
could easily understand how the Russians, a few years
later, in the Japanese war, made a fatal mistake in failing to reckon on the growth of these crops, when making their military assignments for the artillery posts,
these being made when the ground was bare. But, by
the time of actual military occupations, the millet and
sorghum had grown so high that the Japanese could
approach the Russian lines without being observed as
they crawled through the rank vegetation. The productiveness of the country may be judged by the fact
that five hundred thousand tons of beans were annually
sent out of the port of Niu-chuang.

Before the building of the Chinese Eastern railroad
by the Russians, all this inland traffic was by means
of primitive carts. The organization and protection
of these immense caravans as they went back and forth
reveal a condition of things in the Chinese Empire
that is little understood by foreigners. The central
government in China is so weak that almost everything
is left to the local authorities, and they are but the
agents of local public sentiment. " Local option " in
China has been carried to a ridiculous extreme. For

instance, as we were coming down from Shiwantse to Kalgan, we passed through a village which had been visited a few days before by a band of robbers, who had pillaged the public pawnshop, which served as the bank, and carried away a large portion of the goods which were stored there. But they did not take every-thing, and did not disturb the private dwellings. With this the authorities were well satisfied, and made no effort to capture and punish the marauders. Evi-dently they regarded the loot as a sort of a tax for their protection. For if they had pursued the robbers they would have returned and wiped out the whole settlement.

In Manchuria the whole government of the province was practically turned over to a " robber trust," which had been formed by the larger bands. So many small bands had been formed that there was danger that all traffic would be driven off from the road; hence the larger bands formed a trust to put down the smaller bands, and then went to the merchants and offered for a given sum to insure safe conduct for the caravans and their treasures. This was practically all the gov-ernment that existed in Manchuria when we were there, outside of the strip, ten miles wide, bordering the railroad, which was under Russian protection. Similarly, in Kalgan at that time, there was a " beggar trust." The beggars were organized, and had a

" king," who would go to the merchants and arrange with them, for a specific sum, to keep all beggars from infesting the entrance to their stores. The service thus rendered was really a full equivalent for the sum paid. But, after all, this is not much different from the protection which is often secured in our country by the employment of Pinkerton detectives to supplement government agencies.

The railroad through Manchuria seemed to make many curves which were unnecessary in going through a level country. But soon there appeared a reason for this. It was to avoid the desecration of graves, which the Chinese consider most sacred. Much unnecessary ill-will was incurred by the English and Germans through their disregard of this feeling among the Chinese. In this respect the Russians were more considerate than other nations had been. The absence of labor-saving machinery was also noted all along the line of the railroad which was under construction. We did not see a wheelbarrow during the whole journey. The dirt that was removed from the various cuts, and was used to make the equally numerous fills, was all dug up by hoes, placed in baskets hung on the opposite ends of a pole and carried on the shoulders of naked men, who cheerfully trotted back and forth with their burdens, and deposited them where needed. But throughout China human labor is cheap. Ten cents a day in silver was all that was paid, and there were literally, when we were there, hundreds of thousands of men employed in pushing on the work to completion. It was no unusual thing to see a hundred men at work without a stitch of clothes on them. And when off from work, they were often seen wrestling and engaging in other sports. Nakedness was their normal condition in the summer time.

Teling is about thirty miles beyond Mukden and four hundred and thirty miles from Port Arthur. From here to the end of the section which was being built southward from Harbin, there intervened about two hundred miles that must be traversed by private conveyance. Here we were very cordially received by Mr. Cassigeri, the chief engineer, who was constructing the section of seventy-five miles extending northward. His family was with him, occupying a native house, which was comfortably fitted up for the two years' stay during which the work was expected to continue. We were hospitably shown another house, which, with the adjoining garden, we were told was all ours as long as we cared to stay; and a servant was placed at our disposal. Mr. Cassigeri did not speak English. But Colonel Ghenche, the superintendent of telegraphic construction along the whole line, spoke it fluently, and was well versed in every department

of learning. Indeed, he was one of the best informed
and interesting men I ever met. His knowledge of
the conditions of all the countries bordering the Russian Empire on the south was encyclopedic. He was
boarding with the Cossack colonel, whose wife was
with him and was as cordial in welcoming us as was
her husband. She felt quite hurt that we did not make
our home with them instead of the chief engineer. We
could pacify them only by taking one or two meals
with them. Here, as everywhere else where we saw
them, the Cossacks made a very pleasant impression on
us. They are to Russia what the standing army is to
the United States, and are animated by about the same
patriotic and disinterested sentiments of loyalty and
hospitality.

At the dinners in the house of the chief engineer we
were introduced to a Russian custom which we had
much opportunity to observe later. Before sitting
down to the heavily laden table we were expected in-
dividually to go to a side table and help ourselves to
various appetizing morsels, consisting of such things
as sardines, sweet cucumber pickles, crackers, and, if
you were so inclined, a mouthful of " vodka." Colonel
Ghenche usually dined with us, so that there was no
difficulty in carrying on conversation during the meal.
Mr. Cassigeri was a Circassian. I was much touched
when, just before leaving, he asked me into his private

office, and after we were seated took out from his desk
a photograph of a beautiful girl, who, he told me with
the aid of a Latin dictionary, was his daughter, buried
in Petrograd. Sorrow brings all hearts together. The
tears filled his eyes as he shared his feelings with me
for a few moments before we separated.

On Monday, June 11, 1900, we regretfully parted
from our friends at Teling, and set out on our journey of two hundred miles in two carts, each drawn by
three mules, and accompanied by a Chinese driver,
with whom we had arranged to transport us the whole
distance. The journey was to occupy about ten days.
The charge was eighty silver dollars. We still had
with us our Chinese interpreter whom we had engaged
in Peking, and carried our own bedding and a supply
of provisions. None of these, however, were needed
for the first week; since Cossacks conducted us from
station to station of the engineering corps engaged in
constructing the road, and we were everywhere royally
entertained by men of wide information, who fully appreciated the objects of our expedition, and were delighted to see some one from the outside world. An
important sidelight is shed on Russia's power and civilization in that, when a railway eighteen hundred miles
in length was to be constructed in an unknown region,
in the shortest possible time, the large body of trained
men capable of doing the work could be found at once.

Those whom we met were uniformly men of wide general as well as special training; and they were from all parts of the Empire; from Poland, Moscow, Odessa, Circassia, and Armenia. One, Mr. Terovakimoff, an Armenian, who had constructed the section of the Siberian railway from Krasnoyarsk, on the Yenisei River, to Irkutsk, on the Angara, was an accomplished classical scholar, and could repeat with ease large portions of Horace in Latin and of Sophocles in Greek. Nearly all these men were looking forward to a journey home through America on the completion of their work in about a year.

From Teling the valley broadens out till it becomes in the northwest unlimited, and is everywhere, in the vicinity of the railroad, under high cultivation. No part of the prairie region of the United States exceeds it in fertility. Moreover, the distant mountains are covered with timber, in pleasing contrast to those in China. As we proceeded northward I was constantly looking with expectation of finding some indication of glacial deposits, for we were now in the latitude of New England and on the same side of a continent. But the prophecies of finding glacial deposits with which I encouraged my son from day to day proved delusive, and I barely escaped the reputation of being a false prophet. Indeed, no signs of glaciation appeared even when we had reached the Amur River at

Khabarovsk in latitude 48°, nor, later, at Elbazin, in latitude 53°, which is on the same parallel with Hamilton Inlet in Labrador.

At Kwan-Chen-tse we spent the Sabbath with some missionaries from the north of Ireland, who, with others supported by a Scotch society, have had remarkable success in the leading centers of Manchuria. Dr. Gordon, the medical missionary at this place, and his family, entertained us most hospitably, so that it seemed like being at home again. He was both physician and preacher, but unfortunately for us he preached in the language of the people and not in English. His hospital was widely patronized, and evidently was very productive both in the direct good it did and in the indirect influence which it exerted in commending Christianity to the people.

Kwan-Chen-tse is a lively center of trade with Mongolia. Especially is it a great market for horses, which are collected in great numbers. It lies just north of the watershed separating the basin of the Yellow Sea from that of the Sea of Okhotsk. But the grades in both directions are so gradual as to be almost imperceptible. North of the summit the alluvium becomes deeper, the roads worse, if possible, and the soil even more fertile. Across the seventy miles leading from there to the Sungari River, where we met the railroad which was in process of construction south from Harbin, we followed the Chinese roads, and stayed in Chinese inns. The sleeping places in these were common to us with thirty or forty Chinamen, several black pigs, and two or three mangy dogs. But after we had been jolted for twelve hours in a two-wheeled cart without springs, any resting place was acceptable. We reached the Sungari River at two p. m. on Wednesday, June 20, and found it to compare favorably with the Allegheny above Pittsburgh, but more navigable. The river is running here to the northwest, in which direction it continues for more than a hundred miles, where it is joined by the Nonni and turns to the east. The railway crosses in a straight line and meets the river again at Harbin, about a hundred miles by the road, but fully two hundred and fifty as the river runs. The same level fertile plains which we had been traversing by cart for the last two hundred miles continued to Harbin, which we reached safely on Friday, having been thrown off the track once. Harbin was unknown, even by name, two and a half years before we visited it. Then it was a city of ten thousand inhabitants, all engaged in rushing the construction of the railway in three directions, towards Port Arthur, Vladivostok, and towards Siberia. It was located here because it is the practical head of good navigation on the Sungari River, so that material could be transported thither by steamers. An immense amount of material had already been distributed from there,—enough to equip three hundred miles of road, and more was constantly arriving. The most of this was from America. Geologists will be interested to know that at Harbin wells are eighty feet deep in alluvial soil, and that the abutments of the railway bridge go down for foundations through one hundred and eighty feet of clay.

Mr. Yugovitch, the chief engineer of the road, made his headquarters at Harbin. He had heard of our coming and gave us a hearty welcome. On learning that I wished to have the elevations along the road, he at once produced his papers, and read them off to me while I copied them with a pencil. When I asked him questions about the watershed at Kwan-Chen-tse, he saw at once the scientific importance of them and had me write out what I wished done, and telegraphed his engineers to survey and make a profile section along the watershed westward from there to determine what the lowest point actually was. Thus I soon had at command a most important series of facts, which would have been beyond my reach but for Mr. Yugovitch's intelligent interest. I could easily understand why he was chosen to be chief engineer of so vast a work of construction.

DOWN THE SUNGARI RIVER AND UP THE USURI

The importance of the Sungari River will best be

appreciated by Americans when they are told that it
drains an area considerably larger than the basin of
the Ohio, and one that is equally rich in agricultural
resources, and possibly also in mineral wealth and for:
ests. The river is navigable for steamers up to Harbin, a distance of six hundred miles from its mouth,
where it joins the Amur, a hundred miles above
Khabarovsk. In its upper waters an immense amount
of commerce is carried on in Chinese junks. We
were sent down from Harbin on one of the twenty
steamers which had been constructed by the Russians
to bring supplies for the construction of the railroad in
three directions from Harbin. In going through the
yards we were flattered by finding the names of fifteen Ohio firms on the boxes of material required for
their work. Among our companions on the steamer
was Colonel Dessino, the Russian military agent in
northern China. He spoke English readily, and was
able to give us all the information we desired concerning the country.

The scenery along the Sungari is almost unrivalled
in interest. The valley is from twenty-five to fifty
miles broad, with picturesque mountains forming the
sky line on either side. Occasionally these approach
near to one or the other side of the river, but ordinarily they are at the respectful distance which lends
enchantment to the view. The river is everywhere

majestic in its volume, as it rolls along between its green banks and cultivated fields. The scene was also still enlivened by the presence of many native junks, which are slowly propelled by sails, by men pushing with poles against the bottom of the stream, or by others painfully towing them with long ropes from the banks. The natives could yet hardly realize what a transformation steam was to make for them. The junks will, however, always be necessary in the several hundred miles of more difficult navigation above Harbin, and in the various tributaries of the main stream.

We were four days making the trip from Harbin to Khabarovsk; but we were anchored during the darker portions of two of the nights. The hundred miles of the Amur traversed was a repetition of the Sungari, only on a larger scale. From the junction to the sea, the Amur is really one of the grandest rivers in the world. So vast is its basin, and so slightly elevated is the lower part of it, that the gradient is slight. From Harbin to the sea the fall is only about five inches to the mile, while from Blagovestchensk the gradient is still·less.

The view from Khabarovsk in early summer is one of the grandest imaginable. East and west the broad current of the Amur, winding through a valley of luxuriant vegetation, which has no visible northern border, can be traced to the limit of vision, while the broad Usuri comes in from the south through the defiles of the mountain chain which rises in solemn grandeur to limit the vision in that direction. The city itself is also interesting. In 1900 it had fifteen hundred inhabitants. Its museum and geographical society are famous the world over. It is the center of administration for all the maritime provinces of Siberia, and so has a large proportion of intelligent and highly cultivated residents. The completion of the main line of the railroad, through Harbin to Vladivostok, will somewhat limit its future growth; but the prospect of rapid development of the vast tributary region to the west and southwest has already given it a new impulse, which, in a few years, will make it, even more than now, a most attractive place of residence, especially in summer. Yet, strange to say, those who live there go in considerable numbers, every summer, to Kamchatka for variety. Such is the universal anxiety of the modern man to enjoy some change of scene.

Because we had sent our baggage around from Port Arthur to Vladivostok we thought it best to run down there, especially as it would give us a chance to see so much more of the country. But we now began to learn something of the tragedies which were taking place in China, though our inability at that time to read the Russian papers limited our knowledge to the barest outline of facts. In our desperation, however, we had purchased a paper just before boarding the train. Our comrades perceived our difficulty in getting· anything out of the paper, but were unable to assist us. Soon, however, a Russian lady on board learned of our embarrassment and relieved it. She was a woman of about fifty years, and, as we learned afterwards, was the wife of the Military Governor at Vladivostok, and was returning from a visit to Russia. Coming to the door opening into our compartment, she graciously asked us in good English if she should not translate the news to us. Of course we accepted the favor with great pleasure, and learned for the first time of the siege of Peking, and the many other horrors from which we had barely escaped. It is needless to say that this, with several other similar experiences, has given us an exalted opinion of the educated Russian women. The graciousness with which this highborn Russian dame ministered to the wants of two seedy travelers made an impression that can never be obliterated from memory, and led us to wonder if many American women would, or could, give such assistance to Russian travelers in a plight similar to ours.

On arriving at Vladivostok, our first concern was to communicate with those at home to let them know of our safety; for we perceived that, as the last letters they could have received from us were mailed a month before the Boxer outbreak, just as we were starting for Kalgan, there must be great anxiety about us. And so there had been. Telegrams had been sent to China in vain to learn of our whereabouts. The most hopeful surmise was that we were with the missionaries, who had escaped from Kalgan and were making their way across the desert on the camel route to Siberia. To relieve what I knew was their anxiety I paid eight · gold dollars to send two words to my daughters. These were, " Safe, prosperous." After a few days in this beautifully situated naval fortress, we returned to Khabarovsk, to continue our journey homeward by way of the Amur River and the Siberian railroad. An idea of the state of society in this and all other principal towns in Asiatic Russia may be formed from the fact that here we were permitted to attend the production of one of the classic operas, by a company that had come on for a season from Russia, the choruses being performed by a local society, all supported by a local orchestra. The performance was in every way satisfactory.

The distance to Khabarovsk is four hundred miles, and the run was made in thirty hours. A dining car provided excellent meals at a rouble (about fifty cents) each. The second-class carriages had comfortable

sleeping arrangements without charge; but the pas-
senger had to supply his own bedding, as is the case
in . hotels throughout Asiatic Russia. The fare was
only a cent and a half a mile, while on the third-class
cars the charge was less than a cent a mile.

UP THE AMUR

Immediately on returning from Vladivostok, we took
a steamer from Khabarovsk to Blagovestchensk, about
five hundred miles up the Amur River, having been
joined by three interesting traveling companions, Captain Harford, Captain Smith-Dorrien, and Mr. Wettekind. Captain Harford had taken an active part in
the Crimean War, and afterwards was for thirty
years English consul at Sevastopol. He was a great
admirer of Russia and her institutions, and was full
of information of every sort concerning her rulers and
people. Captain Smith-Dorrien had been commander
of the British man-of-war Bonaventura, that had been
stationed at Manila. He had been invited home for
promotion just in time to prevent his partaking in a
most important transaction. Soon after he had left
the ship, it was ordered to Chinese waters, and its
captain had the honor of receiving the surrender of
the Chinese fort, Taku, commanding the entrance to
Tientsin. He is a brother of the General Smith-
Dorrien of South-African fame. Mr. Wettekind was

a member of the great mercantile firm of Kuntz and Albert of Vladivostok. A more agreeable and helpful company of companions it would be difficult to find.

The steamer was crowded with Russian refugees from Manchuria, many of them being families of the engineers who had so hospitably entertained us. Being now under the protection of Russia and in Russian territory we little dreamed of any further difficulty. For two days our steamer wound its way along the tortuous course of the great river, with scarcely anything but the vast plain in sight. The breadth of the stream was fully a mile. On the third day we passed diagonally through the Bureya Mountains, which occupied a width of nearly one hundred miles, furnishing us subdued but very pleasing scenery. Above this at a picturesque Cossack station, called Radeska, we entered a broad prairie region, extending to Blagovestchensk, a distance of about two hundred miles, where the elevation is but three hundred feet above the sea, though a thousand miles from the mouth of the river. Our feeling of security was disturbed by discovering that we had on board two Chinese mandarins, whose baggage contained inflammatory appeals to their countrymen on the south side of the river to rise and destroy their Russian neighbors. We also met a number of steamers and barges, taking down from Blagovestchensk the whole garrison of the city, numbering five thousand, to be used in protecting Russian interests in Harbin and throughout Manchuria.

About one hundred miles below Blagovestchensk, shallow water compelled us to disembark at Poyerkova, and make the rest of our distance on land. After a night's rest, we drove the next day in tarantasses fifty miles to Gulvena, a thrifty settlement of vegetarians (Molokani). The scene was a beautiful one, when, about sundown, the cattle were wending their way homeward from the broad flood-plain of the Amur, and seeking their nightly resting places at each peasant's home. But the people were in a state of great excitement over the report of refugees, that the Chinese had crossed the river a few miles above and burned some Russian villages. Moreover, the silence was broken from time to time by the sound of cannon from the Chinese fort, Aigun, some miles up the river. As a consequence every family in the village packed the women and children and valuable household goods into carts, and in the middle of the night retired into the interior of the country for safety; but we were compelled to camp on the floor of the posthouse and wait the developments of the morning.

As no Chinese had ventured to attack the village, the peasants mostly came back in the morning to attend to their affairs. Two of these we engaged for sixty gold dollars to drive us by a back road to a station twenty miles distant. Here, as the road beyond was reported safe, we engaged teams to take us the rest of our journey at a reasonable price. But around a semicircle of fifty miles, following a curve of the river to the south, majestic columns of smoke were seen to rise from twenty-five or thirty points, and we soon passed the ruins of a small village that had been burned. Not long after, we came to a Chinese settlement of eight or ten thousand inhabitants, which was still burning, and through its streets were compelled to go with the flames roaring on either side and the cinders falling upon us like snowflakes. But we reached the city in safety and brought with us the first news from below that they had obtained for two or three days.

Blagovestchensk was then a city of some 30,000 inhabitants (it is now 70,000) spread out, with broad streets, over an extensive delta terrace between the Zeya and Amur rivers. The kind-hearted and unsuspicious Military Governor had sent the entire garrison of the city to the defense of interests lower down the river. But no sooner was this done, than a Chinese army ten or fifteen thousand strong, appeared on the south side and began to bombard the city. A guard was hastily recruited, which, with their scanty supply of small arms, made such a show that the Chinese did not attempt to cross the river. While we were there, however, shells were bursting constantly in the streets, occasionally killing persons who were exposed; and at one time a bullet came into the dining room in the hotel, on a back street, where we were staying.

It was at Blagovestchensk, two or three days before we arrived, that the reported terrible massacre of Chinese occurred for which the Russians were so greatly blamed. The facts were these: There were between three and four thousand Chinese peaceably living in the city when on Sunday morning the Russians were waked from their fancied security by the bursting of shells from the opposite side of the river, giving them the first intimation that the war was brought to their doors. It was evident at once that it would not do to have Chinese on both sides of them. Therefore all those in the city were ordered to go across the river and join their companions. Rafts were hastily constructed a little above the city, and the Chinese were forced upon them and told to work their way over to the other bank. For reasons not known, the Chinese soldiers on the other side began to cannonade the rafts. A panic ensued, and in the commotion the rafts went to pieces and the whole body of refugees perished in the river. It was full of their floating bodies when we were in the city. I counted a hundred at one time, as I looked down from a protected place on the northern bank. But so far as we could see, and this was the opinion of Captain Smith-Dorrien, it was a casualty connected with a military necessity of self-defense for which the Russians could not be greatly blamed.

Young as was the city, it had every mark of a high civilization. Churches of fine architectural character abounded. There was a large hospital, whose erection had been stimulated by the success of Pasteur's method of treatment. There was a music store, at which I purchased a large quantity of Russian music, which Professor G. W. Andrews of Oberlin had commissioned me to procure for him; while a short time before we were there Saint-Saëns' opera of "Samson and Delilah" had been given in the city, the choruses being sung by local talent while the solos were given by the members of the opera troupe which we heard in Vladivostok.

After remaining about a week in this beleaguered city, we were able, by driving twenty miles across the country, to find a steamer which had brought Russian troops down and sent them overland for the defense of the city. This we boarded on its return trip for more soldiers. But as the Chinese still occupied the south side of the river, we were compelled to take staterooms on the other side of the boat. Progress was slow, partly because of shallow water, and partly from fear of attack. At Ignashina, the most northern point reached by the river, latitude 53° 40', we passed the ruins of the most flourishing Chinese settlement on the upper Amur, which five days before had been burned to the ground. But even at this high latitude we had failed to see any indications of glacial occupation. At Pokrovka, where the Argun and Shilka unite to form the Amur, we turned up the Shilka and proceeded to Stryetensk, where we met the trans-Siberian railroad. At various points below, we had passed many steamers with barges loaded 'with soldiers on their way to the seat of war, and a number of rafts, on which emigrants from Russia, with their live stock and their household goods, were slowly floating down the stream to find homes in the fertile prairies that abound along the middle and lower Amur, the logs of the raft being available for the construction of the favorite Russian house.

On arriving at Stryetensk, the terminus at that time of the Siberian railroad, Captain Smith-Dorrien and Mr. Wettekind separated themselves from us and went forward from this point by express train, and we saw them no more. Captain Harford, however, went more leisurely, so that we met him again at Irkutsk, where we, also, finally separated. But it is pleasant to note that twice in subsequent years he turned aside to visit us in America, while passing to and from his post at Manila.

TRANSBAIKALIA

The distance from Stryetensk to Lake Baikal is about six hundred miles. The railway passes over the continental divide of Asia, rising to about four thousand feet a little west of Chita. The Yablonoi Mountains, forming the crest of this divide, run southwest to northeast, extending continuously from Mongolia to Bering Strait. On the southeast they are bordered by a plateau about twenty-five hundred feet above the sea. This is here about two hundred miles wide, and possesses a climate and flora of its own, both of which are favorable to settlement. All grains ripen readily when there is sufficient water, and everywhere on the uplands there is good pasturage. Immense herds of cattle were visible almost everywhere from the car windows. Though the good land is by no means all occupied, there was already in Transbaikalia a population of about 700,000. It is now 900,000.

Nerchinsk, the first principal town passed through west of Stryetensk, has been for two hundred years a center of mining operations, to which the government has sent convicts sentenced to hard labor. The city had in 1900 a population of 6,700, and the department of 91,000. Chita, a city of 12,000 (it is now 70,000), where we stopped two days, is the capital of the province. One is surprised not only at the beauty of its situation, but at the fertility of the surrounding country. Its public and school buildings were numerous and imposing, but its streets entirely without pavements.

The territory from Chita to Lake Baikal consists in the main of a plateau, three hundred miles wide and about five thousand feet above the sea, in which the headwaters of the Amur, the Lena, and the Yenisei take their rise at a common level. This tract is bleak and well-nigh uninhabitable. It, too, extends from the plains of Mongolia to the vicinity of Bering Strait. But the rivers have deeply eroded its surface, and furnished in their courses long lines of fertile fields. These are specially open to settlement towards the south. The railroad passes over the eastern border into the valley of the Khilok, and for two hundred miles finds productive lands, congenial climate, and prosperous settlements. At Petrovskia we found a large and flourishing village gathered about a blast furnace founded by Peter the Great. The iron ore is near by, and the mountains furnish wood for charcoal to an unlimited extent.

At Verkhni Udinsk on the Selenga River we struck

the great caravan route from Kalgan, China, across
Mongolia. Over this route for hundreds of years the
.tea and many other commodities used in Russia have
been brought on camels' backs. The city had in 1900
a population of 8,000. In midwinter, it is the scene
of an enormous fair, at which millions of dollars'
worth of goods are sold every year. Heretofore the
best time to cross Lake Baikal and for traveling in
general in this region has been in the winter, when it
is frozen over. But all this has rapidly changed now
that the railroad is an accomplished fact.

LAKE BAIKAL

Lake Baikal is one of the five largest bodies of fresh
water in the world. It is more than four hundred
miles long and from sixteen to fifty miles wide, having an area of 12,430 square miles.. It.lies in a longitudinal basin in a vast mountain plateau, which extends in a northeasterly direction from Central Asia
to Bering Strait. The northern half is shallow, being
nowhere much more than two hundred feet in depth,
while the southern part has the astonishing depth of
4,186 feet. As the surface of the lake is only 1,561
feet above sea level, its bottom must be 2,625 feet below sea level. Unlike the Great Lakes of America,
Lake Baikal is not an aid, but a hindrance, to commerce and travel. If the four hundred miles of its

length lay in the line of traffic, it could be utilized with profit for the use of steamboats. But, as it is, it lies directly athwart this line and presents its rugged shores and deep water as an obstruction, which can be overcome only by a detour of about two hundred miles which the railroad is compelled to make around its southern end. Before the days of the railroad, however, it was utilized in the winter by sledges, which crossed on the ice and made it a scene of busy traffic. The great caravan route running from Kalgan in China across the Mongolian desert, passing Urga and Kiakhta, then followed down the Selenga River to its mouth, whence, for several months in the winter, little villages used to dot the surface along the line of the route across the lake, and make everything gay and lively.

The importance of this whole region is little understood by the general public outside of Russia. Lake Baikal separates two of the richest and most populous provinces of Siberia (Irkutsk and Transbaikalai), provinces which have been settled for nearly three hundred years and at the close of the nineteenth century had a population of nearly 2,000,000, only six or seven per cent of whom were exiles, many of whom proved in the end to be most enterprising and patriotic citizens.

In the thirteenth century the region just to the south played a most important part in the world's history.

It was in the valley of the Onon River, near the head-waters of the Selenga, that Genghis Khan was born. After gaining the ascendency over the tribes in his own valley and recruiting his forces from the sympathetic inhabitants of the upper Selenga, this remarkable man conquered China, and, turning, swept with an irre-sistible force over the northwestern frontier of Mon-golia, thence down the depression followed by the Irtysh River and along the irrigated belt at the north-ern base of the Tian-Shan Mountains into Turkestan, and thence onward beyond the Caspian and Black seas to the banks of the Dnieper in Russia, where he won a great victory over the army of that nation. It was the westward wave of the Mongols from the valley of the Onon and the Selenga which drove the Turks across the Bosporus and so permanently affected the history of Europe.

Lake Baikal presents scientific problems which are of great popular interest. One of these is the exist-ence in it of great numbers of arctic seal. As it is now 1,561 feet above sea level, and, as the river runs, two thousand miles from the sea, it is an interesting ques-tion to determine how these seal could have got into the lake. The only satisfactory theory is that there has been a geologically recent depression of land, per-mitting arctic waters to extend all over northwestern Siberia to a depth of 1,500 to 2,000 feet. This would permit the distribution of the seal to Lake Baikal, as well as to the Aral and Caspian seas, where they are also found. On the reëlevation of the land, these seas became separated, both from the ocean and each other, leaving the seal in these remote places.

Another problem on which Lake Baikal sheds light, relates to the date of the great earth movements which took place during the Tertiary period. The depression in which the lake is situated is still the center of important earthquakes. These are especially effective about the mouth of the Selenga River. As late as 1862 an extensive area, covering the delta of this river, disappeared below the level of the lake, thus indicating that the deep water at the south end is caused by the sinking of the bottom. In short, it is a synclinal basin formed during the geological disturbances which, all over the world, produced the moun-tain systems of the Tertiary period. By estimating the amount of sediment which comes down the Selenga River and settles in the southern basin, I have else-where[1] shown that it would have filled the whole basin in 500,000 years. But up to the present time it has accomplished less than one-quarter of this work, giving a maximum date of 100,000 years to the be-ginning of the geological convulsions which formed the lake.

So far as we can see, Lake Baikal in the future is

to render only two important services to the world;
its innumerable sequestered nooks of great sublimity
and beauty will provide summer retreats for the care-
worn and weary multitudes that are destined to fill
the adjoining regions; and it will be an unfailing
reservoir, furnishing a constant supply of water for
the power destined to be developed along the banks of
the rapid Angara River, which descends by a steep
gradient to the city of Irkutsk.

IRKUTSK TO KRASNOYARSK

The gigantic mountain wall which surrounds Lake
Baikal has an opening at one point only. This is well
toward the southern end, and through it the clear
sparkling water rushes with great rapidity, and in
volume more than half that of Niagara. Forty miles
below is the city of Irkutsk, between which and the
lake steamers run with more regularity than is usual in
Siberian waters, for so great is the reservoir that the
depth of the stream varies but little. The descent is
eighty feet, but, as the distance is greatly increased by
the windings of the river, the current is easily overcome by the power of steam. Altogether the trip is
delightful in the extreme. Irkutsk, the capital of
central Siberia, in 1900 was a city of 70,000, in 1908
had increased to 108,000. Its situation is in a beautiful broad valley, through which the Angara, the

principal eastern branch of the Yenisei, flows. The headwaters of the Lena River are not far to the northeast, making the city the commercial center of two of the largest river systems of the world. If we reckon the length of the Yenisei up the Angara to Lake Baikal, and thence up the Selenga to its source on the Mongolian plateau, we have a length of water course which exceeds the Missouri-Mississippi by two or three hundred miles.

Like all Siberian cities, most of the houses in Irkutsk are made of logs. When we were there the principal hotel was of logs. But the city abounds in magnificent churches, and has an opera house equal to anything west of the Alleghanies in the United States, and a museum of imposing dimensions and impressive character. We were invited to dinner by the Military Governor, who told us, as we came away, that the palatial dwelling in which he resided was built by an exile, and was purchased from him by the government. This, with other similar experiences, led us to infer that the exiles had had unusual opportunities to select eligible places for residence, and to build up a civilization that must have gone far to discount the evils connected with the exile system. The fact is, that the most of the political exiles, especially those sent away for conspiring against the inauguration of Nicholas I., about 1825, represented the highest order of intelligence and enterprise of Russia, and carried with them into its wilds such a civilization that when their disabilities were removed they in considerable part elected to remain in Siberia.

In Irkutsk we found bathhouses in abundance and a public reading room with a good supply of English papers and magazines. The boast of the city was that it had no municipal debt and that there was a considerable fund in hand to meet some of the necessary expenses. As an offset, however, it is to be noted that it had no pavements, no waterworks, no adequate sewers, no street cars, and no public electric lights. Doubtless all these conditions will change as a result of the vast movement of population into the whole region since the opening of the present century.

It is six hundred miles in a direct line from Irkutsk on the Angara to Krasnoyarsk on the Yenisei. The old Siberian wagon-road and now the railway traverse this along what was originally a nearly level plain of stratified rock. This area contains twice as much fertile soil as the state of Illinois and is destined eventually to be as thickly populated. The climate, though cold in winter, is warm enough in summer to ripen most varieties of grain. The pastures are green and support large herds of cattle and horses as well as endless flocks of sheep. The streams which cross the plain come down from the Mongolian plateau at the south, and abound in placer mines in their upper portions, so that long ago a line of flourishing towns had existed near where the rivers emerge from the auriferous belt.

At Krasnoyarsk, where a Russian fort was established early in the seventeenth century, we found an attractive city of 20,000 inhabitants, which has since grown to 80,000. The Yenisei is here about the size of the Mississippi above its junction with the Missouri, but in its downward course it has come through very different scenery. For the first seventy-five miles above the city, the river winds its way through a tortuous channel which it has cut across a low mountain range parallel with the edge of the Mongolian plateau, which runs southwest and northeast. In ascending the river on the fine steamboats which ply upon its surface, one is struck with the number and variety of rafts coming down stream, loaded with watermelons, hay, and grain, indicating a fruitful region above. The owners of these rafts, on reaching Krasnoyarsk, sell everything they have, even to the timbers of the raft, and remain in the city till the river freezes over, when they go back upon the ice.

MINUSINSK

After passing through this low mountain range, we emerge, in ascending the river, into an area of comparatively level and very fertile land, about one hundred miles in diameter, which is appropriately spoken of as the Italy of Siberia. This is the district of Minusinsk, which, notwithstanding its secluded position, has been occupied by a highly civilized population from the earliest periods of history. To see the evidences of this in the admirable museum with which the city of Minusinsk is provided, we ascended the river three hundred miles from the railroad.

The museum is a tribute to the enterprise and generosity of one of its leading but most modest citizens, Mr. N. M. Martianoff, a pharmacist of the town, but a botanist of international reputation. In the work of collecting, however, he has been assisted largely by several political exiles, prominent among whom was the brother of Prince Kropotkin, of whose tragic fate Mr. Kennan gives an account. In 1887 there was erected a commodious two-story fireproof building to hold the large number of objects of local interest which were accumulating on his hands. This is now filled with more than 50,000 specimens, scientifically classified and arranged for the inspection of the public. With the exception of a small but excellent pedagogical section, the museum is entirely devoted to the collection and preservation of objects from the vicinity. The rich mining region in the neighborhood supplies a remarkable variety of ores and minerals, while the extensive Silurian, Devonian, Carboniferous, and Jurassic strata of the vicinity furnish a very complete set of fossils for those portions of the geologic record. The flora of the region is also one of the richest in the world. This is represented in the museum by about 800 flowering and as many cryptogamic species of plants; while, of the lower fungi, 1,300 species have been collected, 124 of which, and, perhaps, more, are new.

But to the ordinary visitor the archæological and anthropological collections are of greatest interest. Indeed, so important are these that the societies at Stockholm and Moscow have published elaborate monographs upon them. The palæolithic age is but slightly and doubtfully represented in the collection. The neolithic age, is, however, quite fully and certainly represented by a variety of implements and some pottery which reminds one of the collections of Indian relics in America. But it is in the relics of the bronze age and of its transition into the iron age that the museum can specially glory. These have been collected from the mounds and burial places by the thousand. They consist of swords, knives, daggers, axes, and ornaments of various kinds, all showing great skill in their manufacture and much taste in their design. Among the daggers are some with iron handles and bronze blades, and others with bronze handles and iron blades. Among the objects disinterred are several silver medallions of the Han dynasty, in China, which must be more than 2,000 years old. These, with various other things, indicate a Chinese occupancy at that early day. There are evidences, also, that even then the iron and copper mines of the region were worked. Some of the crucibles of that time are on exhibition in the museum. There are also various early inscriptions of uncertain significance, but evidently in alphabetical characters, gathered from the burial places and ruined shrines. The Post-Pliocene deposits, too, have yielded abundant relics of the mammoth, the rhinoceros, and the gigantic elk that occupied the region during the palæolithic age.

Altogether the museum is one of the most interesting to be found anywhere in the world, and it sheds a flood of light on the bright side of life in Siberia; for all the larger towns of Siberia are supplied with museums which, by their appearance, bear witness not only to the high intelligence of their founders, but to the appreciation of the general public. Already the large room in which was collected the excellent library of this museum was overcrowded with books, and a commodious fireproof library building was nearly completed on a lot adjoining. All this in a secluded town three hundred miles from the main line of Siberian travel.

KRASNOYARSK TO OMSK

From Krasnoyarsk on the Yenisei to Omsk on the Irtysh River is 738 miles, but nearly the whole of the distance is within and directly across the drainage basin of the Obi River. The Chulym River, one of the principal eastern tributaries of the Obi, is crossed at Achinsk, only forty miles west of Krasnoyarsk. Indeed, in one place where the streams are still navigable, the tributaries of the Yenisei and of the Obi are within six miles of each other. It is a singular fact of physical geography that all the long branches of the Yenisei are on the east side, while most of those of the Obi are on the western side. But really the proper continuation of the Obi is its middle branch, the Irtysh, which is in itself a river 1,800 miles in length, whose source is far up on the Mongolian plateau.

The garden of western Siberia (south of the fifty-sixth degree of latitude) lies in the valley of the Obi for a distance of three hundred miles. Here there are 100,000 square miles of well-watered, fertile prairie land, with a climate permitting the ripening of the most important cereals, and in every way as well adapted to cultivation as are the plains of Minnesota. Already there is in this belt a population of nearly 4,000,000. Much of the territory is also underlaid by coal-bearing deposits. Although these are mostly of Jurassic age, and carry a coal that is light—almost lignite—still it promises to supply the want of fuel fairly well, and is being mined extensively. Throughout most of Siberia, wood is still so plentiful that the locomotives ordinarily use it for fuel; but here they use domestic coal.

At all the important places in Siberia touched by the railroad, new cities are growing up about the stations. The old cities are built almost entirely of wood. Even most of the best houses are of logs. But the new cities are growing up like magic out of brick. In due time all will have to follow suit and build of brick, for the wood is rapidly disappearing. Logs are, however, the easiest material from which to construct a house suited to withstand the severe winters of Siberia.

The name of the station where the railroad crosses the Obi River is Ob, which until lately has not appeared on the maps. The old city on the river was called Krivostchekova, and was an important place of 10,000 inhabitants. Connected with this place by steamer up the river are the flourishing cities of Barnaul and Biisk, with populations respectively of 61,000 and 18,000; while a short distance below is Tomsk, with a population of 112,000, and a university of wide renown. One finds, therefore, that in coming to this part of Siberia, he is not out of the world. The mass of the people look and appear much as they do in any European city. The teachers in the schools are highly educated men. More than once, when my Russian and French were insufficient for conversation, I was asked to converse in Latin.

But Omsk, on the Irtysh, is 333 miles west of Ob. Here we found a city, 184 years old, of 42,000 (it is now 130,000) inhabitants, which reminded us more of America than anything else we had seen. Not that the architecture was like ours, for it was not. The houses were nearly all of logs, and the schools and other public buildings of brick in plain style, painted white. The churches, too, were typically Russian, with lofty domes and cupolas. But there was a brisk commercial air about the place, which reminded one of the towns on the Ohio River. Steamboats were coming and going, and the barges they had brought in were busy unloading their cargoes. Numerous rafts had also come down the river loaded with watermelons. In the stores the display of fruit was remarkable. But it was all imported.

As there was no further light to be shed upon the Glacial epoch in western Siberia, we left the railroad at Omsk to visit Turkestan, the road to which would lead us for many hundred miles along the base of the Tian-Shan Mountains, where we might hope to make observations concerning the glacial conditions of the mountainous regions of Central Asia. Here, therefore, is the proper place to say a few words about the general conditions of Siberia. In comparing the statistics at hand in 1900 with those of the present time, one is impressed with the rapid growth of that portion of the Russian Empire. In 1900 the population of Siberia proper was approximately 7,600,0co. According to the available statistics in 1912, the latest at hand, it had risen to 10,800,000. In several of the provinces, the growth has been really phenomenal. The population of Tomsk has increased from 1,929,-092 to 3,855,200; Yeniseisk has increased from 559,-902 to 970,800; the maritime provinces from 220,557 to 572,000.

This growth has been largely through immigration, although the birth rate in Siberia is phenomenally large. The settlers consist of Cossacks and peasants, who have emigrated in villages, carrying with them their communal organization. To a large extent the immigrants have been directed by the government to the outlying portions of the country, especially towards the Mongolian border, where they would provide a natural defense of the country. The Russian government secures remarkably cheap transportation for the immigrants and lends them money without interest for several years until they become established, and only then imposes taxes upon them.

The future of Siberia is one of great promise. Elsewhere (in "Asiatic Russia") I have estimated that nine states of the size of Illinois, and with about equal agricultural resources, could be carved out of the territory of southern Siberia; while the mining interests, the water power, and the facilities for internal navigation render the population independent of outside commerce, except in exchange for various luxuries of the tropics and the products of older civilizations. Siberia alone can easily support a population of 100,000,000.

FOURTEEN HUNDRED MILES BY TARANTASS

The exact distance was 1,406 miles. We did not contemplate quite so long a ride; for our plan was to ascend the Irtysh River from Omsk to Semipalatinsk, and go by tarantass from that city to Tashkent, in Turkestan, which would be a round twelve hundred miles. But the water in the Irtysh River was so low that we had to abandon the steamboat when a little more than half way up, and begin our tarantass experience at Pavlodara, two hundred miles below Semipalatinsk.

The postroads of the Russian Empire are one of its most commendable features. There are 12,979 miles of them in its Asiatic domain. These run from the Ural Mountains to the Pacific Ocean, and from the Caspian Sea to the Peninsula of Kamchatka. So good are these roads, and so perfect are the arrangements for transportation over them, that the delay in building railroads has not been so keenly felt as it otherwise would have been. We have heard much about the rapid traveling in Siberia by sledges in winter, but travel in the summer is equally expeditious.

All along these post routes, stations are established at an average distance of twelve or fifteen miles apart. At each station there is a comfortable house, with two or three public rooms provided with from two to four sofas or mattresses, a few chairs, and a table and looking-glass. A family occupies the house, and is bound to be ready, at very small cost, to provide each company of travelers with hot water and bread; usually, also, with milk and eggs. The traveler is expected to provide himself with tea and sugar, and to carry his own pillows, sheets, and blankets. At each station, also, the government provides a bountiful supply of horses. Over the route of our travel there were from twenty-five to thirty at each station. But that does not always insure prompt attention; for the government is merciful to its animals, and rigidly enforces the rule that the horses shall have three hours' rest between trips. It not infrequently happens, therefore, that the traveler has to spend several of the best hours of the day in waiting for the horses to fill out their allotted times of rest. But, with this exception, the station master is compelled at any hour of the day or

night to provide you with an outfit to carry you to
the next station with the greatest possible despatch.

As to tarantasses, each station has a sufficient supply on hand; but persons who take long journeys usually prefer to have their own, so as to avoid the frequent transfers of baggage. As our journey was a
long one, we decided to buy a tarantass at once. At
the station house at Pavlodara we found a second-
hand, or more probably a fourth-hand, one for sale.
In its day it had been one of the most elegant and
luxurious of its kind. But all tarantasses are essentially alike. The general shape of the box in which
you ride is like that of a modern bathtub. There are
no seats inside. You are expected to have mattresses
and pillows enough to cover the bottom, and to ride
in a reclining position. Thus it is really a sleeping
coach, in which, over smooth roads, one can travel
as well by night as by day.

Our tarantass was provided with a top cover of
leather over the rear end, and an ample leather apron
to pull up before us when necessary to keep out the
rain or dust or wind or cold air. Like all others,
this riding gear was mounted upon a sort of " buck-
board " arrangement which had little spring, but was
very strong. It was all anchored to the axletrees by
large and firmly bolted iron rods. As it had already
seen much service, we thought the weak points had

been well eliminated by a process of natural selection; so that what was left could be trusted to endure to the end. It was a " troika,"—a vehicle drawn by three horses,—one in the shafts to guide the vehicle and hold it back when going down hill, the other two, one on each side, to draw. A bell was hung upon the horses' necks in turn, being changed from one to the other to give new life when the spirits of either began to flag. With the heads of the two draft horses turned outwards to watch the flourish of the driver's whip, we presented the appearance of a Roman chariot race as we galloped along from station to station.

· The tarantass cost us eighty roubles, about forty dollars. We should have paid only about thirty dollars for it; but our haste and lack of familiarity with the language put us at a disadvantage. We expected to sell it at Tashkent at an equal disadvantage. But it was the best we could do; and, even if it were an entire loss, this would not be relatively great, provided it got us safely through. Of one thing we felt confident, namely, that the wheels were strong and sound. But before we were two miles on our way, one of the hind wheels came off as we were going at a rapid rate.

It took us some time to find what was the matter. But at length it appeared that the " box " was loose, and the hub had come off with it, and let the axletree down with a heavy thud. The fact that the axletree was neither broken nor sprung was reassuring. Our driver ingeniously fixed matters up so that we reached the next station safely. There ready hands aided us to wedge the box in so firmly that it gave us no further trouble. It was, however, the cause of much anxiety; for it had dispelled the illusion that there could be no new breaks in our old tarantass, and we were kept constantly on the lookout thereafter to discover any new weak points. Every day revealed some, but they were not serious. We had to see to it that the wheels were well oiled, and take upon ourselves various other responsibilities that would have been borne by the station masters if we had depended on the public vehicles. This was the only drawback to being the owner of the carriage.

The drivers were mostly Kirghiz Tartars, who took delight in displaying their skill in exacting a high rate of speed from their teams, especially when meeting other teams or passing through villages. Whenever the roads permitted it, they drove at a full gallop; and where the roads did not properly permit it, they still drove on at the same rate. This was what brought out the weak points in our tarantass, as well as in our own bodily framework. Ordinarily we drove only by daylight; but we averaged eighty-three miles per day, making the whole 1,406 miles in seventeen days of actual driving. It had taken us the same length of time to come the same distance by steamboats up the Amur River from Khabarovsk to Stryetensk. One day when we drove most of the night we made one hundred and thirty-five miles.

The first two hundred miles, being up the east bank of the Irtysh River, was for the most part uneventful. The roads were smooth; there were no mountains in sight; the Kirghiz Tartars tending their, flocks, or gathering their supply of hay for the winter from the river bottoms, were just what we had seen from the deck of the steamer. After taking the tarantass the monotony was relieved, at one of the first stations, by meeting an officer with his wife and little girl and their household cat. Greatly to our surprise and delight the man was an American, and could talk English. He had been the leader of a band in a Russian regiment for twenty-five years, and had then just come on a furlough from Naryn, a fort on the Chinese border eight hundred miles away. But the meeting was for only a half hour, and we passed on in opposite directions.

We rested a day at Semipalatinsk. Here we found a city of 35,000 inhabitants, about one-half Mohammedans, engaged largely in trade. It came into the possession of the Russians in 1718. The city occupies a most important position on a great river, which comes down from Mongolia through the Sungarian depression, forming one of the main gateways to Central Asia. During high water small steamers ascend two or three hundred miles further and rafts come down from several hundred miles above and bring the produce of the country for exchange; while caravans are continually coming and going between·this place and Kobdo, a Chinese city of much importance on the Mongolian plateau. Much trade is also maintained with the extensive mining region in the Altai Mountains, which lie about one hundred miles to the southeast.

Soon after our arrival at Semipalatinsk, our pass- ports were called for. By this time they were a sight to behold. In addition to having been already frequently viséed by the Russians, they had passed, as before remarked, through the hands of the Chinese at Peking, and there had been almost completely covered with unintelligible Chinese characters, including two immense seal impressions each as large as a man's hand. As it was now a time of war with China, this created suspicion, and we were personally summoned to the police station. Fortunately we had with us also a letter from the Russian Ambassador at Peking commending us and our work to the authorities in Manchuria and Siberia. This paved the way for a gracious reception, and we were speedily sent on our way with a new en-

dorsement on our passports. Instead of being disturbed
by this surveillance, we were really comforted; for it
was evident that all suspicious characters were
watched, and that the strong arm of a Christian civilization was about us to give protection on our further
journey.

The first two hundred miles out from Semipalatinsk.
carried us over the watershed between the Irtysh River
and the basin of Lake Balkash, one of the larger of
the numerous bodies of water in Turkestan which
have no outlets. The watershed is not more than
1,500 feet above the sea, and consists, for the most
part, of a comparatively level surface of very old and
deeply disintegrated granitic rocks, with little depth
of soil. What with this and the absence of rain, the
country is barren, and incapable of settlement. Usually there were no settlements between the stations,
and it had evidently been difficult to find water sufficient to supply their needs. Even the Kirghiz
Tartars, with their movable flocks and felt tents, were
infrequent occupants of the region.

A typical Tartar family is the following, which we
met one day: The Tartar woman, with partially
veiled face, was riding a cow followed by its calf,
carrying in her arms a child, and leading three camels
tied together tandem, upon which were loaded the
tents and all the household utensils of the family.

The man was a little to one side, driving with difficulty a number of horses, while two boys were riding a steer and driving a small flock of sheep. Camels were so numerous that we ceased to count them. During one day when we took pains to count we found that we had met, or passed, 2,500, some of which were carrying iron five hundred miles beyond Semipalatinsk.

At the first station west of Semipalatinsk we met with one of the few delays caused by the merciful regard of the government for their horses. We had to wait three hours in the middle of the day for them to rest. But here we found ourselves in company with two ladies who had come with us on the steamboat from Omsk, and were going by tarantass to Verni, about five hundred miles farther on. They were, it seemed, mother and daughter (the former about fifty, and the latter about twenty-five, years of age) who had been to Moscow on a visit, and took this trip with as little concern as they would have done in the United States the journey by rail from New York to Omaha.

·We kept together to the next station, when, in due time, both our teams were harnessed and hitched to the tarantasses nearly ready to proceed. Suddenly our traveling companions started their horses at a furious rate, and we followed suit. The occasion of this hasty departure was soon evident. The ladies were wiser than we. A tarantass was approaching in the distance. If that should happen to contain an officer with a special commission, and he should arrive before we had started, he could take our horses from us, and compel us to wait another three hours. By starting before the arrival, this danger would be avoided. Hence our precipitate haste. Once past, we paused, and completed the adjustment of our harnesses, and then went on at our leisure.

We arrived at the next station about ten o'clock at night, and made arrangements, as we supposed, to start at half-past three in the morning. But the station master understood us to say three hours, instead of three o'clock, and wakened us at half-past one, with the announcement that our team was ready. As our lady friends were still asleep in their tarantass, waiting a more seasonable hour, we were separated from them, and saw them no more. A day or two later we fell in company with an elegantly dressed and delicate lady, apparently more than seventy years of age, traveling with her son. We were with them two days going over a very hilly road. She rarely alighted from her tarantass, except for meals, but showed no signs of weariness or discomfort.

At Sergiapol, on the Ayaguz River, one hundred and sixty miles from Semipalatinsk, we came into the inclosed basin of Lake Balkash, and continued in it for the next four hundred miles. For the first two hundred of this distance, while passing the eastern end of the lake, the road often led across the bottom of minor inclosed basins which had formerly been filled with water, but were now completely dried up. Lake Balkash is now but an insignificant remnant of what it used to be. It formerly extended over an area of 100,000 square miles or more; whereas now it scarcely covers 10,000. Originally the bottoms of these desiccated areas were smooth enough to furnish the best of roads, but after long use they have been so irregularly cut up by the carriage wheels that they are now the worst of all. The jolting over them was something fearful. It was here that we met a tarantass drawn by seven horses all abreast. The jolting with three horses (the number we uniformly had) was all that we or our tarantass could endure. What the occupants of the seven-horse carriage did was more than we could imagine.

After passing the eastern end of Lake Balkash, we began to cross the series of spurs extending in a westerly direction from the Ala-tau Mountains, which were encountered more or less frequently all the rest of our journey. The first one was what appeared to be a low range of slate hills in front of us about eight hundred feet high. As we approached it over the parched soil of the plain, we saw ahead of us a little spot of green, which proved to be where a small mountain stream was wasting itself in the desert sand. Above, a long line of green marked its course from the hills, and it continually increased in volume as we ascended. Following it into the gorge which it had cut for itself through the escarpment, we soon found ourselves in a most picturesque enlargement, with precipitous walls of rock, three hundred or four hundred feet high, rising on all sides, and surrounding a plot of rich sedimentary soil sufficient for a village site. Here was our station, surrounded by numerous Tartar tents and adobe houses. The gurgling water of the brook, and the trees and grass which grew within its life-giving influence, were in striking contrast to the desolation of the region through which we had been driving. We were not sorry that it was necessary to delay here long enough during the middle of the day to have the tire set on one of our wheels. It was like the lodge in a vast wilderness for which the Psalmist sighed, that he might be at rest.

On following up the stream, we found its explanation. The hills which we saw on approaching this picturesque oasis were covered with mellow soil, which absorbed sufficient water from the winter snows to give out a perpetual supply to the lower portions during the entire summer. The plateau was much higher than it looked to be; and, as height after height was reached, broader and broader valleys opened out, with rich herbage for the sheep and cattle and camels of numerous Tartar settlements.

We stayed that night at a station called Romanov-skia, on the Lepsa River, which in its upper portion irrigates an extensive area at the base of the Ala-tau Mountains, but here it has sunk its channel so deeply in the plain that the water is not available except to a very limited extent along its surrounding flood plain. As we started out in the morning, a new range of mountains came in sight across the whole southern horizon; but, owing, as we thought, to the haziness of the atmosphere, they seemed very dim. Soon, however, we discovered that what we took, at first, for fleecy patches of cloud were glaciers and snowy masses on mountains which towered far above the intervening foothills. With them ever in view, we drove on forty-five miles, past two stations hidden in the troughs of small streams, where alone verdure was found, and changed horses a little before sunset at the base of the first low range. This rose very abruptly from the plain, and here completely shut out from view the lofty peaks beyond. But after winding our way up the steep gradient of a waterworn gorge to a height of 1,300 feet above the station, and 3,800 feet above the sea, the summit of a broad plateau was reached, and the higher peaks burst again on our view in all the splendor of the reflected rays of the setting sun. But we were still scarcely half way to them. Between us and them was another intermediate range still higher than the one we were on, but quite below the snow line. The farther range we had before us was higher than the Alps, having peaks running up to 17,000 feet.

For two days longer we skirted the edge of this mountain range, passing around, through the small but bustling city of Kopal, to the west and southwest sides with its snow-covered peaks ever in view. The glacier-fed streams brought with them fertility to the narrow belt of loam over which their waters were spread. The tents of the Kirghiz Tartars dotted the landscape everywhere, and prosperous villages of Russian peasants, with their thrifty rows of poplar trees, their enormous stacks of grain, and their imposing churches, made us forget the wide desert everywhere surrounding us.

On the third day we lost sight of these mountains; but about noon, after a tedious ride over a long line of sand dunes, we reached the banks of the Ili River, and saw before us another section of the Ala-tau range, as lofty and grand as those we had left behind. This river comes down through a valley many miles wide and by a very gradual descent from the populous district of Kuldja, on the Mongolian plateau, and furnishes another of the important gateways to Central Asia. It is a large stream, several hundred miles long, with its headwaters in the Tian-Shan Mountains, and is the largest tributary to Lake Balkash. But it has worn so deep a trough in the lower part of its plain that its waters are unavailable there for irrigation. Its lower course is simply a hidden streak of green through vast desert wastes.

In the irrigated amphitheater at the base of the mountains that were now before us, Verni, a city of 30,000 inhabitants, lies hidden in a forest of trees which have been planted beside the irrigating channels which here are made to utilize the mountain streams to the utmost. It rained during the night and forenoon. But when the clouds cleared away, the semicircle of peaks rising 12,000 feet above the city were perfectly dazzling in their covering of new-fallen snow. Here, too, five hundred miles from navigable rivers and nine hundred from a railroad, was a busy center of strange life. Caravans of camels and trains of oxcarts were coming and going with their precious loads of merchandise; people of strange looks and stranger manners crowded the streets and thronged the markets; while, over all, was spread the pervading influence of Russian civilization. Christian churches and conspicuous Russian public-school buildings, besides those equally conspicuous for the use of the army and the civil service, are mingled with the minarets of Mohammedan mosques and with the bazaars, where the native population effect the exchange of all kinds of produce and manufacture. The trimly uniformed Cossack, the well-dressed Russian lady, the plain-faced, barefooted Russian peasant woman, the turbaned Kirghiz Tartar on horseback with his partially veiled black-eyed spouse surmounting the entire equipage of their tent packed on the back of a camel, crowd through the streets, jostling each other in a way that is beyond description.

From Verni to Aulieata is 284 miles. The entire distance is along the base of lofty mountain ranges, with numerous peaks 15,000 feet high, and 12,000 feet above the irrigated belt along which the road led. Before we had lost sight of the snow-clad peaks of the Ala-tau back of Verni, those of the Alexander Range, equally high, came into view. Meanwhile we had left the valley of the Ili River and the basin of Lake Balkash, and come into that of the river Chu, reaching Pishpek late in the evening of the second day. This river has its source in the Issyk-kul, a large lake 150 miles long and 50 broad, which lies in a depression of the Ala-tau Mountains south of Verni, 5,000 feet above the sea. The river runs a course of several hundred miles into the desert region to the northwest, between the basins of Lake Balkash and the Aral Sea, and there wastes itself in uninhabitable marshy lagoons which have no outlet. But the upper portion of its valley near the base of the mountains is a picture of fertility. In addition to the frequent clusters of mud houses and felt tents and the countless flocks of the Kirghiz Tartars, there are numerous villages of Russian peasants, with their long rows of poplar trees, their swarms of flaxen-haired children, and, at this season of the year, the immense stacks of hay and grain which bear unmistakable evidence of their prosperity and contentment.

Aulieata on the Talas River is still in the inclosed basin between those of Lake Balkash and the Aral Sea. But its irrigating stream comes down from the opposite side of the Alexander Range, and wastes itself in the Kara Kul marshes before reaching the Chu. The irrigated section, however, supports a population which has created here a bustling city of 12,000 inhabitants. The mobilization of a regiment of Cossack troops the day we passed through the place gave additional liveliness and variety to the scene.

From Aulieata to Tashkent is 160 miles. In the afternoon we ascended the gentle slope of the low mountain range which separates the basin of the Chu from that of the Syr Daria (the ancient Jaxartes), which flows into the Aral Sea. The ascent of 1,200 feet was equivalent, in its effect on the temperature, to going several degrees farther north, so that we found the night air of the last days of September too chilly for comfort, and were glad enough to take early shelter in a comfortable station house, and wait for the morning sun to pour its genial rays upon us.

The second morning from Aulieata brought us to Chimkent, a city of 10,000 inhabitants, on a tributary of the Syr Daria. Here our postroad was joined by the great road coming from Orenburg, 1,000 miles to the north, and passing to the east of the Aral Sea and following up the Syr Daria through a number of small cities. Since we were there, however, a railroad has been built all the way from Orenburg. About one hundred miles to the north is the interesting city of Turkestan, with 12,000 inhabitants. Here it is well to remember that each city of that size means a large irrigated tract with a much larger range of arid pasture land surrounding it.

Tashkent was less than seventy miles distant, and with no delay we could easily have driven the distance before night. But as we approached the great centers, the horses were more and more in use, so that delays became frequent, and we were compelled to spend another night in a station house, or rather in two station houses; for, after three hours' rest in one, we availed ourselves of a fresh team in the middle of the night, to find that at the next station we must wait three more hours. But soon after sunrise we entered the outskirts of the great city, driving for miles between long rows of mud walls and lofty silver poplar trees and across countless irrigating ditches, and with greater and greater difficulty dodging the increasing throngs of loaded camels and horses and donkeys and cattle which filled the streets. In due time, however, we were brought to the broad streets and beautiful avenues of the Russian part of the city, and to the Gostenitza Europanski (European Hotel), where we engaged the best room for fifty cents a day, and where, before noon, we had sold our tarantass for twenty-five roubles ($12.50), and were ready to attend to the sights of the city.

Tashkent is the capital of Turkestan, and had in 1900 a population of 156,414, about 25,000 of whom were Russians. Now its population numbers 271,000. The Russians took the city in 1866, and put an end to the turbulent condition of things which had previously existed. Their own part of the city is luxuriously shaded and provided with parks, and adorned with fine public buildings. Its public library has the largest collection in the world of books on Asia. But the native city is simply a mass of mud walls, inclosing narrow winding alleys, and full of filthy people and bad odors. Their bazaar is famous for both these qualities, but is so interesting that one finds it difficult to keep away. It is simply a block of the narrow streets covered with an awning of matting to keep out the sun, making its general appearance much like some of the lower parts of New York City where shaded by the elevated railway. Here everything the country affords can be had, from a camel to a cambric needle.

Tashkent was the end of our tarantass journey and the beginning of a railroad journey of another fourteen hundred miles to the Caspian Sea. Severe as were some of the experiences, we were sorry to part company with our tarantass and its ambitious horses and jolly drivers. On reckoning up, we found that we had been faithfully served by 276 horses and 92 drivers. Indeed, nothing can be more invigorating than to roll along in a tarantass over the smooth Siberian roads at the rate of ten miles an hour behind three prancing horses urged on by an ambitious Tartar driver. Nor can anything be more impressive and inspiring than to be permitted to divide one's attention between the glacier-clad peaks of the Ala-tau Mountains on the one side and the countless flocks and tents of the Kirghiz Tartars as they fade away into the glamor of the desert mirage on the other. The mountains and the desert are both most mysterious in their inaccessibility, and equally suggestive to the imagination. And they are both present on too grand a scale ever to be deformed by the ruthless hand of civilization. At the present time the railroad is extended eastwards along the route we followed, well on to Verni; aiming to cross Mongolia to Vladivostok.

The fertility and importance of the belt of land which we traversed is indicated by the population which it at present supports, which is not far from 5,000,000. The most of these are Kirghiz Tartars, who are living in the same manner that their ancestors did three thousand years ago. There are, on an average, four sheep to each human being, and two horses, two cows, and a camel to every family. For pasturage they roam widely over the adjoining desert while the vegetation is green, but their main dependence for grain is upon the irrigated belt at the foot of the mountains. In ancient times the irrigation was much more extensive than it is now. But with proper attention and settled government the irrigated area may now be increased threefold. Everywhere the Russians have brought order and increased fertility. The conquest by Russia has exactly reversed former conditions. From having been a center of disturbance from which the warlike Mongols used to roll over into Europe, carrying desolation wherever they went, and spreading terror far beyond the actual limit of their conquest, it has come to be one of the most valuable provinces of the Russian Empire, and one where some of the most interesting problems of modern civilization are in process of settlement.

SAMARKAND

From Tashkent to Samarkand is 175 miles over the Central railroad of Asia. About sixty miles from the city the railroad crosses the Syr Daria River, and is joined by a branch coming down from Andidjan, 170 miles through the fertile province of Ferghana, which is the present limit of the Russian domain in that direction. This is one of the richest and most populous of all the Russian possessions in Turkestan, and is the gateway to the Pamir, which extends southward to Afghanistan and India, over the highest plateau in the world. It is buttressed on its four corners by the Ala-tau, the Tian-Shan, the Hindu Kush, and the Himalaya Mountains, and is appropriately called the "Roof of the World." Nowhere is this plateau less than 10,000 feet above sea level, and much of it is 14,000 feet.

Ferghana itself is a well-watered valley of more than 40,000 square miles, between lofty mountain ranges. It has five cities with more than 35,000 inhabitants each, Kokand, its capital, having 82,000. The entire province tributary to this branch of the railroad has a population of 2,100,000, while the population of the province of Samarkand amounts to 1,200,000. But these statistics give only a faint idea of the vast human interests represented in this desert-encircled area rendered fertile by streams descending from these inaccessible snow-clad mountain peaks. In both these provinces the interests are predominantly agricultural, and those of the nomad population secondary. Manufacturing is also of more varied forms, and on a larger scale. For ages the inhabitants have maintained a high degree of civilization independent of the outside world. But there are nomad Kirghiz Tartars enough in the provinces to give variety to the scene. I believe it is that veracious observer, Mark Twain, who speaks of having seen the natives in Australia plowing with a team of kangaroos. I have not seen anything so wonderful as that, but I have seen a team of camels drawing a plow, and in one case a camel and a horse hitched together to do the same service. Nor is it any uncommon thing to see a man or a woman riding a lusty steer and leading a long string of camels. It will be a great while before the railroad and Russian civilization will banish all such incongruous sights.

The city of Samarkand had in 1900 a population of

56,000, of whom 16,000 were Russians, and the rest
mostly Sarts. In 1912 its population had increased to
90,000. It was taken by the Russians in 1868, and the
growth of their colony gives some idea of the rapidity
with which they are exerting their power in this direction, and of the firmness of their grasp. As in all
the other larger centers, however, so here, the Russian
element lives apart from the native, and constitutes
a city by itself, fashioned in every respect after the best
models of European towns. The well-dressed women
and the fine equipages one meets on the street would
make him forget that he was so far away from the
great centers of civilization, were it not for the constant presence everywhere of the military uniform.
The present government is a military government.
The Russians do not yet trust the native population.
It is not taken into the army. Farther west the Tur-
komans of the Transcaspian province have, to some extent, been drawn upon to fill depleted regiments; but
the Sarts and Kirghiz Tartars of this region have not
as yet been thus honored. The general interest in
army affairs was exhibited in Samarkand one Sunday
evening in a fair held by the Red Cross Society for
the benefit of the suffering soldiers in China. The
fair was in the well-shaded park of the Russian city,
which was brilliantly illuminated. An admittance of
twenty-five cents was charged, but the fair was

crowded by natives as well as by Russians. I believe
that the admission was less for the natives, and it must
be added that one of the attractions was a lottery, at
which the daughter of one of the high officials presided.

Samarkand is in every respect the most interesting
city of Turkestan. Surrounded on three sides by
snow-covered mountains, but itself in a verdure-clad
valley of great productiveness, it has from ancient
times been called the Eye of the World. About the
close of the fourteenth and the beginning of the
fifteenth century, Timur the Tartar, more commonly known as Tamerlane, established his capital
here, and from it well nigh ruled the world, extending his dominion from Russia to the Persian Gulf,
and from Constantinople to the Ganges. Timur
likewise made Samarkand a great center of learning,
and he and his successors adorned it with buildings
whose proportions and beauty challenge, even in their
ruins, the admiration of the world. Four hundred
years of neglect and numerous earthquakes have well
nigh destroyed two or three of these splendid edifices,
but they all now rear their domes and arches and campaniles high above the mud dwellings of the present
wretched city, and look down upon the Babel of an
Eastern market place where everything is sold, from
cotton and wool and silk, to perishable fruit, old

clothes, and scrap iron. The best preserved of these is known as the Rigistan. This is a square of two hundred and fifty feet, open to the street on the south side, but inclosed on the other three sides by lofty, well-proportioned buildings, brilliant in harmonious colors of enameled brick. Beautiful-shaped campaniles adorn the corners, and noble archways lead into interior courts surrounded by cloisters for Mohammedan mollahs. During the Middle Ages the tenants of these cloisters carried the study of mathematics and astronomy to a high degree of perfection, and made their city renowned for learning as well as for war. But now these tenants are a miserable set, only waiting for another earthquake to put an end to their whole business. The campaniles are already far out of plumb, and the noise of the market in the square drowns the devotions of the faithful Mohammedans in the crumbling chapels still in use.

A few hundred yards to the northeast of the Rigistan are the still more extensive ruins of the Bibi Khan, the archway and towers of whose façade were pronounced by Vámbéry a model for such buildings. This, too, was richly colored with enameled brick. At one time it is said to have sheltered as many as a thousand students, but earthquakes have nearly completed its ruin. One of its domes and two of its lofty arches still stand, though ready to fall. Still farther east are the graves of Timur's wives and sisters. These consist of a series of domes, with interior decorations of marvellous beauty, crowning successive terraces reached by forty marble steps. They are still in a fair state of preservation, though birds find a welcome home on all the cornices, and the dust-laden winds have free course everywhere. Still, they continue to stand as noble monuments, all the more conspicuous by reason of the repellent character of everything else in the neglected Mohammedan cemetery to which they form an entrance.

A quarter of a mile to the southwest of the Rigistan is the grave of Timur himself. Here, too, recent earthquakes have wrought the ruin of a portion of the noble pile, but have left uninjured the chapel and lofty dome above the grave itself. This is covered with a large piece of rare jade, and the chapel and whole interior of the dome are adorned with elegant arabesques and inscriptions of gold. Everything about it, both outside and in, is most impressive and appropriate. Indeed, in its time, the splendor of this city was unexcelled anywhere in the world. And it was not barbaric splendor, but that of the highest art of the Saracens. Those who would view it, however, even in ruins, must make haste, for time has already nearly completed its destructive work.

After crossing the Amu Daria River, in going from Samarkand to the Caspian Sea, the railroad wends its way for a long distance through the dreary wastes of the desert of Kara Kum; but, on approaching the delta of the Murgab River, enters another scene of fertility dependent on irrigation from streams that come down from Afghanistan and Persia. A large area of mounds, representing what is left of the ancient city of Merv, is passed through before reaching the modern city. Here, as often all along on the journey from Semipalatinsk, we are reminded, by the deserted ruins, of the former fertility of this irrigated belt, along which Tamerlane came with his conquering hosts to establish his empire in Central Asia. It was with a deep thrill of interest that on reaching Samarkand we were reminded that it occupied the site of ancient Maracanda, which Alexander the Great made his headquarters for two years, taking meanwhile for a wife the queen of the country. The railroad trains bringing into the interior vast quantities of petroleum remind us of how Alexander barely escaped the rôle of being the Rockefeller of his times; for it is related that on one of his expeditions, when he had penetrated the bordering desert region for a short distance, to supply his army with water he ordered a well to be dug, which, instead of furnishing a salubrious beverage, yielded a bad-smelling compound of water and petroleum, which the soothsayers declared was a bad omen; whereupon he deserted the region and took a short cut into India.

But Merv was for a century or two the seat of a Greco-Bactrian kingdom, and was reputed to have had at one time a population of one million. It is interesting to note, also, that we are here near the original center of Aryan civilization, dating back as far as that of Egypt and Babylonia. Balkh, where Zoroaster, the founder of the Parsee religion, is reputed to have been buried, is situated one or two hundred miles farther east on this same irrigated belt. Its ruins occupy a space twenty miles in circuit. One hundred miles farther west we reach Askabad, the military center of the region, just at the base of the Kopet Dagh Mountains. It was near this city that, in 1903 and 1904, Professor Raphael Pumpelly excavated some prehistoric mounds, under commission from the Carnegie Institute at Washington. Here he found evidence, as he believed, of the presence of man eight thousand years before Christ, and much evidence confirming the generally accepted opinion that the most of the domesticated animals and cultivated grains now found in Europe were developed in this region.

At Balla Ishem, about two hundred miles farther west, we stopped off a day to study a section of the old outlet of the stream which once flowed from the

Aral Sea to the Caspian. This we found to be about
as wide as the trough of the Niagara below Buffalo,
with perpendicular banks, twenty-five or thirty feet in
height, still so intact as to show that it was not many
thousand years ago that the channel was abandoned.
The story which this channel tells is very interesting
and important in its bearing on the date of the Glacial
epoch. During and shortly after the climax of the
Glacial epoch the supply of water from the melting
glaciers on the vast mountain system of Central Asia,
filled to overflowing the Oxus, the Jaxartes, the Chu,
the Ili, and other smaller streams, and the interior seas
into which they empty, causing the surplus water to
empty into the Caspian Sea. The channel of this deserted stream is called the Uzboi. So distinct is it all
the way from the Aral to the Caspian Sea, that Russian engineers proposed to build a canal along its
course so that ships could pass from one to the other,
and surveyed it for this purpose. The only obstacle
to the completion of the plan is that there is not sufficient water coming into the Aral Sea at the present
time to furnish an adequate supply for the canal. Under the fierce summer heat of that desert region, the
water is lifted by evaporation into the heavens, as fast
as the rivers bring it down. Elsewhere [1] I have told
the story of the probable effect of the diminishing of
the glaciers in the mountains bordering Turkestan, in

contracting the oases occupied by man in the Glacial epoch and forcing his emigration into Europe, into vast areas from which glacial ice had at the same time been retreating.

After crossing the Caspian Sea from Krasnovodsk to Baku, the great oil center of Russia, and spending a few days in studying the elevated shore lines of the region, to which reference will be made later, we passed up the valley of the Kur to Tiflis and thence on to Batum on the Black Sea and to Trebizond, where Rev. M. P. Parmelee, the American missionary, had reported to me the existence of an elevated shore line, which he thought important enough to be further investigated. And here I found it as he had reported. At an elevation 650 feet above the Black Sea, on the face of the basaltic cliff which rises 250 feet higher, there is a gravel terrace furnishing in some places excellent building sites. The material in the terrace is such as would have been washed in by the waves when they were at that level, showing unquestionably that it is an old shore line of the sea when the land was depressed to that amount, which by subsequent elevation had been brought to its present position. The unstable position occupied by this beach deposit, and the small amount which it has suffered from erosion, indicates that it is of a comparatively recent geological age.

On publishing an account of this, information was soon furnished me of similar terraces near Samsun, on the south shore of the Black Sea, near its western end, and in the Crimea on the northern shore. Professor William M. Davis, of Harvard University, and Ellsworth Huntington, now of Yale University, subsequently visited Trebizond, at my suggestion, and by their observations fully confirmed the existence of this recently abandoned, high shore line. Furthermore, at Baku on the Caspian Sea, they found evidence of similar shore lines at nearly the same elevation. These, too, my son and I had observed, but we were not sufficiently assured of the facts to publish them. The terrace at Trebizond has since been the subject of much interest to the missionaries there, and Miss Millie Cole tells me that they have found extensions of the deposits at several other places along the shore. The significance of all this is of the greatest interest and importance. As I looked from this beach to the north and reflected that between me and the Arctic Ocean there was no land more than five hundred feet above the sea level, and that all northwestern Siberia and much of Central Asia was below that level, I was overwhelmed with the picture the imagination drew of the effects which were produced by the subsidence of land indicated by these abandoned shore lines; and the story of the Noachian flood became easily credible.

From Trebizond we went back again to Tiflis, and thence over the Caucasus Mountains by the Dariel pass—the only practicable road between Asia and Europe for the eight hundred miles between the Black Sea and the Caspian. A well-built military road, rising to a height of about 9,000 feet, makes the passage easy and delightful, opening as it does scenery amid mountain peaks 2,000 feet higher than Mount Blanc, and passing on the north side, through a deep mountain gorge, the classic gate of Dariel, which is so narrow at one point that it was once actually obstructed by gates like those which guard the entrance to a walled city. In following this pass we had interesting evidence of the former extension of glacial ice in a terminal moraine crossed far down on the south side of the mountain range.

From Vladikavkas on the northern terminus of the road through the Dariel Pass, we started by rail for Moscow, a distance of 1,213 miles. The charge for a first-class ticket was only $15.25, which provided sleeping accommodations in the public saloon of the car; but for one dollar extra, half a private apartment with excellent sleeping accommodations could be secured. For several hours the loftiest peaks of the Caucasus

Mountains to the southwest were full in view, but soon we were too far out on the boundless plains of Russia to have much diversified scenery. After going four hundred miles we came to Rostov on the Don, a well-built city scarcely a hundred years old, with a population of 120,000, of which more anon. For two hundred miles further we rode through the prairie country occupied by the Cossacks of the Don, seeing the many indications of their military organization, and being impressed with the many economies resulting from the collection of the agricultural population in villages and the herding of animals, which dispenses with the cost of building fences. For hours we rode through the black-earth region of southeastern Russia without seeing a fence or a weed. Wheat is the staple product for export and all the railroad stations were provided with immense sheds where the grain was stored in sacks ready for shipment.

On nearing Moscow we left the treeless prairie region, and found ourselves whizzing through frequent stretches of pine and oak forest, and across ill-drained areas, which indicated that we were well within the glaciated region. The soil is less fertile, and one wonders how it came to pass that Moscow should become the capital of this great empire. But like the supremacy of New England, that of northern Russia is that of mind over matter. A certain amount of difficulty to be overcome so stimulates the heroic elements in man, that it serves to facilitate rather than hinder his triumphs.

Of the other great cities of Russia besides Rostov, we visited only four,—Moscow, Petrograd, Kiev, and Odessa. Of these Moscow and Kiev are the most interesting. Petrograd and Odessa are comparatively new cities, having had a recent growth as rapid as that of Chicago. Moscow and Kiev, too, have grown rapidly; but they still have about them the flavor of ancient capitals. It was at Kiev that Vladimer in the tenth century was converted to Christianity, and made his capital the Jerusalem of Russia. It is at the Kremlin in Moscow that the Czars still go to be crowned. So much of historic interest is centered there that there is much occasion for the Russians saying, "Above Russia is Moscow, above Moscow the Kremlin, above the Kremlin only heaven." All these places are now centers of great scientific and intellectual, as well as of commercial and manufacturing, activities. It was this which principally drew us to them, and our expectations were more than met in the wealth of their scientific museums and publications, and in the interest which the professors and the heads of the Department of State took in our investigations.

One of the most touching incidents illustrating the

kindheartedness of the Russian people was witnessed
as we approached Moscow. The November frosts
had already covered the small ponds in the vicinity
with a coating of ice sufficient to invite the children to
play upon it. Hundreds of children of all classes
swarmed out to enjoy the privilege of sliding upon
the glare surfaces. But a large part of the children
were barefooted and could not slide. The children
who had shoes, however, after sliding a while, were
seen to lend their shoes to their barefooted companions
that they might slide. Who shall say that the spirit of
Christianity has not pervaded the masses of the people in Russia?

In Petrograd we remained from the 15th to the
22d of November. During all this time the wonder
continued to grow upon us that so large and magnificent a city should flourish in the latitude of southern
Greenland, where in the middle of November the sun
does not rise till nearly nine o'clock, and sets at half-
past three. But with a population of more than 1,500,-
000, and with streets brilliantly lighted, and endless
art galleries open to the public free of expense, and
with houses doubly protected against the cold, and
well-warmed, life in the city is really most attractive
to all classes. Here we were hospitably entertained
by members of the Geological Survey, prominent of
whom were Nikitin, Tchernyschev, and · Frederick

Schmidt, all of whom expressed great interest in our glacial investigations in Siberia and Turkestan, as they were confirmatory of their own observations. Dr. Tchernyschev, especially, coincided with our inferences as to the extent to which water had been instrumental in distribution of the loess in Central Asia, and concerning the unity of the Glacial epoch. Hilkoff, head of the department of transportation, was especially interested to get our report upon the condition of the trans-Siberian railroad, and of the postroad through Turkestan, which he had recently built. General Rikatcheff, the head of the Weather Bureau, took great interest in consulting with my son, who for some time had been connected with the United States Weather Bureau, and gave us the volume of elaborate maps which the Russian government had recently published, having special value from the fact that the Russian government collects its facts from a larger continuous land area than any other country, and its records in many places in Siberia go back two hundred years.

Our route from Petrograd to Odessa was by way of Vilna and Kiev, crossing near Vilna the route of Napoleon's disastrous retreat from Moscow. The Beresina River, where his army suffered most, is a comparatively small stream running through a swampy region, produced by the imperfect drainage of a recently glaciated area. It is in such a glaciated region, with its innumerable swamps and lakes, that the Russians and Germans have been contending for supremacy in 1914 and 1915. All the way to Kiev we felt at home amid glacial moraines and gravel plains such as one meets continually in central and southwestern Ohio. On reaching Odessa we found ourselves where the sun rose an hour earlier than in Petrograd and set an hour later. Another four hundred miles to the south would bring us to the latitude of New York City, and to the genial winter climate of Constantinople.

We had not planned to visit Kiev, which was some distance off from the main line of Odessa, but the geologists of Petrograd told us that, as Professor Armaschevsky had recently discovered remains of man beneath the glacial deposits near that city, it was important for us to see him. On reaching the city, there occurred the incident, already related, in which Professor Armaschevsky indicated his recognition, when I handed him my card, by taking down from the shelf behind him a copy of the "Ice Age in North America" and laying it before me. This was all the introduction I needed, and as the Professor did not speak English, an interpreter was secured and we were shown the most characteristic mysteries of the region.

Kiev is situated on a bluff rising some three hundred feet above the Dnieper River. The upper fifty feet of this bluff is a glacial deposit, in which I had no difficulty in finding granitic pebbles which had been transported seven hundred miles from Scandinavia. It was at the base of this glacial deposit, that a prehistoric village site containing many relics of man had been found a short time before, thus presenting in Russia substantially the same archæological problems with which I had become familiar in various glacial deposits in America.

I need not pause to narrate the incidents connected with our visit to Constantinople, and of the voyage through the isles of Greece and the eastern Mediterranean to Beirut, since they are so similar to those experienced by ordinary travelers. But from Beirut through to the southern end of the Dead Sea in Palestine, many things came under our observation that are of special importance and interest. And here again I must note a providential circumstance, not of our own devising, upon which much depended. It was now the middle of December and too late for ordinary tourists to make the journey through Palestine on horseback. But fortunately one of the first-class passengers on the steamer, who landed at Beirut (we had taken second-class passage), was Rossiter Scott

of Baltimore, Maryland, who was traveling without
any distinct plan; but on consulting with us he expressed a desire, late as the season was, to make the
overland trip to Jersusalem. While we three were
talking over the plan at the counter of Cook's Bureau,
Mr. Moses Cottsworth, an eminent English actuary,
happened to come in and overhear our conversation,
and at once intimated that he would be glad to join
such a party. This made the requisite number, so
that we at once engaged a guide and set out for Damascus, where a caravan was gathered to conduct us
to Jerusalem.

Mr. Cottsworth was greatly interested in reform-
ing the calendar so that the year should always begin
upon the same day of the week. This he would ac-
complish by having thirteen months of four weeks
each, and an intercalary day at the end of each year.
In the interest of this reform (which certainly would
be of great advantage to business and manufacturing
concerns who have to make monthly payment rolls for
their employees, and monthly calculations concerning
conditions of their business), he needed to gather facts
concerning the early structures in Egypt and Palest'ne
which indicated the methods of determining the exact
days in which the vernal and autumnal equinoxes occurred. He had already found that the pyramid of
Cheops near Cairo was built with such a slant that at

the equinoxes it swallowed its own shadow, and so furnished the Egyptian priests with a sundial, by which they could indicate the exact time at which seed should be sown every spring in the Nile Valley. When we reached Egypt, we saw with him remnants of the old graduated scale north of the pyramid, on which the shadow would indicate the exact elevation of the sun above the horizon. Nothing could exceed the expression of delight when, at Shiloh, amid the hills of Ephraim, Mr. Cottsworth discovered that the slope of the battered wall, at the base of the building erected here by the Children of Israel, had exactly the slant of the Egyptian pyramids, showing that they had brought with them the architectural ideas of the land from which they came. With these congenial companions we set out for our survey of Palestine.

THE GREAT JORDAN " FAULT "

From Beirut to Damascus a narrow-gauge railroad carries one over the Lebanon Mountains and across the valley intervening between them and the Anti-Lebanon range. This valley, known as Cœle-Syria, is about ten miles wide, and, though 3,000 feet above the sea, is bordered by mountains rising from 3,000 to 7,000 feet higher. Baalbek occupies its central portion, being on the divide between the Orontes River, which flows to the north, and the Litany, which runs

to the south as far as the base of Mt. Hermon. On
first looking down upon it one might suppose it to be a
long, narrow lake basin which had been filled with
sediment; but closer attention shows that it is a synclinal depression, open at both ends, which has been
leveled up by subaerial erosion and covered with the
fertile wash from the limestone slopes on either side.
Its productiveness is phenomenal, and it is still capable, as in all past time, of supporting a dense population.

The Litany River, after running about eighty miles
to the south and reaching a level of 2,000 feet above
the sea, suddenly turns to the west and crosses the
Lebanon range, making the descent to the Mediterranean in about twenty-five miles. In this part of its
course it has probably taken advantage of a "cross
fault," of which there are several examples farther
south, which has opened a channel to the sea. But, in
addition to this cause of the sudden deflection across
the Lebanon range, another exists in the enormous
amount of volcanic material which fills the valley west
of Mt. Hermon. We had an excellent opportunity
to see this after coming into the head of the Jordan
Valley at Banias. The basaltic masses of rock here
extend entirely across the valley, and rise in successive
steps as far as the eye can reach towards the north. In
every respect they are in striking contrast to the fruit-

ful limestone strata of the mountain slopes on either side.

At Damascus we took horses on December 17 for Jerusalem. As we had no tents, we depended on finding shelter in the villages wherever we should happen to be. Our first stopping-place was Hineh, a Syrian village on the southeastern flank of Hermon, twenty-eight miles from Damascus, and nearly 5,000 feet above the sea. Our shelter was the house of the Russian priest, who was both pastor of the church and teacher of his native language in the parish school. The house was on the side of a hill, and furnished shelter for animals in the lower story. We ascended to the family residence by ten or twelve stone steps, and found there a platform in front of the door, on which all could sun themselves in pleasant weather. This, like the roofs of the houses upon which we could look on the lower portion of the hill, was covered with dirt, well compacted through use of a stone roller. There were no glass windows in the house. The only way of admitting light was by opening the doors and the close wooden shutters on one side. A young Syrian woman who had been educated at the Scotch Mission in Damascus, and was here as a teacher in the school, was occupying the only spare room in the house. This she vacated for us. But there was no means of warming it, and as a storm came on which

shut us in for all the next day, we had ample opportunity to experience some of the discomforts in the
life of the region. The priest and his family of six
or seven were all living in the adjoining room, where
they slept and ate and cooked and warmed themselves
by an open fire with no chimney to afford escape for
the smoke and poisonous gases. Their only fuel was
a scanty supply of corn cobs. During the evening and
the following day nearly the whole village came in to
see us and to shelter themselves from the driving sleet
and snow. Their cheerfulness under these conditions
was a constant surprise to us.

Among the visitors was a blind girl, about ten years
old, whose father was dead, and who had no shoes or
stockings. My compassion moved me quietly to give
ten francs to the young Syrian woman who was her
teacher, with which she promised to send to Damascus
on the following day and buy shoes and stockings for
the unfortunate girl. But I found later that it would
have taken a fortune to clothe all the bare feet of the
village. When the wind had abated, on the third
day, but while snow was still falling, we ventured
to cross the remaining spur of Hermon. Though the
snow was a foot deep, it was no uncommon thing to
see a buxom lass stalking barefooted through the
streets of a village, with a heavy load on her head.
One of our muleteers had nothing on his feet but slip-

pers, one of which was so loose that it kept coming off. After many vain attempts to keep it on, he at length deliberately took it off and tucked it under a strap which held on his mule's load, and cheerfully waded through the snow barefooted the rest of the day. I noticed, however, that on the next day he was very quick to appropriate a pair of well-worn socks which I cast aside before starting in the morning. It is difficult to estimate the extent to which human beings can inure themselves to the inevitable hardships of life.

On descending to the Jordan Valley above Lake Huleh we reached sea level, leaving the snow line 3,000 or 4,000 feet above us, and rode along the edge of the low plain which extends about fifteen miles to the north of the lake. Near the lake this becomes so marshy that it cannot be crossed, but the most of it is cultivated by the Bedouins, who were already out in great numbers putting in seed, with their oxen and plows. On passing one of their numerous villages of black tents, we were accosted in good English by a native, who said he had been in America, and asked us to stop and take coffee with him. Twice before we had been thus accosted by Syrians who had been in the United States. At the annual meeting of the Presbyterian Mission in Beirut, which we chanced to attend, much was said about the tendency of their converts to emigrate to America. In one group of churches containing a membership of 400 or 500, 130 had gone to America. The woman in the Jewish colony at whose house we stayed one night, later on, told us that her husband was in America, and she should follow him as soon as possible. The difficulty of keeping the leaven in the country which is so necessary for its regeneration, is one of the most discouraging factors in the problem of Turkish civilization.

Lake Galilee is more than 600 feet below the level of the sea. One of the most marked of the "cross faults" of the region extends westward from the Jordan Valley a little south of the lake. This is known as the Plain of Esdraelon, and falls down in its highest part to about 400 feet above sea level. The north side of this "fault" appears as a series of precipitous cliffs running east and west and a little south of Nazareth. Mt. Tabor is an outlying block projecting part way into the plain.

The feature in the Jordan Valley to which we gave special attention is the terrace of fine sediment, about 650 feet above the level of the Dead Sea, which completely surrounds it, and stretches far out beyond each end. This, however, attains its full height only near the margin of the valley. Towards the middle of the valley it descends, either by a gradual slope, or by a succession of more or less well-marked terraces, of which we counted twelve near the south end. Where the shores are precipitous and no streams are entering from the sides, the material consists of coarse débris, somewhat waterworn, which has fallen from the cliffs. But, whenever a watercourse comes in from the surrounding highlands, there is a delta-like extension corresponding in extent to the size of the stream which has contributed the material. These are, however, not characteristic of the north end of the shores, for the reason that the sea is here so deep as to have swallowed up all that the shores have heretofore brought within its reach. The delta-like extensions of the terrace are very pronounced about the southeast, the Lisan being most prominent of them all. It is clear enough that in a recent geological age, the water level in the valley stood for some time about 700 feet higher than now, and has gradually receded to its present level.

The cause of this fluctuation in the level of the Dead Sea opens an interesting field of speculation. By most recent writers it has been connected with the Glacial epoch, as in that of the filling up of the Salt Lake basin in Utah. As long ago as 1862 Sir Joseph Hooker announced that the cedars of Lebanon were growing on a terminal moraine. But I could detect no evidence of glacial action anywhere in the Lebanon region which we visited. There was certainly no gen-

eral glaciation of the region. Still, as it is probable
that the Glacial epoch was characterized by increased
precipitation and diminished evaporation over a bordering area of considerable extent, it affords an easy explanation of the rise of the water in the Jordan Valley.
I observed, also, near the south end of the Dead Sea,
evidence that the silting up took place to a large extent during a gradual rise in the water. The coarse
material near the bottom was frequently so far out
from the old shore, and so covered with thick strata
of fine sediment, as to render no other supposition than
this possible. The Glacial epoch affords the best explanation of this.

At Jerusalem we were met by my Old Andover
friend, Selah Merrill, then United States consul. His
experience in the survey of the country east of the Jordan, and his long residence in Jerusalem, were of great
service in our subsequent excursions in Palestine. After
visiting Jericho and the region around we planned,
under his direction, a trip to the unfrequented south
end of the Dead Sea. In this we were joined by Mrs.
Theodore Bent, whose extensive travels with her husband in Ethiopia, southern Arabia, and Persia, had
not only rendered her famous but fitted her in a
peculiar manner to be a congenial and helpful traveling companion. She had her own tent and equipment

and her own dragoman, and her presence added greatly
to the interest of the trip.

After stopping a day at Hebron, we passed along
the heights till we descended to the shore of the Dead
Sea at the north end of Jebel Usdum, through the
Wadi Zuweirah. Here we found indications that,
during the rainy season, tremendous floods of water
rushed down from the heights of southern Palestine,
through all the wadies. Such had been the force of
the temporary torrents here, that, over a delta pushed
out by the stream and covering an area of two or
three square miles, frequent bowlders a foot or more
in diameter had been propelled a long distance over a
level surface. At the time of our visit, the height of
the water in the Dead Sea was such that it everywhere
washed the foot of Salt Mountain (Jebel Usdum),
making it impossible for us to walk along the shore.
A few years before this, however, Professor Hull and
Major Kitchener, when conducting their survey at
the same time of year, camped on the shore here on
a sandy beach fifteen or twenty feet above sea level;
while Professor Schmidt of Cornell University did the
same a few years later. These variations of level,
however, are due to local and temporal causes, rather
than to such secular variations as produced the great
changes connected with the Glacial epoch.

The extent of this delta, and that of many others

which we had observed in our journey along the west shore and which we had seen at the north end, opened up a chapter in the history of the Dead Sea that never before had been adequately considered. Instigated by these discoveries, on returning home I prepared a paper, for the Society of Biblical Literature and Exegesis, in which I presented abundant evidence to show that, owing to this encroachment upon the original area of the Dead Sea, the level of the water had risen greatly since the time of Joshua. For, supposing that the supply of water coming into the sea had been constant for that period, the evaporating surface must have been kept constant in order to secure the equilibrium. As the larger surface in the northern end of the sea was encroached upon by these deltas, the water was compelled to rise and overflow the southern portion, which is very shallow (scarcely more than twenty feet deep anywhere), thereby maintaining the required evaporating surface. This supposition not only has the support of the evidence of the necessary causes at work, but also is confirmed by the statements given in the book of Joshua (xv. 2, 5, 6; xviii. 19) of the boundaries at the northern and southern ends. It also conforms to the tradition that the site of Sodom and Gomorrah is under the water at the south end of the sea. These views have been embodied, also, in an article on the Dead Sea in the International Standard Bible Encyclo-

paedia, and accepted by such high authorities as Dr.
Dalman and Clermont-Ganneau, who had previously
maintained that in Joshua's time the water was two
hundred feet higher than now, while on my theory it
was then forty or fifty feet lower, with a much larger
basin in the northern part.

Near the mouth of Wadi Zuweirah, we observed a
nearly complete section of the 600-foot terrace of fine
material, displaying the laminæ deposited by successive floods during the high level maintained by the
water throughout the Glacial epoch. From these it
was clear that this flooded condition continued for several thousand years. On the road along the west
shore to Ain Jiddy (En-gedi) we observed (as already indicated) ten or twelve abandoned shore lines,
consisting of coarse material where the shore was too
steep, and the waves had been too strong to let fine
sediment settle.

From all the evidence at command it appears that,
at the climax of the Glacial epoch, the water in this
valley rose to an elevation of 1,400 feet above the
present level of the Dead Sea, gradually declining
thereafter to the 600-foot level, where it remained for
a long period, at the close of which it again gradually
declined to its present level, uncovering the vast
sedimentary deposits which meanwhile had accumulated over the valley of the Jordan, north of Jericho.

But probably this cycle in the history of the valley had already been accomplished long before the appearance in it of the Israelites on their return from the land of Egypt.

Our ride from Ain Jiddy to Bethlehem was notable in more respects than one. The steep climb (of 4,000 feet) up the ascent from the sea to the summit of the plateau was abrupt enough to make one's head dizzy. But as the zigzag path brought us to higher and higher levels, the backward view towards the mountains of Moab, and towards both the north and the south end of the Dead Sea, was as enchanting as it was impressive. Across the sea, up the valley of the Arnon, we could see the heights above Aroer and Dibon, and back of El Lisan, the heights about Rabbah and Moab, and those about Kir of Moab, while the extensive deltas coming into the Dead Sea along the whole shore south of us fully confirmed our inferences concerning their effect in encroaching upon its original evaporating area.

After passing through the wilderness of Jeruel and past Tekoah, as we were approaching Bethlehem, a little before sundown, the men of our party wished to hurry on to get another sight of the scenes amidst which Christ was born. As Mrs. Bent was already familiar with those scenes, she preferred to come along more slowly with the caravan, and told us to go on without any concern for her safety. But soon after arriving at Bethlehem, the sheik who accompanied our party overtook us, and told us that Mrs. Bent had fallen from her horse and suffered severe injury; whereupon we all started back over the rocky pathway, to render the assistance that seemed to be needed.

On reaching a point where two paths to Bethlehem separated, we were told by a native that he thought our party had proceeded along the other path from that we had taken, and that it would be found to have already reached its destination before us. We therefore returned to Bethlehem. But, soon after, the dragoman came in great haste, saying that Mrs. Bent had indeed fallen from her horse and broken a limb, and that he had left her unprotected in an open field to await assistance. Again, therefore, but accompanied by six strong natives with a large woolen blanket, on which to convey her, we proceeded to the place where the accident occurred. Here we found her where she had been lying for about two hours under the clear starlight. But, instead of complaining, she averred that it was providential that she had been allowed to rest so long before undertaking the painful journey made necessary by the accident; and that all the while she had been occupied with the thought that she was gazing upon the same constellations in the heavens from which the angel of the Lord had appeared to the shepherds to announce the Saviour's birth.

The task of giving her relief was not altogether a simple one. The surrounding rocky pastures did not yield any vegetable growth from which a splint could be made to stiffen the broken leg. An inspiration, however, came to my son, who suggested that we could take her parasol for one side and the sound limb for the other, and with the girdle of one of the men bind them together so that the journey could be effected safely. No sooner said than done. The sufferer was laid upon the blanket and slowly carried to Bethlehem by the strong arms of our native escort. From here she was conveyed by carriage to Jerusalem where we arrived between one and two o'clock in the morning, taking her to the English hospital, of which she had been a liberal patron, and where she was acquainted with all the staff; but, alas! this hospital was established exclusively for Jews, and as she was not one they refused to admit her, advising her to go down to the hospital conducted by German sisters. This, however, she flatly refused to do, declaring that rather than do that she would camp on the steps of the English hospital. At this two of the lady members of the staff, who were her special friends, vacated their room and she was provided for.

Respecting the sequel we would simply say that her limb was successfully set, and with cheerful confidence she assured us that she would reach London before we did and that we must be sure to call upon her there. She did indeed reach London before we left the city, but it was on the last day of our stay, and, as our tickets had been purchased for the noon train going to Plymouth, we were unable to accept her invitation to dine that evening. Some years afterwards, however, when visiting the city with Mrs. Wright, we found her at home, and had great enjoyment in repeatedly visiting her and studying the rare collections with which she had filled her house upon returning from the various expeditions in which she had accompanied her artistic husband.

Upon leaving Jerusalem we visited Egypt, ascending the Nile as far as Assouan; but, as Egypt is familiar ground, we will refer simply to the fact that in the vicinity of Thebes we were permitted to study the abandoned delta terrace of one of the streams coming into the Nile at that point, in which Professor H. W. Haynes many years before had found palæolithic implements (with some of which he had enriched my collection), indicating an occupation of the valley by prehistoric man long anterior to the construction of the oldest monuments.

From Egypt we sailed to Athens and spent a week in visiting the centers of greatest archæological interest in Greece, driving down from Corinth to visit the ruins of Mycenæ and Tyrens, so fully explored and described by Schliemann.

Crossing to Italy, a week was spent in the vicinity of Naples, whence we made an excursion to Palermo to visit the cavern of San Ciro, from which twenty tons of fresh bones, representing hippopotamus, deer, ox, and elephant, and individuals of all ages from the fetus to the full-grown animal, were found and excavated in 1830, and exported for commercial purposes. The bones were so fresh that they were cut into ornaments and polished, and when burnt gave out ammoniacal vapor. At the time of the discovery, all the facts were carefully collected and described by Abbate D. Scinà, and by Dr. Turnbull Christie in 1831. The only explanation of this remarkable collection of bones is, that, in a comparatively recent subsidence of land which had previously been elevated above its present level, this incongruous mixture of animals had been driven pellmell by the rising water to take refuge in the cave, which is now two hundred feet above sea level. It is an impressive picture that the imagination brings up, of this rising tide of water entering the beautiful amphitheater in which Palermo is situated, and driving before it the terrified horde of

animals that could find no other escape. Palermo itself, with its interesting museum, is worthy of more
attention than it gets from the ordinary tourist.

Pausing at Rome, Florence, and Genoa, we entered France through Turin by way of the Mount
Cenis tunnel, and, after a short stop in Paris, reached
London, where I met again the large circle of geologists and archæologists who had entertained me on
my first visit to England, and read a paper before the
London Geological Society (later published in their
Proceedings), summarizing the results of our observations in crossing Asia. We also visited Mr. Cottsworth in his home at York, where we were permitted
to study the various objects of archæological interest
in that city and vicinity. Returning to London, we
engaged passage on a steamer from Southampton, just
in time, as before remarked, to miss meeting Mrs.
Bent, our unfortunate traveling companion in Palestine.

HOME AGAIN

After returning from our fourteen months' trip
around the world, my spare time was occupied for two
or three years in preparing and publishing the results
of my observations. The most important publication
was " Asiatic Russia," in two volumes, issued by Mc-
Clure, Phillips & Co., in 1902. This work was

abundantly supplied with illustrations from the photographs which my son had taken, and with several
new maps, and presented the subject from every point
of view,—from that of physical geography, history,
sociology, economic and political conditions, geology,
climate, flora and fauna. It has received highest praise
from both English and Russian sources. In spite of
the high price of $7.50, the edition has been entirely
exhausted. So highly was it appreciated in Russia,
that, just before the outset of the present war, arrangements were in progress for the translation into
Russian of a new edition, incorporating the latest statistics; but, like so many other things, this plan was
cut short by the absorbing interest of Russia in her
preparations for the great European war. Meanwhile
I contributed to the Geological Society of America a
paper of considerable length, on the " Origin and Distribution of Loess in Northern and Central Asia,"
and an article to *McClure's Magazine* on " Geology
and the Deluge," giving a full statement of the facts
which indicated a recent subsidence of the land in
China, Central Asia, and northeastern Europe.

Soon after, much interest was excited by some remarkable discoveries in the valley of the Missouri
River. One of these was that of a cluster of Canadian
bowlders at Tuscumbia, Missouri, thirty miles south

of the glacial border, which had been established as
following the line of the Missouri River up to a considerable distance west of Tuscumbia. Moreover,
Tuscumbia was sixty miles above the junction of the
Osage River with the Missouri.

Here was indeed a problem. Had geologists made
a mistake in limiting the movement of glacial ice, at
this point, to the northern bank of the Missouri River?
To attempt a solution, I made two separate excursions
into the region for the purpose of testing theories
which might account for the abnormal facts. First, I
surveyed again the region south of the Missouri River,
and found that there had been no mistake in our
former inferences concerning the extent of the glacial
ice to the south. Glacial ice had not crossed the Missouri River east of Jefferson City, so these bowlders
could not have been brought there by direct glacial
action.

A second possible theory was that the ice had
crossed the Kansas River and penetrated the headwaters of the Osage, whence floating icebergs, broken
off by the glacial flood, had brought the bowlders
down to Tuscumbia. Hence I went up into Kansas
and surveyed the region between these rivers, and
found that there had been no mistake of the geologists
in limiting the glacial boundary there to the Kansas
River. So that hypothesis was eliminated.

A third supposition was, that there were outcrops of rocks in Missouri from which these bowlders might have been derived. Consequently, in company with Professor E. M. Shepard of Drury College, who was then state geologist, I went over the Archæan area, where such an outcrop might properly be found, and was assured that there were no such rocks in Missouri.

The only remaining theory was one of extreme interest, and of the most startling character. This is that in the closing stages of the Glacial epoch, when the ice was rapidly disappearing, the upper Missouri River was supplied with about twenty-five times the amount of water which now annually comes into it, and all this during the summer months. Calculating the width of the trough of the river below the mouth of the Osage, it was easy to see that this would produce annual floods, at that point, 200 feet in height; while the Osage River, being entirely outside the glaciated region, would have no abnormal addition to its water supply to produce floods perceptibly larger than those which occur annually. As a result the 200-foot flood in the Missouri would set a current up the Osage River sufficient to bear small icebergs, containing northern bowlders, to Tuscumbia, where they would be left on the subsidence of the water. The first announcement of this theory was made in an article published in the New York *Nation*. It was interesting, a few years later, when I called on Mr. Salomon Reinach in the museum at Saint-Germain-en-Laye, near Paris, to find that he had translated this article into French and had it published in a French periodical.

Another discovery which claimed my attention about this time was that of two human skeletons, found by Mr. Concannon at the base of the loess, in Lansing, near Leavenworth, Kansas, in a portion of the bluff which here borders the Missouri River. This was brought to the notice of the world by Mr. M. C. Long, an enterprising archæologist of Kansas City. The problem was to determine whether the tunnel in which Mr. Concannon found these skeletons was in the original undisturbed deposit of loess. Upon this point there was considerable diversity of opinion. To satisfy my own mind I made as many as three visits to the region, studying the loess deposits of Kansas City, Leavenworth, and St. Joseph. At St. Joseph, I was greatly assisted by Miss Luella A. Owen, who had made a careful study of the region, and who was a member of the International Geographical Society. Under her guidance I visited the remarkable deposits of loess at St. Joseph, where subsequently she found a palæolithic implement embedded in what was without any doubt the original loess deposit. With her and Mr. Long I also visited the Lansing locality. Subsequently, Professor N. H. Winchell and Mr. Warren Upham made two visits to the region, and collected evidence that seemed to establish beyond reasonable doubt, that the Lansing skeleton was found in loess that had not been disturbed since its original deposition. In an elaborate joint article prepared by Miss Owen and myself, and published in the *American Geologist* (vol. xxxiii), the evidence of the antiquity of these skeletons was fully, and, I think, satisfactorily, collected and presented. I also published an illustrated popular article in *Records of the Past,* which brought out the facts clearly.

The principal objection to the glacial age of these skeletons is due to two misapprehensions—(1) to the assignment of extreme antiquity to the closing scenes of the Glacial epoch. This creates unnecessary adverse presumptions, unfavorable to the genuineness of the discovery. (2) The resemblance of the skeletons to those of modern man leads those who are devoted to extreme evolutionary views to reject the evidence without due examination. But on the other hand, Dr. Arthur Keith, of London, finds the evidence of the full development of the human skeleton during the Glacial epoch in England, to coincide and confirm the glacial age of the Lansing skull, which he has no difficulty in accepting as genuine.[1]

SUMMARY OF THE RESULTS OF THE ASIATIC TRIP

1. My scientific lectures in Japan were instrumental not only in interesting a very wide circle of hearers, but also, I was told years afterwards by a missionary (not connected with my own denomination), in securing for them a much more favorable hearing than they had before been able to obtain. The Japanese were duly influenced by the fact that scientific culture did not necessarily interfere with Christian belief. This to me is one of the most gratifying results of my lecture tour in Japan.

2. My extensive intercourse with Russians of all classes gave me a more favorable impression of the Russian people and government, and a more hopeful view of their future, than I had been led to entertain by the various writers whose books and articles had come to my notice. Instead of finding the Russians of all classes given over to the drinking of vodka and to bacchanalian carousals, I found an unusual proportion of the people were total abstainers from alcoholic beverages. My first contact with a high Russian official in Japan was with an attractive young man, who, though offering me cigarettes, did not smoke himself in my presence. The missionaries assured me that he was a total abstainer from alcohol, and co-

operated heartily with them in promoting total abstinence. The colonel of high rank to whom we had
an introduction, and whom we met at Port Arthur,
turned down his glass when the wine came aro:.nd at
the dinner table, as did two brilliantly decorated
young members of the governor's staff with whom we
dined at Irkutsk. A fair proportion of the Cossacks
who conducted us from station to station through
Manchuria neither drank nor smoked. Practically all
the steamboats upon the Siberian rivers are owned and
run by " Raskolniks," a religious sect estimated to
number more than 12,000,000 individuals, one of
whose cardinal principles is abstinence from alcohol
and tobacco. Repeatedly, also, in our tarantass rides
through Siberia, we found ourselves in villages of this
sect, where it was not possible to get anything to drink
stronger than milk and water.

3. We were impressed with the general dissemi-
nation of knowledge throughout all the Russian com-
munities. In every city of ten or twelve thousand inhabitants there was a museum open to the public,
which conveyed ethnological and historical facts in
such a way that those who could not read could yet
understand; while the educated classes with whom we
came in contact, and who were found in every community, were very highly educated. As already noted,
we were repeatedly requested by engineers, high-school

superintendents, and curators of museums to converse with them in Latin, when other languages were not available. The common soldiers, whom we met everywhere, were able, in connection with our maps, to make us understand what they believed to be the destiny of their Empire, in reaching open ports on the Pacific and the Persian Gulf, and in getting free passage through the Dardanelles.

4. The religious situation in Russia put on a new aspect to us as we mingled with the priests and people, and attended services in their churches. The priests are required to be married, and though evidently not of uniformly high intellectual attainments still fill the rôle which is most needed. They are kind and sympathetic, and their families for the most part exemplary; while the liturgy of the Church brings to the minds of the people the richest truths of the gospel. A large portion of their church service consists in the reading of Scripture, and the Bible is everywhere freely circulated. Repeatedly in Siberia we encountered colporteurs, coming upon the train and offering us Bibles for sale. In the ninety-three posthouses at which we stopped in going through Turkestan we found upon every table a portion of the Scriptures translated into the language of the region, and bearing the imprint of the Petrograd Bible Society, acting in conjunction with the British and Foreign

Bible Society; and we learned that the agents of the Bible Society had free passes from the government, for both themselves and their baggage, over the entire railroad system.

5. Russian church music is the best in the world, and most effective in bringing home to the hearts of the people the essentials of the doctrines of Christianity. On purchasing a large collection of their church music at Blagovestchensk, I found that it ha 1 all passed through the hands of the eminent Russian composer, P. Tchaikovsky. He also had composed a considerable amount. Among his compositions was the music for the Liturgy of St. John Chrysostom, one of the most precious relics of early religious literature. Tchaikovsky's setting of music for the Liturgy was so highly valued by my musical associates at Oberlin, that I translated the words into English and adjusted them to the music, so that our choir could make use of it. On learning what I had done, Jurgenson, the principal musical publisher of Moscow, requested the privilege of publishing an edition with my words. This he did, and I consider it one of the most gratifying accomplishments of my life that I should have secured the association of my name with that of Tchaikovsky, in the following title-page: Liturgy of St. John Chrysostom. Set to Four-Part Choral Music for Mixed Voices. Composed by P. Tchaikovsky. Words trans-

lated and adjusted to Music by G. Frederick Wright. Op. 41. Moscow and Leipsic: P. Jurgenson.

The composition consists of fifteen pieces, and is as varied in its character as are the themes of the Liturgy itself, leading up, from what in the Latin mass is the Kyrie, to a magnificent Hallelujah chorus, which celebrates the completion of the redemptive work of Christ. The Liturgy includes a cherubim song which is peculiar to the Greek Church; the Lord's Prayer; and the entire Nicene Creed.

This Liturgy is everywhere used in the Russian churches, and of itself is sufficient to bring the entire circle of Christian truth home to the hearts of the people. The music is rendered by male voices, without instrumental accompaniment, the singers being a part of the church officials. Let one go into any church whatever throughout the Empire, and he will hear this Liturgy sounded forth in the noblest and most appropriate harmonies conceivable. There are no seats in the Russian churches, so that rich and poor, high and low, officers and subalterns, all crowd in together in the most democratic fashion. It is a most touching scene to see, as we frequently did, a horny-handed peasant and his care-burdened wife come into a magnificent church together and stand with the tears rolling down their cheeks when the choir sounds out the sublime words of the Nicene Creed: ' I believe in Jesus Christ the only

begotten Son of God ... who for us sinful men came
down from heaven ... and became like unto men, and
was crucified under Pontius Pilate, and he suffered
and was buried, but he rose on the third day according to the word, and ascended into heaven most high
and now sitteth at the right hand of God.' But it
was a still more impressive scene to encounter far out
in the Siberian wilderness a church car provided with
a priest and choir and all the necessary preparations for
a church service, and to see the people gathered from
their lonely fields of labor, and the third-class passengers of our train, taking part in a service as noble
and beautiful as any that is rendered in the largest
and richest cities of the Empire. In no country in the
world are the common people more completely imbued with the principles and truths of the gospel than
in Russia. Through all the formalism of the church
services, the truths of the Christian system shine with
irresistible power, illustrating the statement of the
Evangelist concerning Christ's ministry, that "he
could not be hid."

6. When wandering about in the vast fertile fields
and riding through the dense forests and rich mining
regions of Siberia, and noting the boundless opportunities for irrigation in Turkestan, where the Tian-
Shan Mountains, rising thousands of feet higher than
the Alps, and with twenty times their mass, keep the

water in cold storage, to be let down in unfailing
quantities throughout the spring and summer when it
is needed, it was easy for us to foresee an immense
immigration following upon the opening of the country by the building of the trans-Siberian and Trans-
caspian railroads. And, as already noted, such an
immigration from Russia has taken place during the
last decade on an enormous scale; and village com-
munes of Russian settlers are rapidly transforming
Turkestan and southern Siberia into densely populated
centers of modern civilization. The future of Asiatic
Russia is boundless in its possibilities, and its development is rapidly becoming actual. Even in 1900, in a
small bookstore in Omsk on the Irtysh River, I purchased books of as high a grade as could be found
upon the counters of the largest bookstores of the Middle West in America. There are single libraries in
Siberia and Turkestan that compare with the best
we have in America outside the Atlantic Coast and in
some of our largest universities in the Interior.

7. With reference to the scientific objects of my
trip, the following conclusions seem worthy not only
to be put on record, but also to be emphasized, lest
they fail to receive proper recognition:

(1) As already stated, the glaciated areas in Mongolia and in the Transbaikal region as marked on the
maps in James Geikie's last edition of "The Great

Ice Age," proved to be non-existent. There may have been limited accumulations of ice upon the Vitim plateau, east of Lake Baikal, which rises to the height of 5,000 feet above the sea. But it is certain that glaciers did not descend from it into the broad and beautiful valley which runs north from Chita along the eastern border of the plateau. My observations to this effect were, as already stated, emphatically seconded by the Russian geologists I afterwards met in Petrograd. It was also evident that no glaciers ever came down into the plains north of the Tian-Shan Mountains to become confluent, as they did from the Alps in Switzerland during the Glacial epoch, though the Tian-Shan Mountains, as we have said, are vastly higher and more massive than the Alps and in the same latitude. As already noted, also, later direct observations by Professors Davis and Huntington brought to light the fact that the glaciers in the Tian-Shan Mountains never descended below the level of 7,000 feet, while at the present time they are limited to the level of 12,000 feet.

(2) As to the origin and the distribution of the loess, my observations supported the theory that it is of glacial origin, and that its distribution has been accomplished by both wind and water. In northern and western China it is found on mountain passes 5,000 feet above the sea, where it could have been

brought only by the agency of wind; while, in the bordering plains and valleys at lower levels, it has very clearly been distributed by water during a period when the land was depressed considerably below its present level. The erosion of the loess in the higher levels is now progressing rapidly, and its redeposition is taking place on the flood plains of the Yang-tze and the Hwangho, and some of the smaller rivers farther north, while immense bordering shoals of it are being built up along the whole northeastern coast. These deposits are known to have encroached upon the sea for a distance of many miles.

If, however, the glacial origin of the loess is maintained, the source of the Chinese material must be looked for in the vast mountain masses which surround the basin west of the desert of Gobi, where, in the Himalaya and Tian-Shan mountains, the glaciers are still slowly grinding out their grist of loess to be carried by the streams of the plains below, where it is taken up by the westerly winds and transported for thousands of miles to the eastern border of Mongolia. But during the Glacial epoch these loess mills were far more active than now, so that we may well believe they could have supplied the material which, transported by the winds, became entangled in the network of low mountain chains and tortuous valleys which characterize northeastern China, whence the ever-active streams have, until now, been transporting and spreading it out at lower levels, to serve the varied interests of that populous empire. In Turkestan, likewise, the immense deposits of loess about Tashkent and Samarkand may be traced to the glaciers in the Tian-Shan Mountains, where the rivers rise which still fertilize those populous historic regions. In southern Russia, too, the fertile wheat-bearing black belt is a loess deposit, related to the Glacial epoch in Europe as the prairies of the Mississippi Valley are to that epoch in North America.

(3) I was permitted, also, to add something to the evidence, already existing, of great recent changes of level throughout western Siberia, Central Asia, and eastern Europe. The southern end of Lake Baikal is shown by my calculations to be a very recent geological depression, whose age can be estimated in tens of thousands rather than hundreds of thousands of years, thus supporting the general contention that some of the vast geological changes which took place in the closing stages of the Tertiary period date from less than one hundred thousand years ago. The evidence of an extensive postglacial depression of the region extending from Lake Baikal to central Europe is such as cannot be reasonably questioned. In addition to that derived from the presence in Lake Baikal of arctic seal, much specific direct evidence was brought to light in the

course of our journey through Turkestan. For nearly a thousand miles we drove along the base of the Tian-Shan Mountains, at an elevation of about 2,000 feet above the sea. Wherever the numerous mountain streams debouched upon the northern plain there were apparently deltas of loess such as would be formed if the water stood at that level when the silt-laden streams entered it. Subsequently as the land was elevated these deltas were very much dissected by the erosion of the stream; still, not so much so as wholly to disguise the original formation. On reaching Trebizond on the south shore of the Black Sea, we found still clearer evidence. Here, at an elevation of 650 feet above the sea, as already detailed, there is an extensive deposit of gravel clinging to the sides of the volcanic mass of rock at whose base the city is built. Its situation on the steep declivity of the mountain is such that it could not have remained there indefinitely.

The significance of these facts I will not here discuss; but in "Asiatic Russia," "Scientific Confirmations of Old Testament History," and "Origin and Antiquity of Man," I have presented the theory, that this depression is connected in some way with the account of the Deluge, both in the Sacred Scriptures of the Jews and in the cuneiform inscriptions unearthed in Babylonia.

CHAPTER XII

THIRD VISIT TO EUROPE

In the fall of 1904, my first wife having died five
years before, I was married to Florence E. Bedford, a
Quaker lady, who had become deeply interested in my
scientific investigations; and in the following year,
with her, I made my third visit to Europe. This
time, after landing in Liverpool, we spent a week or
two with the Cottsworths in York, revisiting the
scenes of geological and archæological interest in that
region, and then went to Kilmarnock to visit my
friend and coadjutor, Rev. James Lindsay, a philosophical student of wide repute, and a most highly es-
teemed coworker in editing the *Bibliotheca Sacra*.
Dr. Lindsay had then been for a long time pastor of
the Old Scotch Kirk of the town, and thus was able
to introduce me to the work and aims of that branch
of the Presbyterian family. After a very profitable
visit with him and his mother and sisters, with whom
he was then living, we sailed from Leith to Copenhagen, where we had the great privilege of meeting
Dr. Fausböll, Professor of Sanskrit in the University,
whose daughter we had met while governess in the

family of Governor Bistrup in Greenland. Professor Sophus Müller, the eminent archæologist in charge of the museum at Copenhagen, also gave us a cordial reception and was very helpful in facilitating our plans to visit the kitchen middens in the vicinity, where we could see for ourselves the elevated shell heaps in which the oldest indications of man's presence in Denmark are to be found. The most important of these was at Frederickswerke, which was typical of all the kitchen middens, showing a considerable elevation of land since the deposits were made. Near this place also was a typical dolmen, showing an immense flat stone resting upon stone pillars three or four feet high, making it difficult to surmise how such an immense stone could be elevated and made to rest in so unstable a position. The solution provided by the King of Denmark himself is probably correct, being the same as that relating to the elevation of the great stones in the Egyptian temples, namely, that the earth was piled up around the pillars, forming a mound of gradual slant, up which the flat covering-stone could be pulled by main strength and let down upon the pillars, after which the earth would be removed and the imposing monument left to appear with all its impressiveness.

In the museum at Copenhagen it was gratifying to see a collection of palæolithic implements found by Dr. Abbott in the gravel deposits at Trenton, New

Jersey. Altogether Copenhagen left upon us the pleasantest impression of any city which we visited. Its museum is well-nigh unrivalled, both in the amount and in the arrangement of the treasures which it contains. Its art galleries, especially that of Thorwaldsen, are crowded full of most interesting objects. Its people are well educated and contented, and are not separated by the extremes of wealth and poverty as in most other cities.

With regret that we could not remain longer, we left Copenhagen and crossed over to Malmö in Sweden, where Professor N. O. Holst of the Geological Survey had asked us to meet him, to see some of the interesting glacial phenomena of the region. Dr. Holst had visited Greenland and published most important observations upon its glacial phenomena, and had also been sent to Australia to study the evidence of a glacial epoch in that continent which occurred many millions of years ago in the early geological ages. He had also visited me in the United States and familiarized himself with my discoveries here and with a wide range of the glacial field in America.

Provided with a midday lunch, and accompanied by Professor H. G. Simmons (who, as botanist, had accompanied the Sverdrup expedition to Greenland), we proceeded into the interior, partly by train and partly by hand car. At Tapplelargo, twelve miles east from

Malmö, we came to an area of several acres covered with an overwash deposit from the terminal moraine, which is a mile or more distant. In a stratum of clay, about seven feet thick, many species of shells and plants are found, indicating peculiar conditions which can be accounted for only by supposing that during the final melting away of the ice the summers became very warm, so as to allow temperate species to flourish close up to the ice front, thus allowing them to mingle with arctic or subarctic species.

It is evident from inspection of the stratum that these species lived and were deposited contemporaneously, and not by an advance. of the ice after an interglacial period. This would seem to meet the case of the commingling of temperate and subarctic species which Professor Coleman has described in the vicinity óf Toronto, and so greatly simplify our interpretation of glacial phenomena in the northern United States and in Canada.

We were also taken to the most remarkable glacial bowlder that has ever been reported. This was a mass of chalk, five miles east of Malmö, which extends three miles in a northeast and southwest direction, averages 1,000 feet in width, and from 100 to 200 feet in thickness, being, so far as I know, the largest bowlder, or glacially transported mass, that has been described. It is everywhere covered with till, and al-

most everywhere has till underneath it. Its position
is between what we should call the upper and the
lower till, the upper till being yellow and the lower
blue. But in one place, which I examined, the lower
or blue till was both above and below it.

While the chalk is together in one mass, it everywhere shows signs of immense pressure and disturbance, being broken up into small cubes, and having its
flint nodules cracked and arranged in lines simulating
stratification. The upper part of the chalk has also
been extensively sheared off and mingled with the till.

This mass of chalk has been brought fully to light
through its commercial value, eight or ten companies
having mined or quarried it for many years. It belongs to the true soft chalk of Cretaceous age, and
had been supposed by nearly all of the earlier geologists to indicate a Cretaceous area, where it was least
to be expected, since the chalk which mainly underlies
the peninsula belongs to the Trias or Lias. The determination of its glacial transportation has therefore
solved a very difficult problem. It must have been
picked up bodily from the shores or bed of the Baltic
Sea, and transferred westward many miles to its present position.

Dr. Holst detailed to us here an account of a discovery of the remains of prehistoric man which had

long been discredited by the Professor of Geology at Lund, by reason of his distrust of the honesty of the workmen who had found the objects. These workmen were engaged in quarrying the chalk, and they averred that they found in the quarry implements made from the horns and bones of animals which still occupied the region. These stories the Professor tossed aside as pure fabrications, but events proved that the workmen were honest and told the facts as they understood them. It seems that prehistoric man had discovered the value of the flints for making implements, and had dug through the sheet of till, which overlay the deposit containing these flints, and had made extensive excavations in the chalk, to obtain the material for their tools and weapons. But when man had emerged from the stone age to the use of bronze and iron, these quarries were neglected, and in time were filled up with sediment carried in by heavy rains and melting snow. It was, therefore, true that, when the workmen of later times were quarrying away a perpendicular face of the chalky mass, these implements of bone and chipped flints fell out upon them, coming to all appearance from the body of the chalk. A little more patience in interpreting the evidence would have saved the credit of the workmen for honesty, and have earlier led to the important archæological discoveries which Dr. Holst had just made.

Being unable himself to leave his geological work, Dr. Holst sent his nephew along with us in our journey to Solvitsborg, sixty or seventy miles farther north, to visit a typical section of the postglacial raised beaches which were near his own home. These we found to be most impressive from every point of view. Several miles back from the sea and 170 feet above it, in a recess on the side of the mountain, there were vast windrows of pebbles, many of them a foot or more in diameter, which had evidently been washed into position by the tumultuous waves of the ocean when it stood at that level. The fine material had all been washed away, and, as the land rose, three or four lower windrows of pebbles had been formed. While these raised beaches are only 170 feet above the sea, others, found far to the north, are 1,000 feet above the sea, indicating a postglacial elevation of the land there to that extent.

Space will not permit me to speak of the delightful days spent in Stockholm, the Venice of the north, except to say that here we were just in time to see some of the recently discovered chains of gold, which had been dug from some of the mounds of the region and had belonged to a prehistoric princess of high rank. The possession of such a mass of gold, far away from the mines from which it must have been extracted, was no less surprising than it was instructive concern-

ing the high development of the prehistoric race that
inhabited the peninsula.

Sailing through the countless islands that guard
the entrance of Stockholm, and pausing for a short
time at Helsingfors in Finland, we at length reached
Petrograd, where we were both surprised and delighted that they allowed us to land without looking
at our passports or examining our baggage. On
reaching the hotel, however, our passports were sur-
rendered, and no more was thought about them till
we left the city. But on account of them we felt a
safety which is not always appreciated by travelers in
Russia, but which is illustrated by an interesting experience of Professor Charles M. Mead who, as he
told me, at one time had lost his way in Petrograd,
and had forgotten the name of his hotel. At last it ·
occurred to him to report himself to the police department. On doing this, they looked up his pass-
port and were able immediately to give him the needed
directions.

After a few days spent calling on the geologists,
(when we found that Nikitin had passed away and
that Tchernyschev was promoted to the head of the
Survey); visiting the museums and art galleries
(where we found ourselves elbowing our way amid
a crowd of which no small proportion were peasants,

in their homely costume); and attending operas,
(where again we encountered a large company of
plainly dressed people, consisting of families with
their children), we took train for the 400-mile ride
to Moscow.

This was the time of the Russo-Japanese war, and
Russia was under military rule, and in the throes of
the revolutionary attempts of that critical time. The
students in the university at Moscow were on a
strike, demanding permission to bring into the class-
rooms socialistic lectures of their own choice. But
good order prevailed, and we were not in any measure discommoded by the condition of things. One
morning after we had been two or three days in our
quarters at the Slavonsky Bazaar, the clerk came to
me with a letter from William T. Stead, saying that
he was to arrive the next day and desired the
reservation of a suite of rooms with "a southern
exposure." As the clerk was doubtful about the
significance of the word "southern," he came to me
for help, which I readily gave him.

The advent of Mr. Stead was an event of great interest, for he had been invited by the Czar to come
from England to visit him and give him advice in the
present crisis, and act as an intermediary between him
and the revolutionary forces. Mr. Stead told me that
his interview with the Czar was extremely satisfac-

tory, that he had had a heart-to-heart talk with him, such as he had never had with anyone else. He said that he found the Czar a man of alert mind, well-posted on all affairs connected with his position, and evidently anxious to do what was best for all parties concerned. The only criticism he had to make of the Czar was that he was inclined to agree with the last man who talked with him, "which, by the way," Mr. Stead remarked, "is not a bad quality in a constitutional monarch."

When Mr. Stead was in Petrograd he exercised great freedom in associating with the Liberal party, and urged the authorities to free the distinguished agitator Miliukov from his imprisonment, which was done at his request. Soon after, at a meeting of the Liberal men of the city, both native and foreign, at which Miliukov was present, much to their astonishment, there was free discussion as to the course which should be pursued by the government. Among those present to take part in the discussion was Lewis Nixon, former head of Tammany in New York, who was now in Russia to assist in the building up of their navy. In emphatic manner Nixon asserted that the thing most needed in Russia was a series of Tammany Halls. In reporting this, Mr. Stead looked up with a very knowing expression on his face and said, "Perhaps Nixon is not so far off as he might seem; for, paradoxical as it may appear, I am not sure but the political corruption of New York and Chicago is destined to be the salvation of America; for the foreigners emigrating to America are mostly imbued with anarchistic ideas and are opposed to all government, but they are cordially received by Tammany, assisted to homes and occupations, and aided in times of trouble; while all that is required in return is that they vote the Tammany ticket." "And why shouldn't they," said Nixon. "Then they become good citizens," continued Stead, "and are made conservative by the responsibility that rests upon the governing power."

Mr. Stead had come down to Moscow to attend a meeting of the Zemstvos and convey to it the greetings of the Czar and his desire for coöperation. From the subsequent turn of affairs, it would seem that Stead's mission was by no means fruitless. The first Duma was so impractical that the country would have been torn to pieces if it had been allowed to have its way. The courage and constancy shown by the Czar, in holding on to the reins of government until a new Duma could be chosen which could be trusted to preserve the unity of the Empire while gradually introducing the safeguards of a constitutional government, have never been fully appreciated.

Nor has the outside public ever given full credit to the government and the higher classes in Russia in their general efforts to promote the welfare of the masses of the people. At this time in Russia, the sale of intoxicating liquors had been taken out of the hands of the saloon keepers and was wholly under the direct control of the government, and liquors were sold only in sealed packages to be used off the premises. No drinking was allowed at the place of sale. This method was adopted with the hope that it would diminish the sale of vodka. But, as we now know, it did not do so. Still, the adoption of this plan by the government rendered possible the wholesale prohibition of the sale of vodka, which was made at the beginning of the present war.

In connection with the closing of the saloons, the government established, as a temperance measure, numerous clean, cheap, lodging places in the cities, where nourishing foods and temperance drinks were furnished at a low cost, and connected with them halls where cheap public entertainments could be provided for the people. These consisted of lectures on various practical and entertaining subjects, of stereopticon entertainments, and musical performances of a high order. I attended one of these in the outskirts of Moscow. But, being a little late, when I applied for a ticket of admission I was surprised to find the charge was seventy-five cents, which seemed to me not a very popular price. On entering, however, my mind was disabused of this misunderstanding. The hall would hold about one thousand, and in the back part there was standing room for a hundred persons who could obtain admittance for two cents and a half apiece. This was filled, some of the occupants being women with children in arms. The back row of seats were sold at five cents apiece; the second row at seven and one half cents apiece, and so on increasing up to the front row, where I purchased my seat at seventy-five cents. The opera that evening was Glinka's " Life for the Czar," the music of which is of the highest order, and the whole opera the most popular in Russia. The performance was by a cast of the best soloists of the city, accompanied by a first-class orchestra. The enthusiasm of the audience was a fine tribute to the musical education of the masses in Russian cities.

It is a long ride from Moscow to Rostov on the Don, requiring two nights on a sleeping car. On going to our first meal in the diner, we were seated opposite a dignified-appearing, elderly military officer accompanied by a lady of slight frame and intellectual countenance, thirty or forty years of age. In our efforts to order food from the waiter we elicited the sympathy of the lady, who, perceiving our difficulty, asked us in perfect English if she could not render assistance, which of course we gladly accepted. This opened the way to an acquaintance, which, aside from being most agreeable, was a revelation respecting Russian society. Mrs. Rubeyny was the wife of a Cossack colonel stationed at Askabad in Turkestan, but she had come home to accompany her aged father to Petrograd for an operation upon his eyes, with the hope of restoring his failing sight. He was the commissary general of the whole Caucasus region, but did not understand English. This, however, did not prevent his scrupulous attendance upon our wants, directing the waiters when he saw they might be neglecting their duties. His fatherly interest in some of the young soldiers who were on the train was indicative of what I had elsewhere observed was characteristic of Russian officers. Mrs. Rubeyny was well-read in English Literature and was thoroughly informed in all matters concerning the Russian Empire, of which she was a most loyal subject. In passing through the Donnetz coal fields, she was able to give us all the desired information as to the quality and quantity of the coal and the difficulties of getting it to market. She, like most of the Russian officers we met, was depressed by the recent peace with Japan, "We ought to have been allowed another campaign. But," she said, "we are a great people and very patient." The remarkable intelligence and high character of Mrs. Rubeyny were typical of those of many others whom, first and last, I was permitted to meet in Siberia and in European Russia.

At Rostov on the Don we remained several days for the purpose of studying the loess deposits in the vicinity, which we found to confirm our previous observations indicating the agency of water as well as of wind in its deposition. Here we were greatly furthered in our plans by the English consul, but especially by Herr Reidel (the German consul though a Russian by birth), who had visited America and was now the agent of one of the large companies in America manufacturing harvesters. Herr Reidel was very much interested in the archæology of the region, and in the general evidence concerning changes of land level in the Caucasus region. One day he accompanied us in a drive of twenty miles, northeast, to visit the ruins of a Greek city, to which archæologists had paid little attention. Its foundation dated back some centuries before the Christian era; and the piles of débris displayed, around the eroded surfaces, abundant fragments of vases and statuary, inviting thorough exploration. But after walking over these remains for an hour or so we were compelled to return to Rostov, lest darkness should overtake us and expose us to robbers who were crawling about the outskirts of the city. As it was, however, darkness did overtake us. But Herr Reidel was well-armed and had taken pains to have his coachman drive in a separate carriage close behind us, which evidently was all that saved us from an attempted robbery by a small band that stopped us on the way, but wisely concluded that we were too many and too well-prepared to be successfully waylaid.

Our plan was to go from Rostov to Tiflis over the Dariel Pass, stopping at Armavir to study the extensive loess deposits to be found in that vicinity. We had heard, however, that the Caucasus tribes were restless and were disturbing trains and travelers. But Mrs Rubeyny had assured us that it would be perfectly safe to make the journey, "since," she said, "doubtless you do not carry money with you but a letter of credit, so that there will be no temptation for highwaymen to rob you." The consuls at Rostov, however, advised us strongly against the trip, especially as a train had recently been held up at Armavir and shots interchanged, by which several were killed. "But," we explained, "we have a letter of introduction from the Russian embassy at Washington to the Governor General of the Caucasus, which certainly will protect us." " That is just the thing that will not protect you," they replied, " for it is the Governor General they are trying to kill." Whereupon we changed our plans and proceeded down the Don River, which for a long distance wended its way through the countless river boats which had come with supplies of wheat and wool for export to the Western world.

After a short stop at Tagnarog, where steamers of all nations receive their cargoes to be taken to the ends of the world, we crossed the shallow Sea of Azov, and paused for a day or two at Kertch, where a fortress guards the narrow outlet from the Sea of Azov to the Black Sea. Here, too, is the site of an ancient Grecian city, but in this case the ruins have been extensively excavated and countless treasures of Grecian art taken to Petrograd. However, sufficient are left to fill a museum of great interest, while upon the summit of an overlooking hill, where it is reported that Mithridates was buried, public-spirited Russians have erected a temple in imitation of the Parthenon, which is so like it in shape and position that one can easily imagine, on entering the harbor, that he is approaching Athens itself. Some miles out from the city there is an abandoned aqueduct, whose purpose it is difficult to imagine from the present lack of water supply. An extensive artificial mound which we visited, reminded us, in appearance, of that at Miamisburgh, in Ohio. On excavating it, it was found that the pile of earth completely enveloped a rock-built inclosure, drawn to a point at the top, which is almost a duplicate of one at Mycenæ in Greece sacred to the memory of Agamemnon. For nearly two thousand years this mound had concealed the treasures of art that had been deposited in the inclosure.

After pausing at Theodosia, where a replica of the Grecian temple at Kertch crowned the hill overlooking the city, and visiting the celebrated gallery of paintings that a public-spirited citizen of fine taste had furnished at great expense and donated to the public, we proceeded to the noted watering place of Yalta. At Lavidia, adjoining it on the west, the Czar has a splendid palace, amid extensive grounds, looking down upon the blue surface of the Black Sea; while Yalta itself has attracted the aristocracy of the whole Empire, making it a resort of unrivalled interest. This charming spot is surrounded by a semicircle of mountains, several thousand feet in height, which protect it from northern winds and secure a climate that, even in winter, is very grateful to the people of the north. The only approach to it is by water and by a military road, running westward along the flanks of the mountains and keeping about 2,000 feet above the sea to Sevastopol, a distance of sixty miles. Over this well-kept road we drove in a private carriage in a single day. Words cannot express the charm of that drive, as we dashed in and out of the recesses of the winding roadway, now with the weird form of the cloud-capped mountains before us and now with the picturesque hamlets and private residences coming to view on the seashore, 2,000 feet below us. When about two-thirds of the way, we stopped for dinner and rest at the summit, where the road leaves the sea; then, after passing through the vale of Bidar, celebrated for its vineyards, and being driven down the sloping fields where the fatal " charge of the six hundred " took place, with Balaclava on one side, and the Malakoff on the other, we entered Sevastopol, with galloping horses, some time before the close of day.

A week at Sevastopol is all too short to familiarize oneself with the objects of historical and archæological interest in the city and its environs. A commodious harbor, protected by surrounding hills, has predestined it to be for all time a military fortress of greatest value to the Russian Empire, while every portion of the city itself and the country immediately surrounding it were made forever interesting by the scenes attending its siege during the Crimean War. Here, English, French, Turkish, and Italian soldiers struggled in fierce and deadly conflict with Russians during many long and weary months. How strange the combination, in view of the alignment of forces in the great war which is now convulsing Europe!

On the promontory just west of Sevastopol are the ruins of the ancient Greek city of Chersonese, which a Russian archæological society has explored with great thoroughness, filling the local museum with innumerable interesting objects of early Grecian art. Going through the scenes of the battle of Inkerman, and about twenty miles beyond, one reaches Bakhtchi-Saraï, the capital center of the Tartar tribes of the Crimea, near which are large numbers of the most interesting prehistoric cells, dug into the sides of the mountains and occupied for ages by monks of various kinds. Two or three miles east of Bakhtchi-Saraï, on an inaccessible promontory covered with ancient ruins, is a settlement of Caraite Jews, who here maintain a theological school and preserve ancient manuscripts of great value. The Russian government has greatly favored this Jewish sect and we found in their schoolroom, covered with artistic woodcarving, life-size portraits of the Czar and Czarina, which they had presented. In the morning when we reached Bakhtchi-Saraï the streets were full of life and animation, the shops were all open, and wagons, loaded with fruit and melons and various other products of the surrounding country, made the passage through the city slow and difficult. But, on our return after sundown, we found the streets deserted, and the shops closed; and it seemed to us that something terrible had happened, foreboding evil for those who passed through. But we were comforted to learn that it was all due to the strict habit of the Moslems to close the day's work at sundown and all return to the privacy of their homes.

SYRIA AND PALESTINE

So much is written about Constantinople that it is not worth while to give details concerning our visit there, except to say that Robert College, Constantinople College for Women, the Bible House, and Mrs. Marden's school are centers of influence whose value cannot be overestimated; and that, by a process of natural selection, the personnel of those carrying on the work of these institutions is raised to the highest degree of efficiency. One incident, however, is so illustrative of the capacity of Turkish officialdom, that we cannot refrain from mentioning it. When our trunk was undergoing inspection at the customhouse in Constantinople, nothing attracted the attention of the inspectors until they reached an atlas of the world which already had a history. It was a German publication of high character, giving in detail the physical and political geography of all nations. I had purchased it in a bookstore in Omsk, Siberia, just as I was starting, in 1900, on my tarantass ride through Turkestan. On returning home from that trip I had laid it aside in some handy place, for consultation, and there it had lain till we were about to start for the present trip. But at the last moment I threw it into the trunk, as probably what we should need for consultation in various emergencies. On finding this in our possession, the inspector, after faithfully turning over the leaves, shook his head, as though in doubt what to do, and passed it to another, who did the same. But the third inspector knew just where to look for treasonable matter, and, opening the leaves at four different places, proceeded with his penknife to scratch off some objectionable name, which being done he closed the atlas, threw it back into the trunk, put down the lid, and shoved it through the lines. It is needless to say that at our first opportunity we examined the atlas to see what had been done, and found that the word Armenia had been erased wherever it occurred. There were " Armenians," but " Armenia " had ceased to exist. So it was ruled, and so it was believed to be.

Soon after, while we were in Beirut, the Scotch engineer connected with the city waterworks told us

an equally characteristic story of Turkish incompre-
hensibility. Some part of the engine which he was
erecting, and which had been sent from England, was
missing, and he went to the office to send a telegram
to have it forwarded immediately. In describing the
missing part he had to say that it must make two
thousand revolutions a minute. The Turkish officials
were horrified, since one revolution was more than
they could permit, and two thousand was beyond all
reason.

.When I had passed through Beirut in 1900, I had
hoped to visit the cedars of Lebanon, but it was so
late in the season (the first of December) that it was
impossible, because of the snow that already enveloped
the heights of the mountain ranges. But on this visit
an unrivalled opportunity opened for accomplishing
the purpose. Professor Alfred E. Day, the accomplished geologist of the Presbyterian College at Beirut,
was permitted to suspend his classes for a week, to
conduct me over the ground which had long been
familiar to him. As we learned that Professor Benjamin Bacon, of Yale Theological Seminary, was at
Sidon with George H. Driver, one of his honor pupils,
we sent them an urgent invitation to accompany us.
This they did, and one of the most enjoyable and
profitable weeks of my life was spent under the direc-

tion and tutorage of Professor Day. We were provided with horses to ride, and accompanied by a
manager, who supplied tents and provisions for food
while we worked our way diagonally along the western flank of the Lebanon Mountains, up to the vast
amphitheater (6,000 feet above the sea) at the base
of the highest peaks of the mountains, 4,000 feet
higher. Here was a vast and characteristic terminal
moraine, deposited and deserted by the ice thousands
of years before, on which a grove of four hundred
magnificent cedars, surrounded by a wall, are guarded
and protected. The natives undertook to unsettle the
higher critical positions of Professor Bacon by assuring him that these cedars were planted· by Christ
himself, quoting Psalm civ. 16-17, where we read,
" The trees of the Lord are full of sap; the cedars of
Lebanon, which he hath planted; where the birds make
their nests."

On the way from Beirut to the cedars, we passed
a number of ruins where Greek and Roman inscriptions were to be seen upon the walls and fallen pillars. To the traveler who has made the diagonal
journey from Beirut to the cedars, memory fills in
innumerable details which are concealed from vision
at any one time. He has crossed *Nahr el-Kelb* (" Dog
River "), near its mouth, where he has seen Egyptian
and Assyrian inscriptions dating from the time of

Sennacherib's invasion. Ascending this river, after passing numerous villages surrounded by mulberry and olive groves, vineyards, and fields of wheat, and pausing to study the ruins of a temple dating from Roman times, and having crossed a natural bridge at *Jisr el-Hagar* with a span of one hundred and twenty feet, rising seventy-five feet above the stream, he arrives, at the end of the second day, at the ruins of the famous temple of Venus destroyed by the order of Constantine on account of the impurity of the rites celebrated in it. Here, too, is a famous spring, typical of many others which gush forth on either side of the Lebanon range from beneath the thick deposits of limestone which everywhere crown its summit. The flow of water is enormous, and at certain seasons of the year is colored red with a mineral matter, which the ancients regarded with mysterious reverence. The lower part of the amphitheater is covered with verdure and a scanty growth of pine and walnut trees, but the upper part merges in the barren cliffs which lie above the snow line. Onward, alternately through upturned limestone strata, left by erosion in fantastic forms, and through barren areas of red sandstone, where the cedars of Lebanon would flourish if protected from the depredations of man and his domestic animals, he crosses by turns at higher and higher levels the headwaters of the Ibrahim, Fedar, Jozeh, Byblus, and Botrys rivers, and at length reaches, on the fourth day, the Kadisha, five miles below the cedars of Lebanon.

Ascending the summit of Lebanon, to the east of the cedars, we find ourselves in the midst of snow fields which never melt away. But here there bursts upon us, to the east, the Anti-Lebanon range of mountains, rising on the other side of Cœle-Syria, a valley a few miles wide forming the continuation of the great Jordan fault and containing, almost at our feet, the marvellous ruins of Baalbek. But on descending the precipitous pathway we find extensive ruins, far older than those of Baalbek, going back even to pre-Mosaic times, and representing the religious culture of the original inhabitants of Syria and Palestine. Dusty and weary with our travels, we were joined at Baalbek by Mrs. Wright and Mrs. George Doolittle, who, with her husband, was engaged in missionary work à few miles away at Zahleh, at the eastern base of the Lebanon range. With them and Mr. Driver we spent two days in Damascus, when we returned to the Doolittle home, where Mrs. Wright had been entertained during the week of our trip to the cedars.

We have space to note but two or three things in connection with this mission station. As one looks down upon the city from the Doolittle home, one's attention is attracted by a large number of red-tile roofs, which we were informed were for the most part residences of Syrians who had been to America and accumulated sufficient fortune to come home and live in style among their former companions. The city, also, like many other places in the Lebanon Mountains, is a favorite summer resort for Egyptian families who are unable to endure the monotony of the climate in the delta. ·

A side light upon Syrian life is illustrated by an incident which reminds one of what we have already said about the robber and beggar trusts in China. As we were at the station at Zahleh, awaiting a train, a disreputable looking, one-legged man circled around us at a respectful distance; but, to my surprise, he did not stretch out his palm for baksheesh, or alms. The reason for his good behavior we afterwards learned was, that Mr. Doolittle paid him a beshlik (about eleven cents) a month not to beg from his friends. Mrs. Wright informed me that, during her stay at Zahleh, this one-legged beggar hobbled all the way up the hill, a mile long, to receive his monthly stipend.

After leaving Beirut, the few hours we spent at Jaffa, on the way to Egypt, are memorable for the privilege we had there of meeting again my old friend Selah Merrill, who was still consul at Jerusalem, but in broken health, and was spending a few days at Jaffa to recuperate. We found him and his wife (an old friend of Andover days) quietly spending their vacation upon a housetop, surrounded with manuscripts and photographs of an extensive volume which he was soon to publish upon Jerusalem. From no other place could we have received such an impression of the abruptness of the escarpment of the Judean plateau, which rises but a few miles back from the sea. Beth Horon and Aijalon, where, in the midst of a destructive hailstorm, the sun was obscured long enough for Joshua to annihilate the army of the five Amorite kings, were near enough to enable us to distinguish the promontories and mountain gorges in which the Amorites were entrapped. Palestine itself was surrounded by natural walls, far more effective for defense than those built around China by the Mongols.

Lower Egypt must be passed with a simple reference to the trip to Suez for the purpose of verifying the theory, already entertained during the previous visit with my son, that the place where the Children of Israel crossed the " Red Sea " was just to the south of the Bitter Lakes, from ten to twelve miles north of the present Gulf of Suez. More perfectly to assure myself of the situation, we engaged a Mohammedan guide, who provided a small boat to be hauled by a mule through the entire length of the fresh-water canal, to the head of the Bitter Lakes. Everything confirmed the theory. Here was a plain, sufficiently

large to accommodate the hosts of Israel, protected by
a narrow passage between the lakes and the desert
plateau stretching out from Jebel Geneffeh, where
doubtless at the time of the Exodus the land was depressed sufficiently to permit a narrow arm of the sea
a few feet in depth, extending from the Gulf of Suez
to the Bitter Lakes, to intervene between the Israelites
and the Asiatic shore. The situation was one in which
it was easy to see that the strong east wind spoken of
in the Bible would lower the water sufficiently to permit the passage of the Israelites. So perfect is the
conformity of the physical facts in this region to the
conditions involved in the Biblical account, that no
one who adequately understands them can doubt the
truthfulness of the Bible story.

Sailing from Alexandria, we stopped at Messina,
sufficiently long to see enough of the city and its situation to be especially impressed and shocked by the de-
vastation of the earthquake that occurred soon after.
It is needless to dwell upon incidents connected with
our visit to Naples, Rome, and Florence, from which
latter city, passing through Milan, we entered Switzerland through the Simplon Pass, and made our way
northward through eastern France (where now the
horrible scenes of war are being enacted), to Calais
without visiting Paris. Thence we went to London

for a few weeks' stay before returning to America for me to take up the regular routine of my work.

SCIENTIFIC CONFIRMATIONS OF OLD TESTAMENT HISTORY

In 1904 I was invited to give the Stone Lectures at Princeton Theological Seminary. The subject chosen was " Scientific Confirmations of Old Testament History." Two years later, with the information gathered in my third visit to Europe, I rewrote and prepared them for publication. The book was issued by the Bibliotheca Sacra Company, in 1906. In this volume the general authenticity of the history found in the Old Testament is supported by the circumstantial evidence which is supplied by an examination of the physical conditions involved in a number of occurrences, reported in the Old Testament, which seem at first sight very improbable. The object of the book is to show that the setting of these occurrences among complicated physical conditions, about which little was known in ancient times, but upon which modern science sheds a flood of light, is so perfect that the stories could not have been invented, nor could they have been materially enlarged by legendary accretions, as these would certainly have introduced incongruous elements.

The book received cordial recognition from the highest sources. A translation of it was made into Dutch, accompanied by a commendatory introduction by Dr. A. Kuyper. An edition was immediately sold in England, while Dr. Koenig of Bonn gave it a very favorable review, and Professor George Macloskie of Princeton wrote in the *Princeton Review,* " This volume bids fair to be recognized as the standard work on the important subject of Pentateuchal physics," while the *Expository Times* said, " For a long time to come every one who has to write upon the Deluge, or touch that wider subject of the attitude of the Old Testament to the phenomena of nature, will require to know what is written in this book." A third edition, with slight additions, was issued in 1913, and the sales are continuing in undiminished numbers up to the present time. Like " The Ice Age in North America," the volume deals so directly with facts of which I have personal cognizance, that there will be little need of modifying conclusions for a long time to come.

In the publication of this book I was in danger of being misunderstood by both conservatives and radicals. On the one hand, there was danger that the conservatives would charge me with totally discrediting miracles. I was therefore much relieved to find so staunch a conservative as Dr. Kuyper, in his introduction to a Dutch translation, writing as follows:—

"It is hoped that no offense will be taken at the attempt of Dr. Wright to make clear the passing of the Jews through the Red Sea, and through the Jordan, by invoking the aid of irregular operations of nature. The belief in God's wonderful might does not require that in explanation of the wonders we should exclude the operations of nature which would have taken place in any event.

"When I say that, even if Ahab and Elijah had not existed, a fire would still have fallen down at the same moment and on the same place where Elijah's sacrifice was offered, I do not say that it was not a wonder. The objective as well as the subjective wonder exists. The objective wonder is the falling down of the fire just on the same place and at the same moment of the historical event. The subjective wonder is that Elijah without knowing anything of the position of affairs in nature dared supplicate for it and had faith to believe that the fire would come.

"In this way Dr. Wright writes about some of the great wonders in the history of Israel. I dare not say that he always has taken the right view of what happened, but even if in a single instance he might be mistaken I still praise his endeavors to connect wonders in the history with the course of the operations of nature. That his own belief in the wonders does not waver, he states on more than one page."

Prominent among the miracles which I specially treated in these lectures are the crossing of the Red Sea, the parting of Jordan, the destruction of Sodom and Gomorrah, and the Noachian Deluge, which is thought to be connected with the changes of land level accompanying the Glacial epoch. In all these cases and in many more which might be considered, the phenomena are those connected with the special direction of secondary causes. The events are narrated in a direct historical manner. To the historian, the question is not whether they are miraculous but whether the narratives are true. The agency of the divine element is a subsidiary question; but the divine agency is by no means ruled out by the discovery of the means through which God accomplishes his design. The famous law of parsimony may be used in interpreting divine actions even better than in interpreting human actions. This law, known from the fourteenth century as Occam's razor, is variously stated. Its essence is contained in the following expressions: "Assign no other causes than suffice to account for the phenomena." "Nature knows no waste." All that is necessary to constitute a miracle is, to show that the use of secondary causes is on such a scale and of such a character as clearly to reveal a power over nature which is nothing less than divine. With reference to the wind which, according to the

Bible account, was the secondary cause of opening the
Red Sea before the advancing hosts of Israel and closing its waters to the pursuing Egyptian army, we do
not necessarily suppose, in order to make the event miraculous, that they were produced out of the ordinary
course of nature, though such a supposition is by no
means absurd. It is as easy for the Lord to produce a
hurricane as it is for a housewife to produce a wind
sufficient to blow the dust from her mantel. God is
no less a free agent in the use of nature's forces than
is man. Man, certainly, does in innumerable ways
make new combinations, producing effects which were
not originally incorporated in the forces of nature.

In 1907, according to the rules of the college, I was
placed upon the retired list and given the Carnegie
Pension, which, though much less than my regular
salary had been, was sufficient to give me reasonable
support, and allow me to devote my attention to the
completion of my literary plans. The first th'ng
undertaken was the preparation of a fifth edition of
the " Ice Age in North America." The task of such
a work will be better appreciated by referring again
to the fact, that thirty closely printed pages were required to simply enumerate the articles which had
appeared in scientific journals since the first edition
was published.

CHAPTER XIII

FOURTH VISIT TO EUROPE

THE autumn and winter of 1907 and 1908 were
spent in another visit to Europe, in which, landing at
Antwerp, we reveled for a week amid the art treasures of that interesting city, and then visited Holland
and Brussels, from which trips were made on the one
hand to Bruges and on the other to Waterloo. Thence
we went to Paris, where, among other privileges, was
that of meeting Salomon Reinach in the great museum,
of which he is the director, in Saint-Germain-en-Laye
and discussing with him the character and age of the
palæolithic implements found in northern France.
By him I was given an introduction to M. Commont,
principal of the schools in Amiens, whose collection of
palæoliths from the gravels of that vicinity is larger
than that of all others put together. So carefully has
he made his collection, that he is able to classify them
into lower and higher, according to their occurrence
in different elevations of the bank, and to compare
their relative stages of culture. His publications upon
the subject are of the highest value. It was a privilege
to visit again the gravel pits of this celebrated locality,

under the guidance of such an authority, and at the same time it was a surprise to see the extent to which the gravels had been excavated without exhausting the supply of palæoliths. Still, in view of the facts about the rapid accumulation of river gravel during the exceptional conditions of the Glacial epoch, one may well hesitate to assign them to the extreme antiquity demanded by many of the European archæologists. The question of age will be found discussed in my later volume " Origin and Antiquity of Man," to which the reader is referred.

One object which I kept in view was to visit the localities in northern France and southern England where Professor Joseph Prestwich (one of the ablest geologists and most painstaking observers of England) supposed that he had found evidence of an extensive but brief subsidence of the region, followed by a sudden emergence of the land from the water, producing the deposits referred to as " rubble drift " or "head." The classic localities for the study of these deposits are Sangatte, France, a few miles west of Calais, and Brighton, England, on the opposite side of the Channel. These places I visited, and studied with considerable care, not with the expectation that I could add anything to the very careful descriptions given by Professor Prestwich, but to see with my own eyes these remarkable and puzzling phenomena upon which he has based his startling inferences. As clearly and briefly as I can state the facts they are as follows:

Both at Sangatte and at Brighton, there appears, ten to fifteen feet above the present sea level, an elevated beach consisting of a stratum of well-worn pebbles. But overlying this beach there is a deposit of coarse, irregularly stratified material, with a thickness at Sangatte of forty feet and at Brighton of fully eighty feet. This is what is called rubble drift. Near the base of this rubble drift, on both sides of the Channel, there have been found a few palæolithic implements, and numerous mammalian remains characteristic of Post-Tertiary time, among them those of species of elephant, rhinoceros, reindeer, hippopotamus, horse, hog, and ox.

This rubble drift is evidently not a deposit of running water, but shows clear marks, in some places, of rapid and tumultuous accumulation, while in other places there is seen the fine lamination produced by tranquil water action and deposition. Both at Sangatte and Brighton large blocks of rock with angles but slightly worn appear at irregular intervals in the drift. One of these at Brighton, measured by Professor Prestwich, was 8 by 2 by 2 feet. The material in this rubble drift is all of local origin, and is derived from the immediate vicinity. At Sangatte, the highland from which the material in the rubble drift had been derived lies to the south and west, while in Brighton the highland furnishing the material lies to the north and east. This would make it difficult to explain as a glacial deposit, as some have surmised. Furthermore, no scratched stones have been observed in it. In many other localities in which Professor Prestwich has found the same class of deposits, it is found to be distributed in all directions from a central elevation, but not in deltas, as would be the case if it were deposited by a running stream of water. In the Jersey Islands, which I also visited, this drift had been carried over a very low gradient, a long distance from its source.

Thus it will be seen that these facts present a very puzzling problem. After eliminating all other causes, as insufficient to account for all the phenomena, Professor Prestwich presents what he believes is the only sufficient explanation. He believes that all the phenomena can be accounted for only by supposing that after a continental subsidence which had submerged the region to the extent of several hundred feet, the land was suddenly reëlevated by a series of violent earthquake shocks, like that which brought the tidal wave into Lisbon in 1755, or like that in San Francisco, in which the instantaneous vertical movement was ten feet, or that on the Alaskan coast in 1899,

where the paroxysmal elevation was from thirty to
forty feet. Such a series of sudden elevations would
be sufficient to produce a current, in all directions from
the higher elevations, of sufficient force and character
to account for all the facts. I have been unable to detect any flaw in Prestwich's reasoning, and have
ventured to introduce it as part of the evidence in support of a postglacial deluge causing widespread destruction both of man and animals throughout western
Europe, and so indirectly supporting the story of the
Deluge as told in the Bible.[1]

While in England during the winter following,
numerous opportunities were afforded to lecture upon
the archæological relations of the Glacial epoch. The
most of these were delivered in London, where, also,
a paper was read before the Geological Society. One
invitation, also, came from Cambridge, where I was
cordially received by Professors Hughes and Marr,
and where I had the opportunity of meeting the Lewis
sisters, whose discovery of the early Syrian manuscript
of the New Testament on Mount Sinai created such
a sensation in the scholarly world, and of the results
of which I had made considerable use in my lectures
on the " Scientific Aspects of Christian Evidences."
But at Cardiff, in the lecture which I gave before the
Natural History Society, including most of the Uni-

versity professors, I was able to put in shape a theory which had been cherished ever since my visit to Central Asia. This, which I have already partially outlined, was that the influence of the Glacial epoch in Central Asia was the predominant factor both in developing and in dispersing the human race. It was during the climax of the Glacial epoch that conditions were most favorable to life in the vast oases of Central Asia, irrigated by the streams which came down from the glacier-covered mountain masses of the region; while it was the elevation of land all over the Northern Hemisphere at that time which favored the dispersion both of man and of the animals originating with him in the same region. At the same time, during the closing stages of the Glacial epoch, while the habitable oases of Central Asia were rapidly contracting by reason of the diminished water supply, the fairest fields of Europe, which had been overborne by glacial ice, were being relieved of their glacial envelope and were inviting that westward movement of population which is even now going on into the glaciated areas of the United States and Canada.

On returning to America, I set to work at the task of rewriting in the light of all subsequent observations the Lowell Institute Lectures on the "Orig'n and Antiquity of Man," which I had given in Boston

twenty years before. A portion of these lectures had
been enlarged and embodied in " Man and the Glacial
Period," published in 1892 in the International Scientific Series. But in " Origin and Antiquity of Man "
I endeavored to present and properly estimate the evidence coming from every quarter, treating in successive
chapters of Methods of Scientific Approach; the Historical Evidence; the Linguistic Argument; Origin of
the Races of Europe; Origin and Antiquity of the
American Indian; Significance of the Glacial Epoch;
Man in the Glacial Epoch; Man and the Lava Beds
of the Pacific Coast; Remains of Glacial Man in Europe; Supposed Evidence of Tertiary Man; Glacial
Man in Central Asia; the Physiological Argument;
the Psychological Argument; the Biblical Scheme;
Summary and Conclusion, in which emphasis is laid
upon the fact, that the theory of evolution by a uniform and gradual process is contradicted by innumerable facts and cannot be made a basis for estimating
the length either of geologic or of historic time. So
far as we have evidence, palæolithic man had a brain
equal in size to that of modern man, while the intellectual qualities which he displayed were such as compare favorably with those which modern man possesses.
Evidence, which it is well-nigh criminal for anyone
now to neglect, is adduced concerning the recency of
the Glacial epoch and the abnormal conditions con-

nected with it, which render of no value the arguments for the extreme antiquity of man asserted by many who assume to be authorities upon the subject. The changes in the glaciers of Alaska during the last thirty years are greater than those in the glaciers of the Alps, which German authorities assume to require 15,000 years and proceed to make the basis of their chronology; while Baron de Geer and Professor Holst have demonstrated that glacial ice did not disappear from southern Sweden until about 7,000 years ago.

CHAPTER XIV

EDITORIAL WORK

AMONG the important responsibilities which Providence has thrown upon me, is the editorial work connected with the *Bibliotheca Sacra* and the *Records of the Past*. Professor Edwards A. Park of Andover was known to say that the two things in which his success in life was most evident were the editing of the *Bibliotheca Sacra* and the Sabbath Hymnbook. In 1844 the *Bibliotheca Sacra* was founded in Andover, Massachusetts, under the editorship of Professors Bela B. Edwards and Edwards A. Park, with the special coöperation of Dr. Edward Robinson and Professor Moses Stuart. Professor Park continued as its principal editor until the close of its fortieth volume in 1883, since which I have been its leading editor. Thus this Quarterly has had a longer continued existence than any other in America. From the beginning the aim of the editors has been to publish articles of permanent value only, and by following this policy it has become one of the most important repositories of theological material in existence.

The circumstances which threw upon me a leading

part in the perpetuation of the Quarterly are of sufficient interest to warrant a somewhat detailed statement of facts. As already said, I had become, soon after settling in Andover, a prominent contributor to its pages. For the most part my contributions during this period were related to the theological questions raised by the prevalence of Darwinism. Soon after my removal to Oberlin. in 1881 occurred the great theological convulsion at Andover known as the " New Departure," the essence of which was that some of the professors claimed the right of holding their positions and keeping their salaries while teaching doctrines that were in positive contradiction to the creed which they specifically signed on entering, and re-signed thereafter every five years. The specific point which came before the public was that of the future probation of the heathen, a doctrine which was categorically denied in the Andover Creed. And here it should be noted that the signatories to the Andover Creed were not let off like those to the Westminster Confession, by assenting to it for "substance of doctrine," but prefixed every section of the Creed with, " I believe."

Soon after the outbreak of this revolution, Professors Henry M. Thayer and Charles M. Mead resigned their chairs rather than be implicated in the manifest dishonesty. The remaining members of the revolutionary party proposed the publication of an organ called the *Andover Review*. Without consulting with the editor, Professor Park, or Mr. Draper, the publisher, they proceeded to advertise their review extensively, and in due time launched it upon the public, evidently expecting that it would undermine the *Bibliotheca Sacra* so that its subscription list would fall into their hands. But their expectations were not realized. On the contrary, the result was that in 1883, at the beginning of the forty-first volume, the *Bibliotheca Sacra* was removed to Oberlin to be conducted by an editorial board consisting of G. Frederick Wright, Judson Smith, and W. G. Ballantine with " Edwards A. Park, W. M. Barbour, E. C. Bissell, F. B. Denio, C. F. Thwing, D. W. Simon, and Archibald Duff Associate Editors." I had for two years already been one of the associate editors. The outcome of it all was, that after three or four years the *Andover Review* was discontinued, while *Bibliotheca Sacra* has continued, up to the present time, to command a constituency sufficient for its support without the aid of any endowment or subsidy.

While the editorial staff has changed more or less from time to time, I have been the one who has succeeded in giving the magazine its continuity. When Judson Smith was appointed secretary of the American Board, his removal from Oberlin and assumption of other duties naturally led to his resignation. Professor Frank H. Foster, Professor Smith's successor in the chair of Church History, naturally took his place on the editorial staff. Some years later, when Professor Ballantine was elected President of Oberlin College, and Professor Foster was called to Pacific Theological Seminary, they both resigned; and Mr. Z. Swift Holbrook, at once an enterprising business man, a sound theologian, and an ardent promoter of sensible views of Christian sociology, joined me in the purchase of the magazine from Mr. E. J. Goodrich, the former Oberlin publisher. Mr. Holbrook's business ability gave a new impulse to the publication, which it has felt ever since. But on his removal by death the whole responsibility fell on me, and since 1900 I have been the sole responsible editor. Various efforts were made at different times to induce me to consent to a popularization of the magazine. At one time it was proposed to make it an organ of Oberlin affairs. At other times it was proposed to make it a monthly, and to give it a more popular character; but fortunately I have been able successfully to resist these shortsighted plans, and have kept it to its original purpose of publishing only, or at least mainly, thorough discussions of fundamental themes which would be of permanent value. The result has been that *Bibliotheca Sacra* has maintained a cosmopolitan character, both in its circulation and its contributors, more fully than any other American publication has done. It is bound and indexed in all the leading libraries of the world, and hence has become a favorite channel for writers of eminence, who had something important to say to the leaders of thought in all centers of influence.

I should not fail to mention the inestimable services rendered by Miss Annie S. Davis, a member of my church in Andover and a graduate of the Salem Normal School, who, forced by ill health to abandon her chosen profession, had temporarily served an apprenticeship in the printing office of Warren F. Draper, the publisher of *Bibliotheca Sacra*. When the magazine was brought to Oberlin she was induced to come to take charge of the details of keeping the books, preparing the manuscript for the printers, and being responsible for the proof reading. This she has done now for more than thirty years, to the satisfaction of all parties concerned, relieving the editor and publisher from the burdensome work connected with the details.

While I have continued to write largely for the magazine, both over my own name and in unsigned critical notes and book reviews, my chief work in connection with it has been to draw and direct to its pages articles from competent scholars, supporting, in the main, the evangelical system of church doctrines.

Marked success has attended this effort. Archæology
has been treated by Professor M. G. Kyle, recognized
as an authority on the archæology of Egypt the world
over; the authority of Scripture by Dr. Huizinga and
Professor Estes of Colgate University; the Babel-
Bible controversy by Dr. Notz; the influence of the
Bible on intellect, conscience, scholarship, criticism, and
science by Rankin, Stimson, Kuyper, and Hitchcock;
the relations of the body to man's spiritual nature by
Boardman, Goddard, and Bixby; the land and people
of the Bible by Curtiss and Beecher; the diseases of
the Bible and the plagues of Egypt by Dr. Merrins;
the nature, character, and work of Christ by Hillis,
Keen, Wright, Merrins, Howland, Burton, Mc-
Laughlin, Thomson, Wendell, Crannell, Sewall,
Shaw, Boardman, Hutchins, Weston, Fairfield, Met-
calf, Thwing, Gardiner, and Magoun; on creation
and modern science by Warring, Magoun, Howland,
Cooper, Gulick, and Wright; on the Deluge by
Prestwich, Adams, Bishop, Whitney, Magoun, Res-
telle, and Wright; demoniacal possession by Merrins; evolution by Wright, Simon, Mackenzie,
Thurston, Reeve, Hawkins, and Campbell; freedom
of the will, Foster, Wright, Potwin, and Howland;
higher criticism, Hayman, Wright, Wiener, Kuyper,
Lamb, Dewart, and Griffiths; inspiration by Wright,
Foster, Bartlett, and Jarrel; Isaiah by Caverno, Lias,

and Osgood; John's Gospel, Ferguson, Rishell, Lias, Juel; Jonah by Macloskie; man, origin and antiquity of, Upham, Wright, Miss Owen, Macloskie; miracle by Wright, Blake, Warring, Greene, and Lamb; Paul's life and work by Foster, Gilbert, Bosworth, Marsh, Merrins, and Williams; Pentateuch by Haman, Wiener, Potwin, Bartlett, Barton, Dahse, Aalders, Koenig, Troelstra, and Noordtzij; philosophy by Lindsay, Campbell, and Neighbor; theism by Morton, Bascom, Gardiner, and Wright; textual criticism by Hoskier, Buchanan, and Wiener; Wellhausen school by Wiener and Margoliouth. This partial list of subjects with their authors gives but a faint idea of the whole collection of material found in the pages of the Quarterly.

It is difficult to estimate the influence exerted by such a publication as *Bibliotheca Sacra*. To judge of it correctly one must take a long look. For the last quarter of a century it has been defending those doctrines of theism, of the Bible, and of theology in general, which have been commonly believed through all the Christian centuries, and which have served to give continuity to the Christian Church. Since the beginning of the nineteenth century this system of truth has been largely supplanted by a materialistic form of evolution, which has taken possession of many of the

seats of learning and influence and to a large extent
is permeating the centers of scientific thought, while
a monistic theory of the universe, equally destructive
with pantheism of the true theistic view, is to a la-
mentable extent controlling many centers of theological thought. In eliminating the idea of second causes
and referring everything to the direct activity of God,
the prevalent doctrine' of divine immanence is under-
mining the whole Christian system, by relieving man
from the responsibility of sin, charging it upon the
Creator himself; and by obliterating the whole distinction between natural and supernatural, and referring everything to the direct action of God, is destroy-
ing the whole conception of miracles, since it renders
everything miraculous.

In the controversy that has been going on, it is of
course impossible to single out any one cause as having
been predominant in controlling public opinion; but it
can be said in truth that the theistic view of the universe, as outlined and defended in the articles of *Bibliotheca Sacra* prepared by me while in close conference
with Professor Park and Asa Gray and published
more than thirty years ago and repeatedly supported
by articles in later years written by various scholarly
authorities, is that which both the scientific and the
theological world are again coming more and more to

entertain; while, in the defense of the Mosaic authorship of the Pentateuch, and in getting back to the
original text of the New Testament, the influence of
Bibliotheca Sacra has been phenomenal.

To this end the work of Harold M. Wiener and
E. S. Buchanan have contributed most largely; and
the way in which both these scholars have been led in
their investigations, and to the choice of *Bibliotheca
Sacra* as the main channel through which to reach the
public, deserves a brief record.

Harold M. Wiener is an orthodox Jew, between
thirty and forty years of age, who was graduated from
Cambridge University (England) with highest honors
several years ago, and who distinguished his gradua-
tion by publishing an important volume entitled
"Studies in Biblical Law." In due time he was admitted to the bar, and became an active barrister, with
his office in Lincoln's Inn, London. Soon after, Dean
Wace, of Canterbury, pressed upon the attention of
a leading Jewish rabbi of London the duty of the Jews
to come to the defense of their hero, Moses. "Why,"
he pointedly asked, "should you leave the defense of
your hero to the Christians?" The challenge was
taken up by Mr. Wiener, who, above all other men,
had the all-round preparation for undertaking the task.
He is a lawyer, and so is qualified to consider a legal

document such as the Pentateuch is. He is a faithful Jew, and knows the Jewish literature by heart. He has command of all the languages necessary to obtain the facts shedding light upon the subject. Profoundly impressed with the truth of his cause, Mr. Wiener has entered the field, and has already accomplished striking results.

He has shown in the first place, that the higher critics have neglected textual criticism, and that if the text is restored to its probable condition before the Septuagintal translation almost all the contentions of the higher critics fall to the ground.

Secondly, he has shown that the higher critics, not being lawyers, have introduced inextricable confusion by not distinguishing between legal terms and not discerning the processes by which laws come into operation. The whole of the Priestly Code is what the lawyers would call "procedure," which, instead of being relegated to Ezekiel's time, almost necessarily came into existence with the first promulgation of the law.

Thirdly, the higher critics have not distinguished between an "altar of sacrifice" and a "sanctuary," and thus have made confusion worse confounded in their reasonings. Other errors are pointed out too numerous to mention.

Rev. E. S. Buchanan is an Oxford scholar, who at

the beginning of his career was taken under the tute-
lage of Bishop Wordsworth of Salisbury, who in his
lifetime was the ablest exponent of the importance of
the Old Latin manuscripts of the New Testament.
At the instigation of the Bishop, Buchanan has devoted
his life to the prosecution of investigations concerning
these manuscripts. In preparation for his work he
visited the chief libraries in Europe, where the earliest
manuscripts of the New Testament both in Greek and
in translation were contained, and studied them with
painstaking care. He then began the editing and
translating of the numerous Latin translations of the
New Testament which had been found in out-of-the-
way places in Ireland. Before this work had proceeded very far, it became evident that these represen-
tatives·of the text of the New Testament were two or
three hundred years nearer the original than that which
is found in the received Greek text, from which our
English version was made, or the Sinaitic and Vatican
texts, which Westcott and Hort accepted as practically
infallible where they agreed. It appears that these
Greek texts are in practical agreement with that followed by Jerome when he made the Vulgate translation in 382 A.D.

But that the very earliest Latin versions of the New
Testament were likely to be found in Spain, France,

and Ireland, on the west coast of Europe, was made
probable from the fact that Paul in Romans (xv. 24,
28) twice intimated that he expected to visit Spain.
This would indicate that there was a well-known
body of Roman emigrants, consisting of soldiers and
commercial men, to whom he hoped to carry the gospel in the middle of the first century. This inference
is also supported by the fact that at this time Rome had
more commercial intercourse with Spain than it had
with Greece. As illustrating the adage, It never rains
but it pours, Mr. Buchanan's attention was later
drawn to a most remarkable Spanish manuscript,
which Mr. J. P. Morgan bought for a large sum
($30,000) in 1910. What attracted Mr. Morgan
was the size and beauty of the work. It was a large
folio containing 184 leaves of thick vellum, each leaf
measuring 21 inches by 14 inches; its binding was
elaborate; and it contained 110 richly colored minia-
tures. The manuscript was the work of a Spanish
Presbyter named Beatus; and the work was written
in the latter part of the eighth century, and in substance is a commentary upon the Apocalypse and the
book of Daniel, containing innumerable quotations
from the New Testament. On examining the text,
Mr. Buchanan found that in numerous places the
original readings of New Testament texts had been
erased and the Vulgate reading written over them.

His task was to recover these original readings, and in this he has developed remarkable skill. The original readings, thus reproduced, were of the greatest interest and importance. From his investigations it appeared that the Vulgate readings superimposed upon the original, very uniformly magnified the ecclesiastical pretensions of the church authorities, to the depreciation of the purer spiritual teachings of the erased texts. For example, the passage in Matthew xvi. 18, 19, which in our received text reads, "Thou art Peter; and upon this rock will I build my church; and the gates of hell shall not prevail against it. And I will give unto thee the keys of the kingdom of heaven: and whatsoever thou shalt bind on earth, shall be bound in heaven; and whatsoever thou shalt loose on earth, shall be loosed in heaven," appears in the Spanish text without any reference to Peter, or the Church, or to the keys, but reads simply, " On this rock shall be built up by the Holy Spirit his disciples." And instead of the binding on earth and the loosing in heaven being given as the prerogative of the Church, it is in this text given as the prerogative of the Holy Spirit. And so in a large number of cases it is evident that the original text of Beatus had been erased, and the Vulgate text inserted, in the interest of the ecclesiastical pretensions of the Church authorities.

Scarcely had the work of translating and editing

the Beatus Manuscript been completed, when Mr. Buchanan's attention was directed to the Old Spanish manuscripts which Mr. Archer M. Huntington was gathering in his Hispanic Museum in New York City. Almost immediately his eye fell upon a Latin translation of the New Testament, which was made in Spain in the twelfth century, but which originally contained practically the same readings which had been erased in the Beatus Manuscript and written over with the Vulgate text. Matthew xvi. 18, 19 was originally the same as in the Beatus Manuscript, and like it had been made to conform to the Vulgate text, which introduced the reference to Peter, the Church, and the keys. Pretty uniformly, also, this text, like that of Beatus, contained readings which magnified the work of the Holy Spirit to the depreciation of the ecclesiastical authorities.

The significant thing in regard to these discoveries is that they support the readings peculiar to what was called the " Western Text," which Westcott and Hort treated as of little critical worth. But the value of these readings is confirmed in a remarkable manner by the discovery, in Egypt, of a Greek manuscript older than the Sinaitic and Vatican, which was purchased by Mr. Freer of Detroit, and which has been edited and published by Professor Sanders of Ann Arbor. This manuscript, which Mr. Freer has deposited in Washington and has insisted should be called the " Washingtonian Manuscript," is recognized on all hands as of the greatest importance in determining the original Greek text of the New Testament; and it, too, in general supports the readings of the Western Text.

That Mr. Buchanan, like Mr. Wiener, should have chosen *Bibliotheca Sacra* as the best channel through which to reach the scholarly public interested in determining the original text of the Bible, is a striking witness to the importance of my influence in keeping the Quarterly up to its original scholarly standard. On consulting the back numbers, it appeared that Dr. H. C. Hoskier, the highest authority on the Genesis of the Versions of the New Testament, had also chosen *Bibliotheca Sacra* as his favorite channel through which to reach the scholarly public interested in this most important work; and that, at his request, Mr. Buchanan, as far back as 1911, had published a lengthy review of Dr. Hoskier's volumes " Concerning the Genesis of the Versions of the New Testament "; hence his appearance as a contributor in the recent volumes was not the result of a sudden afterthought, but of a matured conviction based on solid evidence.

Soon after returning from my trip to Asia, I joined

with some others, including my son, Frederick Bennett Wright, in establishing at Washington the *Records of the Past,* a highly illustrated, beautifully printed monthly, in quarto form, designed to bring before the public the most important facts brought out by archæological excavations and studies the world over. Later it was issued bi-monthly and so continued for twelve years, when an elaborate index both of the articles and the illustrations was published, and the magazine was absorbed by *Art and Archæology,* published by the Archæological Institute of America, and covering nearly the same ground. While my son was the managing editor, I coöperated with him to bring the magazine up to a high standard. In this we succeeded fairly well, so that the twelve bound volumes, as they are scattered widely both in public and private libraries, constitute a storehouse of archæological information, which is of the greatest value, not only for imparting general information but incidentally in emphasizing the archæological facts which support the credibility of the Bible.

CHAPTER XV

ARCHÆOLOGICAL AND PROFESSORIAL WORK

NOT the least enjoyable and important work in which I have been engaged is that connected with the Ohio State Archæological and Historical Society, which was organized in 1885, and of which I was elected president in 1907, following an eminent list of predecessors, namely, Rutherford B. Hayes, Allen G. Thurman, Francis C. Sessions, and Roeliff Brinkerhoff. My interest in the archæology of the State was greatly increased during my survey of the glacial boundary, which led me through many sections containing prehistoric mounds and earthworks. Later, I took occasion to make a tour of the State in company with Judge C. C. Baldwin, for the purpose of visiting all the most important localities in Ohio where these prehistoric works were to be found. This was before any systematic attempt had been made by the State to preserve them. When in England, my interest was stimulated further by a visit to the Blackmore Museum in Salisbury, which then contained the most important collection in existence of the relics of the mound builders in Ohio. This of course was very humiliating to American archæologists, especially those of Ohio.

The way it came about that such a collection should be there was on this wise: About 1840, Squier and Davis made an extensive survey of the mounds in the Mississippi Valley, partially excavating them, and making a very rich collection of relics. The account of their work formed the first Smithsonian report, entitled the "Ancient Monuments of the Mississippi Valley." But their collection of relics was not sufficiently appreciated, either in Ohio or in the United States, to be purchased and preserved for inspection in any museum here. Mr. and Mrs. Blackmore from England, however, so fully appreciated the collection, that they purchased it entire, and made room for it in the Blackmore Museum in Salisbury, where for some decades American students were compelled to go to study the archæology of their own country. A large number of the articles in this collection were never duplicated in any American museum until 1915, when discoveries were made which put us on an equality with England, in the possession of mound builders' relics. Of this we will speak later.

Meanwhile parties outside the State, to our shame, were much more interested in exploring the mounds of Ohio than were the citizens of the State. The Smithsonian Institution at Washington was continually making sporadic collections of mound builders' relics, while the Peabody Museum at Cambridge, under the judicious management of Professor F. W. Putnam, was systematically exploring some of the most important sites of the mound builders and taking the collection to Cambridge, Massachusetts. In 1893, the promoters of the Columbian Exposition in Chicago put several thousand dollars into the hands of Warren K. Moorehead to explore one of the Ohio mounds, which yielded an immense number of relics, all of which were taken to Chicago, and remain in the possession of the Field Columbian Museum. At the same time, public-spirited ladies of Boston raised several thousand dollars to purchase the farm in Adams County on which was situated the famous Serpent Mound, and to enable Professor Putnam thoroughly to explore it and restore it to its original condition.

For many years we found it impossible to arouse the legislature to such interest in our work as would induce them to provide us with adequate means for carrying on our explorations effectively and systematically, and, what was equally important, to provide facilities for displaying the results of our explorations.

But at length, after more than twenty years, public interest was thoroughly aroused; and the results have been all that we could expect, and almost all that we could ask. Although it seemed at first that we had but the gleanings of the field, the systematic work of

our curator, William C. Mills, has shown that this
was not the case, for we have secured results exceeding
those of all other investigators combined. From the
mounds in the vicinity of Chillicothe, collections have
been made of implements and ornaments of argillite
from the Rocky Mountains, of copper from Lake Superior, of mica from North Carolina, and of shells
from the Atlantic Ocean and the Gulf of Mexico, thus
indicating a prehistoric commerce as wide as the continent. In one of these mounds was found a collection
of fresh-water pearls, which experts said would be
worth $10,000 if they were fresh. But still more
interesting was the collection of counterfeit pearls,
which consisted of clay balls covered with malleable
mica giving the appearance of real pearls. In 1915,
Mr. Mills explored what had been thought to be an
effigy mound, representing an elephant, in the vicinity
of Portsmouth, Ohio, but which has proved to be a
vast crematory, at one end of which was unbared the
surface where the bodies were burned, while adjoining
it was a broad depression filled with bones and ashes
resulting from the fires, and still beyond was an immense collection of broken pipes and other exquisitely
carved ornaments, which more than duplicated the
unique collection which we had been accustomed to
make pilgrimages to Salisbury, England, to study.

As our Society grew in influence its opportunities

rapidly increased. The State purchased for us Fort
Ancient, in the valley of the Little Miami, in Warren
County, the largest and most elaborate earthwork on
the American continent. The Serpent Mound in
Adams County was given to us by Harvard University, who had come into possession of it. Various other
historic sites have been given to us for preservation,
including the famous elm tree under which the Indian
Chief, Logan, made the speech that has been so widely
copied in school readers; and last of all Spiegel Grove
in Fremont, a plot of twenty-five acres of the original
forest, in which President Rutherford B. Hayes had
built his residence, was given to us by his son Colonel
Webb C. Hayes, on condition that the State would
build a fireproof building to hold his father's library,
consisting of the most complete collection of Ameri-
cana in existence, and of the accumulation of documents connected with his father's military and political
career as governor of the State and president of the
United States. Such a building, costing $50,000, was
provided for by appropriations from the legislature in
1911, and at the same time $100,000 was appropriated
for a building in Columbus, in which we could display our general collections. These two buildings are
now completed, and form attractions of the greatest
interest to the State and the country. It is difficult
to overestimate their educational value. In doing my

small share in bringing about these results, my association with men of like mind, from different parts of
the State, has furnished one of the joys of my life,
bringing me into contact, as it has, with a body of
men keenly interested in promoting the higher ideal
interests of the people, and men whose gratuitous services place them above the suspicion of having any personal interest to serve. The names of them all are
too numerous to mention. But among the most conspicuous are the following: Mr. Roeliff Brinkerhoff,
Mr. George F. Bareis, the late Mr. C. H. Gallup,
General J. Warren Keifer, Dr. Walter C. Metz,
Mr. E. F. Wood, the late Mr. A. J. Baughman,
William C. Mills, Honorable D. J. Ryan, Mr. L. P.
Schaus, Rev. H. A. Thompson, Mr. H. E. Buck,
Colonel Webb C. Hayes, President W. O. Thomp-
son, Honorable F. W. Treadway, Rev. N. B. C.
Love, the late Honorable J. W. Harper, Honorable
Myron T. Herrick, Professor M. R. Andrews, Pro-
fessor B. F. Prince, Mr. E. O. Randall, Mr. W. J.
Sherman.

It is believed that, as time goes on, the citizens of
the State, and of the country at large, will more and
more appreciate the work which this Society has done,
and that, in seeing what prehistoric man accomplished
with crude implements made of stone and bone, they

will feel for them greater respect, and will be stimulated to more earnest study of all the records of the past. Except in the possession of the accumulated wisdom of the centuries, and the labor-saving machinery of modern invention, prehistoric man was the equal of modern man, and moved by all the aspirations and sentiments which animate existing races. They erected defensive works that demanded for their execution a highly organized society; they carried on an extensive commerce; they had a high appreciation of the beauties of nature, as shown in their selection of village sites; they had cultivated tastes, as shown in their collection of ornamental pearls gathered from far and near, and in the exquisite carvings upon their pipes of peace, and by their successful attempts to counterfeit pearls when the natural supply was not sufficient; and finally, they honored the dead and worshiped the Great Spirit.

One of the things which I have taken special delight in accomplishing has been the preparation of a booklet of a hundred pages, entitled " See Ohio First," in which a condensed account is given of the geology, physical geography, archæology, and history of the State, to which are appended thirty-nine itineraries, by which the tourist may, with as little waste of time and expense as possible, visit all the places of special interest in the State. It is a " consummation devoutly to be wished," that our teachers and our citizens in general should be induced to appreciate the interesting things about their own doors, before wasting their time and treasure in long journeys to get hasty glimpses of foreign fields.

Before closing this narrative, a few words should be said concerning the work which I have done as teacher at Oberlin. From 1881 to 1892 I filled the chair of New Testament Language and Literature in the Theological Seminary, being associated with an exceptionally able corps of instructors. James H. Fairchild filled the chair of Systematic Theology; Albert H. Currier, that of Homiletics and Pastoral Theology; Frank H. Foster, that of Church History; William G. Ballantine, that of Hebrew and Old Testament Literature, and William B. Chamberlain, that of Elocution and Rhetoric. At the same time an English department under the instruction of Edward I. Bosworth drew a large number of earnest students. This was a combination of ability, both for scholarship and skill in imparting knowledge, such as it is difficult to excel. The attendance in the classical department rose to upwards of sixty, all of whom studied the Bible in Hebrew and Greek; while the English department numbered forty or fifty.

From 1892 to 1907 I occupied the chair of Harmony

of Science and Revelation, created specially for me.
During this period my instruction was equally divided
between theological and college classes,— a special
course being given in glacial geology. Of the success
attending my work as teacher I will not venture to
speak. Information on that point must be looked for
in the development of the hundreds of pupils who were
in my classes. This Story, which I now bring to a
close, contains the " substance of doctrine " which it
was my aim to impart. Having, in 1907, already
passed the age at which it was decreed that professors
who were to receive the Carnegie pension were to re-
tire, I have since been freer than before to devote my
time to the work of preparing, for the general public,
the statement of facts and truths relating both to the
material and the spiritual world which I have endeavored to impart to my classes.

In surveying my life I am more and more impressed with my constant dependence on the help of
others. At every stage of progress I have been but a
single factor in coöperation with many others in bringing about results. And over all a kind Providence
has preserved me from the natural fruits of my own
perversity and ignorance, and brought about good results which my own plans would have failed to ac-
complish. My lines have indeed fallen to me in

pleasant places, and I have had a goodly heritage. I have had sufficient difficulties to overcome to duly develop my powers, I have had a favoring Providence to shield me from irretrievable error, and a host of friends to help me on my way at every important juncture of my life. What I have accomplished must be judged by the test of its endurance in the future. What more could I ask except that I be spared a few more years to show " to the generation to come the praises of the Lord, and his strength, and his wonderful works that he hath done "; and that I be able cheerfully to resign myself in due time to meet the last ordeal, and enter with the Christian's hope on the untried scenes of the future life, when that which is perfect is come and that which is in part shall be done away; and when I shall know even as I am known.

CHAPTER XVI

MY CREED

1. *I know that I exist, experience certain sensations, and put forth exertions to explain and coördinate these sensations so that they shall form a basis for a system of beliefs by which to guide my conduct. I know that I ought to shape my conduct with reference to the highest good of being.*

2. *I believe that the primal, self-existent, eternal reality was spiritual and personal, rather than material and impersonal.*

Something must be self-existent and eternal. The only problem is whether that something is personal or impersonal. The supposition, that an impersonal force should have filled nature with the utilities and adaptations which we observe, and should at last have evolved the personality of man, is as near an absurdity as can be conceived. That a self-existent personality should have planned and created nature involves no such an absurdity. Even in regard to matter, its creation is by no means an absurdity, for we know nothing of it except its manifestations. Matter is changeable in form, fugitive in its effects, and is known by man only on its outside. Any theory of its ultimate composition leads to a profound mystery. Atoms and molecules are merely combinations and bundles of force. It does not remove, but multiplies the mystery, if, with some modern physicists, we invest the atom with all the qualities and capacities attributed by theory to the Deity himself.

3. *I believe that God is a creator and has established a system of secondary causes, both material and spiritual. The doctrine of monism and of the immanence of God as set forth by its extreme advocates overlooks the plainest facts of experience.*

At one time I was invited to address a large ministers' meeting in which I was preceded by an extreme advocate of the divine immanence. The speaker had maintained that everything in the outside world was a direct creation of God. There were no inherent forces in the material that constituted the table before him. The table was merely a phantasmagoria, kept on the screen by the direct action of the Creator. Our own actions were the product of immediate divine agency. God worked in us directly to produce all our good impulses. At the outset of my address, I turned to the speaker and asked him if he held God responsible for all the mean things he had ever done. Being an honest man, he confessed that he did not. Whatever was the source of the good in him, the meanness in him was his own creation, thus acknowledging himself as a secondary cause, endowed with power to resist the will of God. That admission made, the existence was granted of secondary causes, which, properly conceived, are centers of various kinds of forces which the Creator voluntarily permits to act within their sphere by their inherent capacities. From these spheres of action he has, in the act of creation, voluntarily withdrawn his direct agency.

4. *I believe that, in the beginning, God created the elements out of which have evolved, under his direction, the heavens and the earth; in other words, that he gave to the ultimate particles of matter the qualities of inertia which permit them to be segregated into the various masses which appear in the universe; that he imparted to these particles and masses the motions appearing in the infinite variety of combinations incident to a progressive universe, and, over all, imposed the mysterious power of gravitation. How these things were done, I have no idea. They belong to the mysteries, no less of science than of theology.*

5. *I believe that in due time the principle of life came into the world as a new creation.*

This belief rests partly upon the fact that its effects are contradictory to those of the other forces of nature. Gravitation pulls every thing down. The friction of the elements wears away the rocks, and reduces everything to a level; whereas life builds up new structures, which defy the power of gravitation, and, in animals, moves them hither and thither without any regard to the inertia of their component particles. I maintain this belief in face of the assertion of Huxley that he believed that somewhere in infinite time, and amid the infinite series of changes through which matter has been called to pass, life with all its possibilities did somehow originate from material forces. But, though Huxley was a scientific man of high degree, this was not a scientific conclusion, since he had just admitted that the theory of spontaneous generation had been shown, by a great variety of experiments, to · be without foundation. But even if we should suppose that, in the creation of material forces, God had endowed them with power automatically to bring forth at a certain stage of development what is described in Genesis as plant-life, "whose seed is in itself," it would still be a creative act, incorporated into the original constitution of things, to develop only in due time when conditions were ready for its perpetuation. But this is as nearly inconceivable as anything can well be.

6. *I believe that, after the introduction of life into the world, there was an orderly progress from lower to higher forms, as, in the geological ages, conditions*

became favorable for their maintenance. But I do not have sufficient evidence to believe that this progress has been due wholly to the inherent forces of nature.

I would not, however, set hard and fast limits to the power of variation in plants and animals, and to the power of natural selection in preserving variations adapted to new conditions. Since we know that man, by selection and protecting care, can produce in species such varieties as we have in domestic plants and animals, we would not say that the Creator may not go farther in the use of natural forces to produce variations which we should call species,— the difference . between varieties and species being largely one of definition.

7. *I believe that, whatever may be true about some organic connection between man and some unknown species of anthropoid apes, man with his present physical and spiritual characteristics appeared suddenly on the earth, at no very distant period, as geologists count time.*

The peculiar characteristics both of mind and body which constitute man are too numerous and peculiar to have come in by slow increments. The average human brain weighs three times as much as the average brain of the gorilla. The average brain capacity of the earliest prehistoric skulls yet discovered is equal to that of existing races. The upright position of man; his free and shorter arms, with the delicately adjusted thumb and fingers upon the extremity; his well-developed lower limbs, and the broad-soled foot with the stiff projecting big toe; the absence of a hairy covering, together with the mental capacities enabling man to make fire at will, to construct implements of stone and bone and wood, create spoken language and means of perpetuating his thoughts by hieroglyphs and alphabetical characters; especially his powers of inductive reasoning by which he learns the courses of the stars and studies the history of the earth in its rocky strata, and through a variety of sciences learns the history of man in the past and forecasts his future both in this world and the next,— such a combination of bodily and mental characteristics could not have been produced by piecemeal. Without the mental characteristics those of the body would be disadvantageous. Without the bodily characteristics, the mental developments would be useless. Such complicated accidental combinations are inconceivable. They can occur only as the product of design, which is equivalent to creation.

8. *I believe in a Glacial epoch, the magnitude and complication of whose effects few as yet begin to comprehend.*

It would seem incredible, if the evidence were not overwhelming, that the warm climate of the Tertiary period should have been succeeded by climatic conditions which compelled the snows of the north to accumulate till they pushed the vast mass of glacial ice, a mile thick in North America, down to New York City, Cincinnati, Carbondale in the southern part of Illinois, and Topeka in Kansas, covering in all four million square miles; and in Europe filling the North Sea and covering the British Isles almost down to the latitude of London, and extending to the mountain barriers south of Berlin to the center of Germany, and to Kiev in Russia, covering, in all, two million square miles. But such are the facts.

9. *I believe that the conditions of the Glacial epoch were so abnormal that they render nugatory a vast amount of reasoning by which archæologists draw, from present conditions, inferences concerning the events of the past.*

In connection with the advance and retreat of the glacial ice there was a great destruction of animal species that were contemporaries of man, and a remarkable development and redistribution of species both of plants and animals. There is abundant evidence that great changes of land level occurred in the Northern Hemisphere, first in its depression during the accumulation and climax of the period, and again in its reëlevation after its close. This postglacial depression amounted to 600 feet at Montreal, and 1,000 feet farther north in America and in corresponding latitudes in northern Europe; while there is distinct evidence of a depression in Central Asia, amounting to 700 feet, and much evidence of its extension to 2,000 feet. At the same time, the floods connected with the final melting of the ice were perfectly enormous in their amount, and incalculable in their destructive effects on animal life. During that period the Missouri River was compelled to handle, during the summer months, twenty-five times its present volume of water, causing floods two hundred feet in height; while the Mississippi River was compelled, at the same time, to dispose of sixty times its present volume. Let him who can, picture to himself the significance of these facts.

10. *I believe that the Glacial epoch continued down to historical times.*

The evidence is such as should convince anyone who candidly considers all the facts, that glacial ice did not retreat from southern Sweden until seven thousand years ago. Nor did it retreat from central New York and northern Minnesota at a much earlier date. It is still retreating at a rapid rate in Alaska, the Muir Glacier having retired seven miles and a half in the last twenty-five years, and nearly all the other glaciers proportionally. Thus it would appear that when the civilization of Egypt, Babylonia, and Central Asia was at its height, the most populous present progressive

centers of the world were buried beneath a glacial
covering. Any one who draws inferences concerning
the earliest history of mankind, without duly considering these facts and others correlated with them, is sure
to be misled.

11. *I believe that the abnormal conditions connected with the Glacial epoch make it impossible,
when the documents are properly interpreted, to discredit the stories of the flood in Genesis and of the
distribution of the human race from Central Asia.*

12. *I believe that with all man's splendid capacities for inductive reasoning, by which he extracts
knowledge from the facts of nature with reference to
the things which are distant in space and time both
past and future, he needs, for his guidance and satisfaction, a supplementary revelation from God.*

The demands of man's ethical nature and the needs
of his moral nature cry out for some more definite
knowledge, both of the Creator's dealings with him in
the past and of his intentions respecting him in the future, than he can obtain from personal experience or by
induction from the complicated facts of the material
universe and of the general history of the race.

It is well that, in making such supplementary revelation to man, God has respected and honored the intellectual capacity bestowed upon him, by which he
weighs and estimates historical evidence and transmits

to the future the truths already thus obtained, enabling successive generations to stand upon the shoulders of their predecessors, and so to secure progress from age to age. It is little less than suicidal for one generation to sunder the historical connection that binds them to the past,— especially to that epoch in history that witnessed the introduction of Christianity.

13. *I believe that in the Bible we have such a supplementary revelation from God of the facts and truths essential to the promotion of true religion.*

The proof of this comes largely from the character and extent of the influence which the Bible has already had in the world. But this presumptive inference is amply supported by every other kind of needed evidence. The first chapter of Genesis stands unrivalled, as a comprehensive and brief statement of the origin of the universe and the development of the world up to the introduction of man. No unaided human intellect could, in the period when the first chapter of Genesis was written, have framed a cosmogony with which modern science could find so little fault. The historical statements of the Old Testament are so amply confirmed by the inscriptions upon the monuments of Assyria, Babylonia, Palestine, and Egypt, and by study of the natural conditions amid which their seemingly incredible facts are said to have occurred, that they stand accredited as fully as could be desired, and more fully than any other extended historical document of ancient times. Disbelief in the statements of the Old Testament is mainly the result, not of superior knowledge, but of ignorance.

14. *I believe that greater care than is wont should be used in the inspection and interpretation of the reported miracles, lest we burden ourselves with unnecessary and harmful incongruities between the alleged facts and the objects to be accomplished.*

An extraordinary interference with the course of nature implies an extraordinary end to be accomplished. We cannot believe that the Creator would invalidate the law of parsimony, and put forth superfluous force for the accomplishment of his purposes. Causing the sun and moon to stand still, in the literal sense, would seem a superfluous expenditure of force to secure so small a thing as a victory over Israel's enemy. It is a relief, therefore, to find that a proper interpretation of the narrative easily brings it within the range of credibility. The words translated " stand still " may as well be translated " be silent," equivalent to stop shining, thus making the prayer a request that the storm, which is said to have been prevailing, might continue until the victory was complete.

Still I would not press this statement to unreasonable lengths: the law of parsimony may be made to work in both directions. The display of a great amount of force in the accomplishment of a purpose, if properly substantiated by evidence, proves the importance of the end to be secured, which may be the accrediting of a witness, or the imparting of force to a figure of speech. In the main the reported miracles of the Bible are made to serve these purposes, and so are indispensable elements in making a divine revelation effective.

Again, the short chronology formerly adduced from the Biblical statements, which seems to conflict with the scientific evidence of the antiquity of man, is shown by Professor William Henry Green to be an incorrect and unnecessary inference from the data. The phrases "son of" and "begat," while indicating direct line of descent, do by no means indicate immediate descent, so that the genealogies in Genesis v. and xi. are indefinite in their time ratios, and can be stretched out to any length required by other evidence which may be at hand.

A large number of the miracles of the Old Testament belong to a class described as "mediate miracles," in which the means employed are evident, the miraculous element consisting in the use of such a degree of power as to indicate in some way the direct presence of the Creator's activity. This is illustrated in the crossing of the Red Sea, where the wind is expressly said to have been the means by which the

waters were parted for the Israelites to pass through
and were brought back again to overwhelm the
Egyptions.   In the destruction of Sodom and Gomorrah, the plagues of Egypt, the opening of the Jordan for Joshua's host, the fall of the walls of Jericho,
the destruction of Sennacherib's host, and various other
miracles, the secondary causes involved are now easily
recognized by scientific investigators.   Whether this
abnormal use of secondary causes involves the direct
interference, by the Creator, with the course of nature, as when a man kindles a fire or blows the dust
from his mantel, or whether it merely involves that
foreknowledge which makes the conjunction of events
a matter of prophecy, is immaterial.   In either case it
becomes a supernatural event, sufficient to accredit the
human agent in whose behalf it takes place.   The importance of the results flowing from the Old Testament miracles amply justifies their introduction into
the course of human history.   For it is through their
influence upon the Jewish race that the conception of
the unity of God has been preserved in the world.
Idolatry prevails everywhere except among Jews, Mohammedans, and Christians, who have felt the direct
impulse of these miraculous interpositions.   Furthermore, the Jewish history prepared by these miraculous
revelations of God has furnished the root upon which
Christianity could be grafted.   These results are cer-

tainly sufficient to justify the means supposed to be employed. The ends accomplished by the Old Testament miracles are as noble and important as the means for accrediting the revelation were extraordinary.

15. *I believe that the books of the New Testament are genuine and authoritative records of the facts concerning Christ's life and the doctrines which are logically connected with that life.*

This belief, too, is justified by the fruits of Christianity. The noblest civilization of the world, and that on which the highest hopes of the future depend, has sprung directly from the life and teachings of Christ, as revealed in the New Testament. Outside of the New Testament we have no facts and teachings of Christ of any importance. All this is sufficient to give presumptive evidence, of the highest value, that Christianity rests upon a foundation of fact.

This presumption is supported by such an amount of additional evidence, of a scientific character, as to establish its truth beyond reasonable doubt. The documents of the New Testament all bear evidence of having been produced so near to the events recorded, that they are first-class witnesses. Some of the Epistles of Paul, witnessing to all the essential facts of Christ's life, were certainly written within thirty years of his death. There is abundant evidence to show that the first three Gospels were written before the destruction of Jerusalem. The Gospel of John, though written towards the close of the century, comes, as an historical document, far within the limit which is set by historians for the competency of traditional evidence. The testimony of the New Testament to the fact of Christ's death upon the cross and of his subsequent bodily resurrection satisfies all the requirements of judicial procedure in courts of law, and is, in fact, not only ample but superabundant to produce a belief in the facts which is beyond reasonable doubt. It is needless to say that the proposed object of Christ's death, and the actual results flowing from belief in it, amply justify the means employed to display the love of God for the human race, and the plan by which its restoration to righteousness and happiness may be secured. This one miracle, of Christ's resurrection, being established by evidence that cannot be controverted, there is no difficulty in believing the story of minor miracles connected with his life.

16. *I believe that we can most effectively preserve the truths of the Christian revelation and promote the unity of the church by adhering, in the main, to the formulas of doctrine wrought out through the experiences of the early church, and incorporated in the Nicene Creed.*

Whatever criticisms may be made of these formulas, they avail little against the fact that they represent

the main springs of the life of Christ's followers, nearest the original fountain of truth, and before the
stream had been polluted by the corruptions of more
prosperous times. I fear that, in the efforts to eman-
cipate ourselves from the misunderstandings incident
to the acceptance of the early creeds of the church,
and to substitute in their place the refinements of modern metaphysical speculations, we shall lose the power
of the great original truths, and waste our lives in a
rarefied air of speculative philosophy, unsupported by
the facts of revelation; and doom our followers to
the fate of those spoken of by the prophets as " walking
in sparks of their own kindling."

I fear that an uncritical acceptance of the doctrine
of evolution will pervert the minds of an increasing
number of the leaders of public opinion in Christian
lands, so as to rob the mass of the people of their precious heritage in the most inspiring doctrines of Christianity. A tissue of myths and fables is a poor substitute for an historical record of divine intervention,
in accrediting messengers who could speak in the
name of the Lord. A Saviour who was not " God
manifest in the flesh " but a being of human origin,
whose character and work is not that which is his-
torically represented in the New Testament, but an
illusion of speculative writers of a subsequent generation, is a feeble substitute for the gospel which is

the power of God unto salvation. I fear, therefore, that before these erroneous and stifling views shall be stayed in their spread from the various centers of learning where they are being propagated, an untold multitude, deprived of the real bread of life, will pine away in a land where spiritual food is scarce, and where faith is by no means "the substance of things hoped for."

I fear that, robbed of "the faith of the fathers," which transformed the Roman Empire, and which, wherever it has opportunity to "run and have free course and be glorified," is still transforming the world, the "powers that be," which are controlling the political and social order of nations, will drive the world to destruction and make the forecasts of the premillenarians a true and welcome prophecy of events that are to come.

17. *I confidently expect that, as the Lord has often, in the past, raised up "judges in Israel" to lead the people out of bondage, so now, leaders will be raised up, whose voices will be effectively heard in defense of the "faith once delivered to the saints."*

18. *I confidently expect that theologians and men of science will in due time come to such mutual understanding that, recognizing their own limitations and giving credit to both the direct and the indirect revelations of the Creator, they will incorporate into their*

*creeds the well-established truths pertaining to both
the material and spiritual worlds.*

We look for a speedy return of the day when lead-
ing men of science, in line with Copernicus, Galileo,
Kepler, Tycho Brahe, Sir Isaac Newton, the Her-
schels, Benjamin Pierce, Angelo Secchi, C. A. Young,
Sir Humphrey Davy, Benjamin Silliman, Michael
Faraday, Clerk Maxwell, Lord Kelvin, Baron Cuvier,
Sir Richard Owen, Louis Agassiz, Sir Robert Murch-
ison, Hugh Miller, Sir Joseph Prestwich, President
Edward Hitchcock, Sir William Dawson, J. D. Dana,
Alexander and N. H. Winchell, Joseph LeConte, Asa
Gray, John Torrey, Joseph Henry, and a host of
others, will duly magnify the facts of the spiritual
world, and fully appreciate the evidence by which they
are brought to our consideration through the revelation contained in the Bible. We look for a new
generation of clergymen, who shall follow in the
footsteps of Dean Buckland, Adam Sedgwick, J. P.
Smith, J. S. Henslow, Peter Lesley, Edward Orton,
and others, who, in addition to their theological training (perhaps by virtue of it), shall greatly enlarge the
range of knowledge in various scientific fields.

19. *I hope and expect that God will make use of
the judgments now falling so heavily upon the nations
of the world, so to exhibit the " exceeding sinfulness
of sin " and so to magnify his grace in the atoning*

work of his Son, that the whole world shall fear and tremble, and that, by mighty outpourings of the Holy Spirit, as on the day of Pentecost, the world shall be convicted of the manifold ways in which they have crucified their Lord afresh, and shall speedily return in humble penitence to the Lord that bought them.

APPENDIX

NOTES

CHAPTER I

NOTE 1, p. 15.—See pages 334-337.
NOTE 2, p. 15.—See page 378.

CHAPTER III

NOTE 1, p. 124.—See page 132-136.

CHAPTER IV

NOTE 1, p. 139.—See "Studies in Science and Religion," chap. v.

NOTE 1, p. 140.—This moraine forms the backbone of Long Island, and furnishes, like a huge sponge, the water supply of Brooklyn and the various cities throughout the length of the Island.

CHAPTER XI

NOTE 1, p. 265.—See Bulletin of the Geological Society of America, vol. xiii. p. 136 f. A more detailed calculation is found in my "Scientific Confirmations of Old Testament History," pp. 208-213.

NOTE 1, p. 306.—"Origin and Antiquity of Man," chap. xi.

BIBLIOGRAPHY

1871

Ground of confidence in inductive reasoning. New Eng 30: 601-15 O

1873

Recent works on prehistoric archæology. Bib Sac 30: 381-4 Ap

1874

Baptism of infants, and their church membership. Bib Sac
31: 265–99, 545–75 Ap, Jl

1875

Indian Ridge and its continuations. Bull Essex Inst 7:
165–8 D

Recent works bearing upon the relations of science to religion. Bib Sac 32: 537–55 Jl

1876

Divine method of producing species. Bib Sac 33: 448–
494 Jl

Dr. Hodge's misrepresentations of President Finney's system
of theology. Bib Sac 33: 381–92 Ap

Recent works bearing upon the relations of science and religion. Bib Sac 33: 448–93, 656–94 Jl, O

Some remarkable gravel ridges in the Merrimack valley.
Proc Bos Soc Nat Hist 19: 47–63 D 20

Book Reviews. Bib Sac 33: 584–90, 773–8 Jl, O
    History of the Conflict between Religion and Science, by
    J. W. Draper; Great Ice Age and its Relation to the
    Antiquity of Man, by James Geikie; Chips from a Ger-
    man Workshop, by Max Müller; Darwiniana, by Asa
    Gray.

1877

A fortnight in South Carolina. Ch Un Mr 28, Ap 4

In memory of John Dove, Esquire: a sermon preached . . .
Nov. 26, 1876. pp. 24

President Finney's system of theology in its relations to the
so-called New England theology. Bib Sac 34: 708–41 O

Professor Max Müller and his American critics. Bib Sac
34: 183–90 Ja

Progress among the Freedmen. Nation 24: 189–90 Mr 29

Recent works bearing upon the relations of science and religion. Bib Sac 34: 355–85 Ap

Book Review. Bib Sac 34: 584–7 Jl
    Geographical Distribution of Animals, by A. R. Wallace.

1878·

Kames in the south part of Rockingham county [N. H.] and in northeastern Massachusetts. N H Geol Sur 3: 167–70

Proper attitude of religious teachers towards scientific experts. New Eng 37: 776–89 N

What the argument for immortality is. Ind Ap 11

What the argument for immortality is not. Ind Mr 28

1879

J. Stuart Mill on the omnipotence of God. Ind S 11

Kames and moraines of New England. Proc Bos Soc Nat Hist 20: 210–20 Ap 2

Book Reviews. Bib Sac 36: 201–4, 398–400, 782–4 Ja, Ap, O
Elements of Geology, by Joseph LeConte; Popular Astronomy, by Simon Newcomb; Human Species, by A. De Quatrefages; Freedom in Science and Teaching, by Haeckel and Huxley; Evolution of Man, by E. Haeckel; Darwinism and Other Essays, by John Fiske.

1880

[Address] at opening of Brigham Academy, Bakersfield, Vt., Aug. 1879. Exercises and Addresses. 7–25

Insufficiency of natural religion. Advance Mr 25

Man and the glacial period. Ind Mr 4

Palæolithic man in New Jersey. Ind D 16

Prehistoric Andover. "Historical Sketches of Andover."

Recent works bearing upon the relations of science and religion. Bib Sac 37: 48–76 Ja

Reverend Mr. Dillaway's reasons for believing in the Bible. Cong S 1

Why Willie should believe in a God. Cong Ag 18

Why Willie should believe in Christ as divine. Cong Ag 25

Book Reviews. Bib Sac 37: 390–5, 577–86 Ap, Jl
Natural Science and Religion, by Asa Gray; Final Causes, by Paul Janet; An Introduction to the Philosophy of Religion, by John Caird; Preadamites, by Alexander Win-

chell; History of Materialism, by F. A. Lange; Early
Man in Britain, by W. Boyd Dawkins.

1881

Attempt to estimate the age of the palæolithic-bearing gravels in Trenton, N. J. Proc Bos Soc Nat Hist 21: 137–45
Ja 19

Book Reviews. Bib Sac 38: 199–206, 394–9, 587–91 Ja,
Ap, Jl
Religion and Chemistry, by J. P. Cooke; Gleanings from
a Literary Life, by Francis Bowen; Creation and Early
Development of Society, by J. H. Chapin; Essays on Art
and Archæology, by C. T. Newton; Island Life, by A. R.
Wallace; Brain as an Organ of the Mind, by Bastian;
Past in the Present. What is Civilization? by Arthur
Mitchell; Relation of Science and Religion, by Calder-
wood; Anniversary Memoirs of the Boston Society of
Natural History.

1882

Physical science in the theological seminary. Bib Sac 39:
190–6 Ja

Book Reviews. Bib Sac 39: 207, 208 Ja
Primitive Industry, by C. C. Abbott; Report upon the
United States Geographical Surveys West of the One
Hundredth Meridian, by F. W. Putman.

1883

Exaggerations of the issues between science and religion.
Cong My 10
Parsonage and the home missionary. Advance Ap 19
Practical bearings of our belief concerning the relation of
death to probation. Bib Sac 40: 694–713 O
Prehistoric man in North America. Advance N 8, 15, 29,
D 13, 27
Recent investigations concerning the southern boundary of
the glaciated area of Ohio. Am Jour Sci 26: 44–56 Jl
Science and life. Overland Mo 1: 279–82 S

Some of the foundations that science cannot shake. Cong
My 31

True and false agnosticism. Cong My 3

Uncertainties of science. Cong My 17

1884

Dr. Ladd on alleged discrepancies and errors of the Bible.
Bib Sac 41: 389–98 Ap

Glacial Boundary in Ohio, Indiana and Kentucky. West
Res Hist Soc Tract 60

Glacial boundary in Ohio. Geol Sur of O 5: 750–72

Glacial man in Ohio. Howe's Hist Coll of O 1: 90–9

Glaciated area of North America. Am Nat 18: 755–67 Ag

Misplaced agnosticism. Cong Ag 7

Niagara Gorge as a chronometer. Bib Sac 41: 369–76 Ap

Prehistoric man in North America. Advance Ja 3, 17, 31,
F 14, 28, Mr 13, 27, Ap 10, 24, My 15

Prof. John Morgan. Advance O 23

Theory of a glacial dam at Cincinnati and its verification.
Am Nat 18: 563–7 Je

What is old may be true. Cong N 6

Book Review. Bib Sac 41: 197–202 Ja
The Doctrine of Sacred Scripture, by G. T. Ladd.

1885

Christian consciousness. Cong My 5

Dr. Ladd's agnosticism. Bib Sac 42: 765–72 O

Man and the glacial period in America. Mag West Hist
1: 289–300 F

Prof. Wright and some of his critics. Bib Sac 42: 351–9 Ap

Book Reviews. Bib Sac 42: 591–600 Jl
Elements of Moral Science, by Noah Porter; On the Dif-
ference between Physical and Moral Law, by William
Arthur; Paradise Found, by William F. Warren.

1886

Has modern criticism affected unfavorably any of the essen-

tial doctrines of Christianity? Hom Rev 11: 307–12 Ap
Wonders of Alaska. Advance N 11, 25, D 9

Book Review. Bib Sac 43: 785–7 O
  Evolution of Revelation, by James M. Whiton.

1887

Age of the Ohio gravel-beds. Proc Bos Soc Nat Hist 23:
  427–36, D 21
American Board and speculative theology. Bib Sac 44:
  707–24 O
Gas wells. Cong Mr 17
Genesis and science. Cong F 24
Importance of the study of the archæology of Ohio. Ohio
  State Arch and Hist Soc Pub 1: 55–60
Muir Glacier. Am Jour Sci 33: 1–18 Ja
Notes on the glaciation of the Pacific coast. Am Nat 21:
  250–6 Mr
[With A. A. Currier] Park's discourses considered homilet-
  ically and theologically. Bib Sac 44: 156–74 Ja
Prof. Smyth and the Andover Creed. Bib Sac 44: 557–
  559 Jl
Relation of the glacial period to archæology in Ohio. Ohio
  State Arch and Hist Soc Pub 1: 174–186
Term "son of man" as used in the New Testament. Bib
  Sac 44: 575–601 O
Wonders of Alaska. Advance Ja 20, 27, Mr 24

Book Reviews. Bib Sac 44: 194–7, 564–7, 729–34 Ja, Jl, O
  Nature and the Bible, by F. H. Reusch; An Introduction
  to the Textual Criticism of the New Testament, by B. B.
  Warfield; Commentary on the Gospel of John, by F.
  Godet.

1888

Age of the Philadelphia red gravel. Proc Bos Soc Nat Hist
  24: 152–7 D 19
A secret of missionary success. Cong Ag 30
Cosmogony of Genesis (Rejoinder to Professor Driver's

Critique of Professor Dana). Bib Sac 45: 356–65 Ap
Debt of the church to Asa Gray. Bib Sac 45: 523–30 Jl
Indian missions as seen upon the ground. Cong Ag 2
Inspiration. Our Day 1: 468–71 Je
Mr. Darwin's religion. Cong Mr 1
Prof. Asa Gray. Advance F 9

Book Review. Bib Sac 45: 366–72 Ap
    Life and Letters of Charles Darwin.

1889

Affinity of science for Christianity. Bib Sac 46: 701–20 O
Darwinism and deism. Ind O 10
Darwin on Herbert Spencer. Bib Sac '46: 181–84 Ja
Dr. Briggs on the higher criticism and its results. Bib Sac
    46: 381–3 Ap
Glacial period and Noah's deluge. Bib Sac 46: 466–74 Jl
Huxley among the false prophets. Advance Je 20
Huxley on the cessation of miracles. Cong Ag 29
Nampa image: correspondence relating to its discovery, with
    explanatory comments, etc. Proc Bos Soc Nat Hist 24:
    424–50 Ja
Peril from glacial reservoirs. Ind Ag 18
Reëxamination of Darwin's theory of coral islands. Bib Sac
    46: 377–81 Ap
Transcendental science. Ind O 3
Union efforts between Congregationalists and Presbyterians:
    results and lessons. Bib Sac 46: 721–5 O
Uses and abuses of an important interpretation. Bib Sac
    46: 304–20 Ap

Book Review. Bib Sac 45: 743–5 O
    Bible Doctrine of Inspiration, by Basil Manly.

1890

Archæological discovery in Idaho. Scrib Mag 7: 235–8 F
Civil wars of science. Ind S 18
Country church. Bib Sac 47: 267–84 Ap

Discovery of a palæolithic implement at New Comerstown, Ohio. West Res Hist Soc Tract 75
Dr. Briggs's " Whither." Bib Sac 47: 136–53 Ja
Glacial boundary in western Pennsylvania, Ohio, Kentucky, Indiana, and Illinois. U S Geol Sur Bull 58
Moraine of retrocession in Ontario. Bull Geol Soc Am 1: 544–6
Mormon muddle in Utah. Nation 51: 338–9 O 30
Mormon question in Idaho. Nation 51: 243–4 S 25
Owen's socialistic experiment at New Harmony. Cong Ap 17
Palæolithic man in Ohio. Nation 50: 331 Ap 24
Statute of limitations. Cong F 20
Truth about Yellowstone Park. Cong O 2

Book Reviews. Bib Sac 47: 159–165 Ja
    Mental Evolution in Man, by G. J. Romanes; Darwinism, by A. R. Wallace; Scientific Papers of Asa Gray.

1891

A catastrophe of the glacial period. Nation 53: 350–1 N 5
Additional notes concerning the Nampa image. Proc Bos Soc Nat Hist 25: 242–6
A geological prediction. Cong N 26
Antiquity of man in the light of recent investigations. Ch Ad D 31
Antiquity of man on the Pacific coast. Ind Ja 15
A Sunday in Cologne. Cong Ag 6
Great Shoshone falls. Bost Tran Ag 8
Lava Beds of Idaho. Sci Am S 19
Lessons from a recent volcanic eruption in California. Ind N 19
Man and the glacial period. Pop Sci Mo 39: 314–8 Jl
Origin of the Yosemite canyon. Ind F 26
Prehistoric man on the Pacific coast. At Mo 67: 501–12 Ap
Recent discoveries bearing on the antiquity of man. Bib Sac 48: 298–309 Ap
Some fallacies concerning higher criticism. Cong F 12
Some will-o'-the-wisps of higher criticism. Cong Mr 12

Supposed interglacial shell-beds in Shropshire, England. Bull
 Geol Soc Am 3: 505–8
Table-mountain archæology. Nation 52: 419–20 My 21

Book Reviews. Bib Sac 48: 185–6, 531–5, 542–3 Ja, Jl
 Eschatology according to the Chronology of the Apoca-
 lypse, by F. G. Hibbard; Change of Attitude toward the
 Bible, by J. H. Thayer; Elements of Geology, by Joseph
 LeConte.

1892

Adjustments between the Bible and science. Bib Sac 49:
 153–6 Ja
An English glacial myth. Nation 54: 318–9 Ap 28
A travesty upon the dominant methods employed in Old Tes-
 tament criticism. Bib Sac 49: 143–9 Ja
Changes in Muir glacier. Ind My 26
Credibility of the supernatural in the Old Testament. Bib
 Sac 49: 149–53 Ja
Excitement over glacial theories. Sci 22: 360–1 D 23
Extra-morainic drift in the Susquehanna, Lehigh and Del-
 aware valleys. Proc Phil Acad Nat Sci 469–84 D 27
Geological time. Cong Ag 4
Man and the glacial period. Dial D 16
Man and the glacial period. Sci 20: 275–7 N 11
Ministers and mobs. Bib Sac 49: 676–81 O
Outlets to the Great Lakes. Nation 55: 217–9 S 22
Pre-Niagara period of the Great Lakes. Ind N 10
President Finney and Oberlin. Advance Ag 25
St. Elias glacial fields. Nation 54: 48–9 Ja 21
Supposed post-glacial outlet of the Great Lakes through
 Lake Nipissing and the Mattawa river. Bull Geol Soc
 Am 4: 423–7
Theory of an interglacial submergence in England. Am
 Jour Sci 43: 1–8 Ja
Unity of the glacial epoch. Am Jour Sci 44: 351–73 N

Book Reviews. Bib Sac 49: 169–72, 351–5 Ja, Ap
 What is Reality, by F. H. Johnson; Evolution: its Nature,

its Evidences, and its Relation to Religious Thought, by
J. LeConte; Elements of Theology Natural and Revealed,
by J. H. Fairchild.

1893

Additional evidence bearing upon the glacial history of the
upper Ohio valley. Am Geol 11: 195-9 Mr
Commerce of the mound builders. Ind N 16
Evidences of glacial man in Ohio. Pop Sci Mo 43: 29-38 My
Glacial man in America. Ind Mr 30, Ap 13
Glaciers of Alaska. Worth Mag 1: 341-54 Ap
Ice Age in North America. Dial Ja 16
Moses and the art of writing. Advance D 19
Mr. Holmes's criticism upon the evidence of glacial man.
Sci 21: 267-8 My 19
Some detailed evidence of an ice-age man in eastern Amer-
ica. Sci 21: 65-6 F 3
Some of Professor Salisbury's criticisms on " Man and the
Glacial Period." Am Geol 11: 121-6 F

Book Reviews. Bib Sac 50: 375-6, 552-7 Ap, Jl
Interpretation of Nature, by N. S. Shaler; Genesis First
and Modern Science, by C. B. Warring; Apologetics; or,
Christianity Defensively Stated, by A. B. Bruce.

1894

Adaptations of nature to the highest wants of man. Bib
Sac 51: 206-30 Ap
Adaptations of nature to the intellectual wants of man. Bib
Sac 51: 560-86 O
Cincinnati ice dam. Pop Sci Mo 45: 184-98 Je
Continuity of the glacial period. Am Jour Sci 47: 161-87
Mr
Geological time. Ind Ap 5
In the Snake river valley. Worth Mag 3: 227-41 Mr
Last trip of the Miranda. Cong S 13
Life in the north Atlantic. Nation 59: 422-3 D 6
Some remarkable fossil fish in Ohio. Ind Ja 4
The Greenland kayak. Nation 59: 213-4 S 20

Two Sundays in Greenland. Ind O 18

Book Reviews. Bib Sac 51: 181-3, 351-3, 522-3 Ja, Ap, Jl
  Letters of Asa Gray; Anti-Higher Criticism, by Howard
  Osgood; Is Moses Scientific, by T. E. Kipp.

1895

Along the route of Burgoyne. Cong O 3

Bad philosophy going to seed. Bib Sac 52: 559-61 Jl

Glacial phenomena between Lake Champlain, Lake George
  and Hudson river. Sci n s 2: 673-8 N 22

Dr. Holst on the continuity of the glacial period. Am Geol
  16: 396-9 D

Geological history of Lake George. Ind N 28

Greenland Christianity. Bib Sac 52: 176-9 Ja

Herbert Spencer on the inadequacy of natural selection. Ind
  Jl 11

Irenicon. Bib Sac 52: 1-17 Ja

Letter regarding Chicago drainage canal. Clev News and
  Her Mr 25

New evidence of glacial man in Ohio. Pop Sci Mo 48:
  157-65 D

Observations upon the glacial phenomena of Newfoundland,
  Labrador and southern Greenland. Am Jour Sci 49: 86-
  94 F

Professor Prestwich on some supposed new evidence of the
  deluge. Bib Sac 42: 723-39 O

The Chicago drainage canal. Nation 60: 320-1 Ap 25

The Chicago ship canal. Ind Je 20

Book Reviews. Bib Sac 52: 369-70, 569-75 Ap, Jl
  Manual of Geology, by J. D. Dana; Foundations of Be-
  lief, by A. J. Balfour; Thoughts on Religion, by G. J.
  Romanes; Historical Geography of the Holy Land, by
  G. A. Smith.

1896

Age of the Philadelphia brick clay. Sci n s 3: 242-3 F 14

Fresh relics of glacial man at the Buffalo meeting of the
  A. A. A. S. Am Nat 30: 781-84 O

Luke as a historian. Ch 16 of " The Bible as Literature"
Mary Lyon and Oberlin. Nation 63: 436 D 10
Memorial of Charles Candee Baldwin, LL.D., late President
of the Western Reserve Historical Society. West Res
Hist Soc Tract 88
The latest concerning Niagara Falls. Ind S 17

Book Reviews. Bib Sac 53: 196–7, 392–4, 397–8 Ja, Ap
Higher Critics Criticised, by R. P. Stebbins; Unity of the
Book of Genesis, by W. H. Green; Darwin and after
Darwin, by G. J. Romanes.

1897

Archæological discoveries made in the gravels at Trenton,
N. J. Sci n s 5: 586 Ap 9
Effects of gales on Lake Erie. Ind N 18
Genesis and geology. Bib Sac 54: 570–2 Jl
Geology of the Yukon river. Ind Ag 19
Harmony of science and revelation. Hom Mo 33: 206–10 Mr
Lyman Abbott rediscovered A.D. 4001. Advance Ap 29
New " sayings of Jesus." Bib Sac 54: 759–70 O
Paradoxes of science. Bib Sac 54: 205–31 Ap
Place of the Sermon on the Mount in the Christian system.
Bib Sac 54: 381–3 Ap
Prehistoric man at Trenton. Ind S 9
Royal road to influence. Ob Rev 24: 173–81 F
Special explorations in the implement-bearing deposits on the
Lalor farm, Trenton, N. J. Sci n s 6: 637–45 O 29
Yukon gold fields. Nation 65: 105–6 Ag 5

1898

Agassiz and the ice age. Am Nat 32: 165–71 Mr
" Beyond reasonable doubt" — a practical principle. Hom
Rev 36: 291–5 O
Dr. Driver's proof texts. Bib Sac 55: 515–25 Jl
First chapter of Genesis and modern science. Hom Rev 35:
392–9 My
Glacial observations in the Champlain-St. Lawrence valley.
Am Geol 22: 333–4 N

Gulick's contribution to evolutionary theories. Ind Ap 7
Nature of miracles. Bib 'Sac 55: 360-1 Ap
Present aspects of the questions concerning the origin and
    antiquity of the human race. Prot Epis Rev 11: 300-24
    F, Mr
Probable rapidity of man's early development. Bib Sac 55:
    359-60 Ap

· 1899

Christian scientists. Bib Sac 56: 374-81 Ap
Dr. Driver's proof texts. Bib Sac 56: 140-47 Ja
New method of estimating the age of Niagara Falls. Pop
    Sci Mo 55: 145-54 Je
Truth about the Nampa figurine. Am Geol 23: 267-72 Ap

Book Review. Bib Sac 56: 589-92 Jl
    General Introduction to the Study of Holy Scripture, by
    C. A. Briggs.

1900

A lecture tour in Japan. Cong Je 7
An inside view of Christian movements in Japan. Bib Sac
    57: 609-13 Jl
Archæological discoveries in Ohio. Jour of Arch Inst of
    Am 4: 165
A sure and short method with the Seventh Day Adventists.
    Bib Sac 57: 609 Jl
Balkash basin. Nation 71: 401-2 N 22
Breach between Russia and China. Nation 71: 247 S 27
Dr. Gulick's field of investigation. Bib Sac 57: 608-9 Jl
Evolutionary fad. Bib Sac 57: 303-16 Ap
Future of China. Bib Sac 57: 738-47 O
Lake Baikal to the Yenisei. Nation 71: 267 O 4
Notes on Japan. Nation 70: 395, 415-6 My 24, 31
Oberlin College. New Eng Mag n s 23: 65-84 S
Prehistoric remains in Japan. Sci n s 990-1 Je 22
Remarks on the loess in north China. Sci n s 12: 71-3 Jl 13
Russians in Mantchuria. Nation 71: 207-8 S 13
Samarkand. Nation 71: 507 D 27

Stretensk to Lake Baikal. Nation 71: 225–6 S 20
Tashkend. Nation 71: 441 D 6
Up the Irtish river. Nation 71: 383 N 15
Up the Yenisei. Nation 71: 285–6 O 11

1901

Across Asia. Ind 53: 772–5 Ap 4
Armenian future. Advance. F 7
Biblical and geological chronology. Advance Ag 29
Caspian sea. Nation 72: 66 Ja 74
Caucasus mountains. Nation 72: 152–3 F 21
Crossing of the Red sea. Bib Sac 58: 570–9 Jl
Flood and Genesis. Ind 53: 1858–9 Ag 8
Geology and the deluge. M'Clure 17: 134–9 Je
Geology of China. Sci n s 13: 1029–30 Je 28
Geology's witness to the flood. S S Times Jl 6
Great Jordan fault. Nation 72:250–2 Mr 28
Oil-fields of Baku. Nation 72: 46–7 Ja 17
Origin and distribution of the loess in northern China and
    central Asia. Bull Geol Soc Am 13: 127–38
Physical preparation for Israel in Palestine. Bib Sac 58:
    360–9 Ap
Possible population of Palestine. Bib Sac 58: 740–50 O
Professor Park. Bib Sac 58: 187–90 Ja
Recent geological changes in northern and central Asia.
    Quart Jour Geol Soc 57: 244–50 My
Religious future of Siberia. Bib Sac 58: 191–94 Ja
Religious future of Siberia. Miss R 24: 211–3 Mr
Russian problem in Manchuria. R of Rs 24: 60–7 Jl
Russo-Turkish border. Nation 72: 211 Mr 14
Trans-Caspian region and its evidences of the flood. Ind
    53: 1361–3 Je 13

1902

Archæological interests in Asiatic Russia. Rec Past 1: 7–
    14 Ja
Case of Professor Pearson. Bib Sac 59: 379–82 Ap
Christian Evolution. Advance Ja 9

Crimea and the Caucasus. Chaut 36: 253–69 D

Geological confirmations of the Noachian deluge. Bib Sac
59: 282–93, 537–56, 695–716 Ap, Jl, O

Geology's testimony to Israel's crossing the Jordan. S S
Times S 27

Influence of the geography of central Asia upon the early
history of mankind. Trans Ohio Coll Assoc

Irrepressible conflict in the East. Nation 74: 187–8 Mr 6

President James H. Fairchild. Bib Sac 59: 375–78 Ap

Rate of lateral erosion at Niagara. Am Geol 29: 140–3 Mr

Reminiscences of President Fairchild. Oberlin Rev 29:
404–6 Mr 27

Uncertainties of biblical criticism. Advance Jl 31

· Uncertainties of science. Advance My 15

Years of plenty and years of famine in Egypt. Bib Sac
59: 169–74 Ja

Book Reviews. Bib Sac 59: 387–91, 584–9 Ap, Jl
Rational Basis of Orthodoxy, by A. W. Moore; Lines of
Defense of Biblical Revelation, by D. S. Margoliouth;
Authorship of the Book of Deuteronomy, by J. W. Mc-
Garvey.

Book Review. Rec Past 1: 195–204 Jl
Oldest Civilization of Greece, by H. R. Hall

1903

Age of the Lansing skeleton. Rec of Past 2: 119–24 Ap

Another glacial wonder. Nation 77: 461–2 D 10

Archæological interests of central Asia. Proc Arch Inst of
Am D 29–31

Destruction of the Taku forts. Nation 76: 454 Je 4

Eastern Siberia and Manchuria. Chaut 37: 245–62 Je

Evidence of the agency of water in the distribution of the
loess in the Missouri valley. Bull Geol Soc Am 15:
575–6

Glacial man. Rec Past 2: 259–71 S

Inspiration of Paul's address at Athens. S S Times Ja 17

Lansing skull and the early history of mankind. Bib Sac
    60: 28–32 Ja
Mediate miracles. Hom Rev 45: 18–22 Ja
Problems confronting Russian statesmen. Bib Sac 60: 765–
    70 O
Revision of geological time. Bib Sac 60: 578–82 Jl
Rights of the community versus the rights of labor. Bib
    Sac 60: 179–81 Ja
Russian rights in Mantchuria. Nation 76: 411–3 My 21
Scientific basis of religious faith. Cong N 28
Signs of the glacial period in Japan. Sci n s 17: 349–50
    F 27
Uncertainties of science and the certainties of religion. Hom
    Rev 46: 413–5 D
Western Siberia and Turkestan. Chaut 37: 144–59 My
What the Bible teaches concerning the flood. Hom Mo 45:
    298–304 Ap
Book Reviews. Bib Sac 60: 587–90, 776–82 Jl, O
    Exploration in Bible Lands during the Nineteenth Cen-
    tury, by H. V. Hilprecht; Old Testament Criticism and
    the Christian Church, by J. E. McFadyen.

1904

American Bible League. Bib Sac 61: 567–71 Jl
Arkansas cotton belt. Nation 79: 332–3 O 27
Balfour on design in nature. Bib Sac 61: 780–3 O
Bone Cave of San Ciro. Rec Past 3: 216–9
Dr. Driver's rope of sand. Bib Stud and Tea 3: 151–7 Mr
Evidence of the agency of water in the distribution of the
    loess in the Missouri valley. Am Geol 33: 205–22 Ap
Geological confirmation of the flood. Hom Rev 47: 256–
    62 Ap
Influence of the Russian liturgy. Bib Sac 61: 166–74 Ja
Old-time Mississippi plantation. Nation 79: 351–2 N 3
Russia's civilizing work in Asia. por R of Rs 29: 409,
    427–32 Ap
Substantiating witness of textual criticism. Bib Stud and Tea
    1: 24–7 Ja

Tchaikovsky's Music set to the Russian Liturgy. Bib Sac 61: 571-8 Jl

Unscientific character of the prevailing higher criticism. Bib Stud and Tea 1: 348-55 Je

Book Reviews. Bib Sac 61: 195-203, 390-2, 588-93 Ja, Ap, Jl
Old Testament History, by H. P. Smith; Ultimate Conceptions of Faith, by G. A. Gordon; Christian Faith in an Age of Science, by W. N. Rice; Teaching of Jesus concerning his own Mission, by F. H. Foster; New Light on the Life of Jesus, by C. A. Briggs.

1905

Albert Allen Wright. Am Geol 36: 65-8 Ag

Ancient gorge of Hudson river. Rec Past 4: 167-71 Je

Antiquities of the Crimea at Kertsch. Rec Past 4: 339-40 N

Application of the golden rule. Bib Sac 62: 782-6 O

A question in casuistry [gifts from Standard Oil Company]. Bib Sac 62: 370-6 Ap

Archæological notes from Sweden. Rec Past 4: 329-33 N

Archæological notes on northern England. Rec Past 4: 312-4 O

Contributions of geology to the credibility of the flood. Bib Stud and Tea 3: 11-5 Jl

Early art in Egypt. Rec Past 4: 367-72 D

Ethics of Standard Oil. Bib Sac 62: 538-559 Jl

Geological confirmation of the biblical history of Israel from Abraham to the Exodus. Bib Stud and Tea 2: 423-30 Je

Glacial movements in southern Sweden. Am Geol 36: 269-71 N

In southern Sweden. Nation 81: 275-6 O 5

Physical conditions in North America during man's early occupancy. Rec Past 4: 15-26 Ja

Professor Shimek's criticism of the aqueous origin of loess. Am Geol 35: 236-40 Ap

Recent date of lava flows in California. Rec Past 4: 195–
    8 Jl
Russia after the war. Nation 81: 295 O 12
Russian peasant. Nation 81: 420–2, 441–2 N 23, 30
Scientific criticism falsely so-called. Bib Stud and Tea 2:
    38–41 Ja
Situation in Mantchuria. Nation 80: 265–6 Ap 6

Book Reviews. Bib Sac 62: 191–3, 398–400, 593–7 Ja, Ap, Jl
    The Gospel and the Church, by Alfred Loisy; Central
    Asia and Tibet, by Sven Hedin; Ethics of the Christian
    Life, by H. E. Robins; Atonement and Modern Thought,
    by J. B. Remensnyder.

1906

Archæological museum of Florence, Italy. Rec Past 5: 59–63 F
Bible and Science, Accord of. New Stan Enc 2
Cedars of Lebanon. Rec Past 5: 195–04 Jl
Geology and Genesis on the creation. S S Times Ja 6
Inscriptions at Dog river, Syria. Rec Past 5: 1–5 Ja
Liberty's limitations — the dead hand. Bib Sac 63: 164–6 Ja
Light from geology upon the crossing of the Red sea by the
    children of Israel. Rec Past. 5: 295–302 O
My recent European trip. Oberlin Alum Mag 2: 179–84 Mr
Politics and popular delusions. Bib Sac 63: 735–40 O
Situation in Russia. Advance Mr 1
Submerged trees of the Columbia river. Rec Past 5: 243–3
    Ag

Book Reviews. Bib Sac 63: 177–83, 364–9, 744–9 Ja, Ap, O
    An Outline of the Theory of Organic Evolution, by M.
    M. Metcalf; Philosophy of Religion, by G. T. Ladd; Ge-
    ology (vol. 3), by Salisbury and Chamberlin; Knowledge
    of God, and its Historical Development, by H. M. Gwat-
    kin; Studies in Biblical Law, by H. M. Wiener.

1907

Albert H. Currier. Oberlin Alum Mag 3: 211–4 Mr
A neglected analogy. Bib Sac 64: 179–82 Ja

Jericho and San Francisco. S S Times O 5

Miracle of the strong east wind. S S Times Je 1

Neglected analogy. Bib Sac 64: 179–82 Ja

Recent geologic changes as affecting theories of man's development. Am Anthrop n s 9: 529–32 Jl–S

Troglodyte dwellings of Bakhtchi-Saraï. Rec Past 6: 13–20 Ja

Where was Sodom? S S Times Mr 3

Book Reviews. Bib Sac 64: 194–7, 591–4, 600–2, 770–7 Ja, Jl, O

Golden Days of the Renaissance in Rome, by R. Lanciani; A Critical and Exegetical Commentary on the Book of Psalms, by C. A. Briggs; Light on the Old Testament from Babel, by A. T. Clay; Babylonián Expedition of the University of Pennsylvania, vol. xx. pt. 1, by H. V. Hilprecht; A Genetic History of New England Theology, by F. H. Foster; Evolution, Racial and Habitudinal, by J. T. Gulick; Systematic Theology, by A. H. Strong; Christian Theology, by M. Valentine.

1908

Alleged collapse of New England theology. Bib Sac 65: 601–10 O

Chronology of the glacial epoch in North America. Proc Geol Soc of Lond Ja 16

Cosmogony. Murray's Il Bible Dict pp 182–3

Fort Ancient. Rec Past 7: 191–8 Jl–Ag

Hebrew Poetry. Murray's Il Bible Dict pp 697–700

Influence of glacial epoch on early history of mankind. Rec Past 7: 22–37 Ja

Influence of the glacial epoch upon the early history of mankind. Trans Vic Inst Ja 6

Jewish temple in Egypt. Bib Sac 65: 170–3 Ja

Latest concerning prehistoric man in California. Rec Past 7: 183–7 Jl–Ag

New serpent mound in Ohio and its significance. Rec Past 7: 220–32 S–O

Poverty and vice of London. Bib Sac 65: 368–74 Ap
Scientific confirmations of the deluge. Friends' Wit 1: 44–6
    Ap
Solar eclipses and ancient history. Rec Past 7: 275–81 N–D
Some other Old Testament miracles. Friends' Wit 1: 55–7
    My

1909

Calvinism and Darwinism. Bib Sac 66: 685–92 O
Great Indian quarry of Ohio. Rec Past 8: 192–3 Jl–Ag
Hittites. Rec Past 8: 308–10 N–D
Mistakes of Darwin and his would-be followers. Bib Sac
    66: 332–43 Ap
More about the new serpent mound. Rec Past 8: 76–7 Mr–Ap
New serpent mound in Ohio. Ohio Arch Hist Pub 18: 1–12
    Ja
Significance of the Jewish temple at Elephantine. Rec Past
    8: 245–6 S–O
Variations of glaciers. Rec Past 8: 113–7 Mr–Ap

Book Review. Bib Sac 66: 362–6 Ap
    Miracle and Science, by F. J. Lamb.

1910

Book Review. Bib Sac 67: 156–9 Ja
    Introduction to the New Testament, by T. Zahn.

1911

Computing age of gravel terraces. Rec Past 10: 332–3 N–D
Geological Light on the interpretation of "the tongue" in
    Joshua 15:2, 5; 18:19. Jour Bib Lit 30: 18–28
Glacial man at Trenton. Rec Past 10: 273–82 S–O

Book Review. Rec Past 10: 283–92 S–O
    Palestine and its Transformation, by E. Huntington.

1912

Logan Elm. Rec Past 11: 264–6 N–D
Postglacial erosion and oxidation. Bull Geol Soc Am 23:
    277–96 Je

Book Review. Rec Past 12: 43-5 Ja-F
  Deciding Voice of the Monuments, by M. G. Kyle.

1913

Age of pithecanthropus erectus. Rec Past 12:93-4 Mr
Crossing the Red sea. S S World n s 53: 340-1 Ag
Dependence of Christianity upon Historical Evidence. Bible
  Champ 16: 3-7, 68-71, 123-127 Ag, S, O
Destruction of Sodom. S S World n s 53: 99-100 Mr
Dr. Matthew on Wright's Origin and Antiquity of Man. Am
  Anthr 15: 704-6
How old is mankind. S S Times 55: 52 Ja 25
Old Fort Sandoski 1745. Ohio State Arch and Hist Soc Pub
  22: 371-80
Recent Date of the attenuated glacial border in Pennsylva-
  nia. Int Geol Cong 12: 451-3
Story of the flood as told on the tablets. West Teach 41:
  62-3 F
Testimony of the monuments to the persecution in Egypt.
  West Teach 41: 293-4 Je
Work of natural forces in relation to time. Nature 92:
  346 N 20

Book Reviews. Bib Sac 70: 538-42, 695-7 Jl, O
  What is the Truth about Jesus Christ, by Friedrich Loofs;
  New Testament Manuscripts in Freer Collection, by H.
  A. Sanders; Spiritual Interpretation of Nature, by J. Y.
  Simpson.

1914

Age of Don River glacial deposits. Bull Geol Soc Am 25:
  205-214 Je
Centennial of Perry's victory. Ohio State Arch and Hist Soc
  Pub 23: 49-80
Evidence of a glacial dam in the Allegheny river. Bull Geol
  Soc Am 25: 215-218 Je
Man and the mammoth in America. Rec Past 13: 103-5 Mr
Man and the mammoth in America. Sci Am S 78: 3 Jl 4

Prehistoric flint quarries and iron workings in Sweden. Rec
    Past 13: 82–6 Mr '
Present aspects of the relations between science and reve-
    · lation. Bib Sac 71: 513–33 O
The War. Bib Sac 71: 675–8 O
Who is Deutero-Isaiah. Bible Champ 18: 178 N
Work of James Orr. Bible Champ 18: 29 Ag

1915

Antediluvians. Int Stan Bible Enc 1: 143
Arabah. Int Stan Bible Enc 1: 211–3
Ararat. Int Stan Bible Enc 1: 224–5
Ark of Noah. Int Stan Bible Enc 1: 246
Cities of the Plain. Int Stan Bible Enc 1: 600–1
Dead Sea. Int Stan Bible Enc 2: 800–11
Deluge of Noah. Int Stan Bible Enc 2: 820–6
Eden. Int Stan Bible Enc 2: 897–8
Euphrates. Int Stan Bible Enc 2: 1038–9
Invincible ignorance. Bib Sac 72: 669–74 O
Jordan [river and valley]. Int Stan Bible Enc. 3: 1732–36
Noah. Int Stan Bible Enc 4: 2153
Paradise. Int Stan Bible Enc 4: 2246–7
Red Sea. Int Stan Bible Enc 4: 2538–41
Tigris. Int Stan Bible Enc 5: 2981
Vale of Siddim. Int Stan Bible Enc 4: 2784–5

Book Review. Bible Champ 20: 90 S
    Bible as Literature, by I. F. Wood.
Book Review. Bib Sac 72: 675–80 O
    International Standard Bible Encyclopaedia.

1916

Geology of [Lorain] County. Stand Hist Lorain Co 1: 1–12
Judge Francis J. Lamb. Bible Champ 21: 115 Mr
J. E. P. R. imposture. Bible Champ 21: 14–7 Ja
Newest things in biblical criticism. Advance Ja 13
Periodicity a law of nature. Bib Sac 73: 302–17 Ap

Book Reviews. Bib Sac 73: 324–30 Ap
  Antiquity of Man, by A. Keith; Men of the Old Stone
  Age, by H. F. Osborn.   .

Mosaic authorship of the Pentateuch. Fund 9: 10–21
Muir Glacier, Alaska, Soc Alaskan Nat Hist and Ethn, Bul 2
Passing of Evolution. Fund 7: 5–20
Relation of the Bible to Science. Monday Club Sermons 6:
  9–31
Sermons for the Monday Club (22)
Testimony of the monuments to the truth of the scriptures.
  Fund 2: 7–23

www.ingramcontent.com/pod-product-compliance
Lightning Source LLC
LaVergne TN
LVHW012207040326
832903LV00003B/175